D1130527

THE UNIVERSAL GOD

THE ETERNAL QUEST IN WHICH ALL MEN ARE

BROTHERS ❧ AN INTERFAITH ANTHOLOGY

OF MAN'S SEARCH FOR GOD

Edited by Carl Hermann Voss

Cleveland  New York

THE WORLD PUBLISHING COMPANY

Library of Congress Catalog Card Number: 53–6645

FIRST EDITION

COPYRIGHT ACKNOWLEDGMENTS

The editor and The World Publishing Company herewith render thanks to the following authors, publishers and agents whose interest, cooperation and permission to reprint have made possible the preparation of *The Universal God*. All possible care has been taken to trace the ownership of every selection included and to make full acknowledgment for its use. If any errors have accidentally occurred they will be corrected in subsequent editions, provided notification is sent to the publisher.

GEORGE ALLEN & UNWIN LTD., for a selection from *Science and the Unseen World*, by Sir Arthur Eddington, copyright, 1929, George Allen & Unwin Ltd.; for a selection from *Masaryk on Thought and Life*, translated by M. R. Weatherall, copyright, 1938, George Allen & Unwin Ltd.; for a selection from *Christianity and the Religions of the World*, by Albert Schweitzer, copyright, 1939, George Allen & Unwin Ltd.; and for a selection from *Toward Democracy*, by Edward Carpenter, copyright, George Allen & Unwin Ltd.

MAXWELL ANDERSON, for selections from *Key Largo*, copyright, 1939, Maxwell Anderson.

ASSOCIATION PRESS, for a selection from *Religion on the Campus*, by Francis P. Miller, copyright, 1927, Association Press; for a selection from *Book of Student Prayers*, copyright, 1946, Association Press; and for selections from *God*, by Walter Marshall Horton, a Hazen Book on Religion, copyright, Association Press.

THE BEACON PRESS, for selections from *Man's Destiny in Eternity*, copyright, 1949, The Beacon Press; and for a selection from *Five Stages of Greek Religion* by Gilbert Murray, copyright, The Beacon Press.

HC 1153

Copyright 1953 by The World Publishing Company. All rights reserved. No part of this book may be reproduced in any form without written permission from the publisher, except for brief passages included in a review appearing in a newspaper or magazine. Manufactured in the United States of America. Design and typography by Joseph Trautwein.

Acknowledgments

G. Bell & Sons, Ltd., for a selection from *The Mystics of Islam*, by R. A. Nicholson, copyright, 1914, G. Bell & Sons, Ltd.; and for a selection from *The Chief Works of Spinoza*, translated by R. A. M. Elwes, copyright, 1900, G. Bell & Sons, Ltd.

Geoffrey Bles Ltd., for a selection from *True Humanism*, by Jacques Maritain, copyright, Geoffrey Bles Ltd.; and for selections from *The Divine and the Human*, by N. Berdyaev, copyright, 1949, Geoffrey Bles Ltd.

Bloch Publishing Co., for a selection from *The Standard Prayer Book*, translated by Simeon Singer, copyright, Bloch Publishing Co.

The Estate of John E. Boodin, for a selection from *Cosmic Evolution*, by John E. Boodin, copyright, John E. Boodin.

Bowes & Bowes Publishers Limited, for selections from *Xapiteσσi*, copyright, 1912, Bowes and Bowes Publishers Limited.

Burns Oates & Washbourne Ltd., for a selection from *The Hound of Heaven*, by Francis Thompson, copyright, 1907, Burns Oates & Washbourne, Ltd.

Cambridge University Press, for a selection from *New Pathways in Science*, by Sir Arthur Eddington, copyright, Cambridge University Press.

The Clarendon Press, for a selection from *The Nicomachean Ethics*, by Aristotle, edited by D. A. Rees, copyright, 1951, The Clarendon Press; for a selection from *Discourses of Epictetus*, translated by P. E. Matheson, copyright, 1916, The Clarendon Press; for a selection from *Hermetica*, translated by Walter Scott, copyright, The Clarendon Press; for a selection from *Sacred Books of the East*, edited by F. Max Muller, copyright, The Clarendon Press; and for a selection from *The SKH Religion*, by Max A. Macauliffe, copyright, The Clarendon Press.

Wm. Collins Sons & Co. Ltd., for a selection from *Cities, Sea Coasts and Islands*, by Arthur Symons, copyright, 1918, Wm. Collins Sons & Co. Ltd.

Columbia University Press, for a selection from *The Book of Hours*, by Rainer Maria Rilke, translated by Jessie Lemont, copyright, Columbia University Press.

The Commonweal, for selections from *The Commonweal Reader*, copyright, 1949, The Commonweal.

The C. W. Daniel Company, Ltd., for a selection from *The Kingdom of the Spirit*, by Claude Houghton, copyright, The C. W. Daniel Company, Ltd.

Arthur Dobell, for a selection from *Centuries of Meditation*, by Thomas Traherne, copyright, 1908, P. J. & A. F. Dobell.

Doubleday & Company, Inc., for a selection from *The Story of My Life* by Helen Keller, copyright, 1903, by Helen Keller; and for a selection from *American Song*, by Paul Engle, copyright, 1933, Doubleday & Company, Inc.

E. P. Dutton & Co., Inc. and J. M. Dent & Sons, Ltd., for selections from *The Mystical Element in Religion*, by Friedrich von Hugel, published by E. P. Dutton & Co., Inc.; for selections from *Readings from Friedrich von Hugel*, selected by A. Thorold, published by E. P. Dutton & Co., Inc.; for a selection from *The Republic*, by Plato, translated by A. D. Lindsay, published by Everyman's Library, E. P. Dutton & Co., Inc.; for a selection from *The Vision of God*, by Nicholas of Cusa, translated by Emma Gurney Salter, published by Everyman's Library, E. P. Dutton & Co., Inc.; for a selection from *Ethics*, by Spinoza, translated by A. Boyle, published by Everyman's Library, E. P. Dutton & Co., Inc.;

and for a selection from *The Wild Knight and Other Poems,* by G. K. Chesterton, published, 1914, E. P. Dutton & Co., Inc.

E. P. DUTTON & Co., INC. and ROUTLEDGE AND KEGAN PAUL LTD., for selections from *The Eleven Religions and Their Proverbial Lore,* by Selwyn Gurney Champion, published and copyright, 1945, E. P. Dutton & Co., Inc.

THE EPWORTH PRESS, for selections from *The Spiritual Maxims of Angelus Silesius,* translated by Henry Bett, copyright, 1914, The Epworth Press.

FARRAR, STRAUS & YOUNG, INC., for selections from *Man Is Not Alone,* by Abraham Joshua Heschel, copyright, 1951, Abraham Joshua Heschel.

VICTOR GOLLANCZ, for a selection from *Man and God,* edited by Victor Gollancz, copyright, 1951, Victor Gollancz.

ROBERT GORDIS, for a selection from "Toward A Renascence of Judaism," by Robert Gordis, reprinted by permission of the author.

HAFNER PUBLISHING COMPANY INC., for selections from *God—Some Conversations,* by Johann Gottfried Herder, translated by Frederick H. Burkhardt, copyright, 1940, Hafner Publishing Company Inc.

HARCOURT, BRACE AND COMPANY, INC., for selections from *The Conduct of Life,* by Lewis Mumford, copyright, Harcourt, Brace and Company, Inc.; for a selection from *The Psychology of Religious Mysticism,* by James Henry Leuba, copyright, Harcourt, Brace and Company, Inc.; for selections from "The Rock," in *Collected Poems,* by T. S. Eliot, copyright, Harcourt, Brace and Company, Inc.; and for a selection from *The Conduct of Life,* by Benedetto Croce, translated by Arthur Livingston, copyright, 1924, Harcourt, Brace and Company, Inc.

HARPER & BROTHERS, for "Heritage," from *Color,* by Countee Cullen, copyright, 1925, Harper & Brothers, copyright, 1953, Ida M. Cullen; for a selection from *American Spiritual Autobiographies,* edited by L. Finklestein, copyright, 1948, Harper & Brothers; for a selection from *Meditations on the Cross,* by Toyohiko Kagawa, translated by Helen F. Topping and Marion R. Draper, copyright, 1935, Harper and Brothers; for a selection from *The Eclipse of God,* by Martin Buber, copyright, 1952, Harper and Brothers; for a selection from *A Catholic Speaks His Mind,* by Thomas Sugrue, copyright, 1951, 1952, Harper and Brothers; for a selection from *Modern Man's Worship,* by Bernard Eugene Meland, copyright, 1934, Harper and Brothers; for selections from *A Testament of Devotion,* by Thomas R. Kelly, copyright, 1941, Harper and Brothers; for selections from *Meister Eckhart,* A Modern Translation, by R. B. Blakney, copyright, 1941, Harper and Brothers; and for a selection from *Vedanta for Modern Man,* copyright, Harper and Brothers.

HARPER & BROTHERS, GEOFFREY BLES LTD., and THE Y.M.C.A. PRESS, for a selection from *The Beginning and the End,* by Nicolas Berdyaev, translated by R. M. French, copyright, 1952, Harper & Brothers.

HARVARD UNIVERSITY PRESS, for a selection from *Select Translations from Old English Poetry,* by Albert S. Cook and Chauncey B. Tinker, copyright, 1926, Harvard University Press; for a selection from *Ad Lucilium Epistulae Morales,* by Seneca, translated by R. M. Gummere, Loeb Classical Library, copyright, 1923, Harvard University Press; for a selection from *The Consolation of Philosophy,* by Boethius, translated by "I. T.," revised by H. F. Stewart, Loeb Classical Library, copyright, 1918, 1926, Harvard University Press; and for a selection

Acknowledgments vii

from *The Communings With Himself of Marcus Aurelius,* translated by C. R. Haines, copyright, 1916, Harvard University Press.

NEW YORK HERALD TRIBUNE, for a selection from *Re-Examining the Foundations of Our Spiritual Life,* by Harry Overstreet, copyright, 1952, New York Herald Tribune. Reprinted by permission of the author.

B. HERDER BOOK Co., for a selection from *The Graces of Interior Prayer,* by Auguste Poulain, copyright, B. Herder Book Co.

JOHN HAYNES HOLMES, for "A Prayer for Peace," by John Haynes Holmes, reprinted by permission of the author.

HENRY HOLT AND COMPANY, INC., for a selection from *Out of My Life and Thought,* by Albert Schweitzer, copyright, 1933, 1949, by Henry Holt and Company, Inc.

HOUGHTON MIFFLIN COMPANY, for a selection from *Accepting the Universe,* by John Burroughs, copyright, 1920, Houghton Mifflin Company.

ALDOUS HUXLEY, for "Door of the Temple," in *The Burning Wheel,* by Aldous Huxley, copyright, 1916, Basil Blackwell.

THE JEWISH PUBLICATION SOCIETY OF AMERICA, for a selection from *Selected Poems of Moses Ibn Ezra,* copyright, The Jewish Publication Society of America; for selections from *Selected Poems of Yehudah Halevi,* copyright, The Jewish Publication Society of America; for selections from *Selected Religious Poems of Solomon Ibn Gabirol,* copyright, The Jewish Publication Society of America; for a selection from *Mesillat Yesharim,* copyright, The Jewish Publication Society of America; and for a selection from *Selected Works of Israel Zangwill,* copyright, The Jewish Publication Society of America.

JEWISH RECONSTRUCTION FOUNDATION, for selections from *Sabbath Prayer Book,* copyright, 1945, Jewish Reconstruction Foundation.

THE JOHNS HOPKINS PRESS, for a selection from *Tongues of Fire,* by Grace H. Turnbull, copyright, The Johns Hopkins Press.

THE ESTATE OF RUFUS M. JONES, for a selection from *The Inner Life,* by Rufus M. Jones, copyright, 1916, Rufus M. Jones; and for a selection from *Pathways to the Reality of God,* by Rufus M. Jones, copyright, 1931, Rufus M. Jones.

HIND KITABS LTD., for selections from *Great Indians,* by S. Radhakrishnan, copyright, 1949, Hind Kitabs Ltd.

ALFRED A. KNOPF INC., for a selection from *Tertium Organum,* by P. D. Ouspensky, copyright, 1923, Alfred A. Knopf, Inc.; and for a selection from *Men Who Have Walked With God,* by Sheldon Cheney, copyright, 1946, Alfred A. Knopf, Inc.

THE ESTATE OF JOSHUA LOTH LIEBMAN, for a selection from "How Can I Believe in God Now?," by Joshua Loth Liebman, copyright, 1943, Joshua Loth Liebman.

J. B. LIPPINCOTT COMPANY and A. P. WATT & SON, for a selection from *Watchers of the Sky,* by Alfred Noyes, copyright, 1949, Alfred Noyes, published by J. B. Lippincott Company. Reprinted by permission of the original publishers, Wm. Blackwood & Sons Ltd.

LONGMANS, GREEN & Co., INC., for a selection from *Spiritual Letters of Archbishop Fenelon,* translated by H. L. Lear, copyright, 1909, Longmans, Green & Co., Inc.; for a selection from *Psychology and Modern Problems,* edited by J. A.

Hadfield, copyright, Longmans, Green & Co., Inc.; for a selection from *God and the Astronomers,* by William R. Inge, copyright, 1933, Longmans, Green & Co., Inc.; for a selection from *The Inward Vision,* by R. A. J. Steuart, copyright, Longmans, Green & Co., Inc.; for a selection from *Religion Without God,* by Fulton J. Sheen, copyright, 1928, Longmans, Green & Co., Inc.; for a selection from *Varieties of Religious Experience,* by William James, copyright, 1902, Longmans, Green & Co., Inc.; for selections from *Human Destiny,* by Pierre Lecompte du Noüy, copyright, Longmans, Green & Co., Inc.; for a selection from *Home Prayers, with Two Services for Public Worship,* by James Martineau, copyright, 1900, Longmans, Green & Co., Inc.; and for a selection from *Critique of Practical Reason,* by Immanuel Kant, translated by Thomas K. Abbott, copyright, Longmans, Green & Co., Inc., for selections from *The Will to Believe and Other Essays,* by William James, copyright, Longmans, Green & Co., Inc.; and for "The Quest" and "Form," in *Poems,* Complete Edition, by Eva Gore-Booth, copyright, 1929, Longmans, Green & Co., Inc.

LONGMANS, GREEN & CO., LTD., for selections from *The Spirit of Man,* by Robert Bridges, copyright, Longmans, Green & Co., Ltd.

LUZAC & COMPANY LTD., for a selection from *Readings from the Mystics of Islam,* by Margaret Smith, copyright, Luzac & Company Ltd.

THE ESTATE OF GEORGE MACDONALD, for a selection from "Lost and Found," in *Poetical Works of George MacDonald,* copyright, George MacDonald.

THE MACMILLAN COMPANY, for a selection from *Christianity and the Religions of the World,* by Albert Schweitzer, copyright, 1939, The Macmillan Company; for a selection from *Religion in the Making,* by Alfred North Whitehead, copyright, 1927, The Macmillan Company; for a selection from *Science and the Modern World,* by Alfred North Whitehead, copyright, 1925, The Macmillan Company; for a selection from *Gitanjali,* by Rabindranath Tagore, copyright, The Macmillan Company; for a selection from "Fruit-Gathering," by Rabindranath Tagore, copyright, The Macmillan Company; for a selection from *Mysticism East and West,* by Rudolph Otto, copyright, The Macmillan Company; for a selection from *Holism and Evolution,* by Jan Christian Smuts, copyright, 1926, The Macmillan Company; for a selection from *Personal Realism,* by James B. Pratt, copyright, 1937, The Macmillan Company; for a selection from *The Religious Consciousness,* by James B. Pratt, copyright, 1920, The Macmillan Company; for a selection from *Pathways to the Reality of God,* by Rufus Jones, copyright, 1931, The Macmillan Company; for a selection from *Rethinking Religion,* by John Haynes Holmes, copyright, The Macmillan Company; and for a selection from *Science and the Unseen World,* by Sir Arthur Eddington, copyright, 1929, The Macmillan Company.

MACMILLAN & CO. LTD., London and St. Martin's Press, Inc., New York, for a selection from *Quaestiones Naturales,* by Seneca, translated by John Clarke, copyright, 1910, Macmillan & Co. Ltd., London; for a selection from *One Hundred Poems of Kabir,* translated by Rabindranath Tagore, copyright, Macmillan & Co. Ltd., London; for a selection from *Masaryk on Thought and Life,* translated by M. R. Weatherall, copyright, 1938, Macmillan & Co. Ltd., London; for a selection from *The Worship of Nature,* by Sir James G. Frazer, copyright, Macmillan & Co. Ltd., London; for a selection from *Nature, Man and God,* by William Temple, copyright, 1935, Macmillan & Co. Ltd., London; for a selection from *Thoughts on Problems of the Day,* by William Temple, copyright, Macmillan & Co. Ltd., London; for a selection from *Gitanjali*, by Rabindranath Tagore, copyright, Macmillan & Co. Ltd., London; and for a selection from "Fruit-Gathering," by Rabindranath Tagore, copyright, Macmillan & Co., Ltd., London.

JOHN MACMURRAY, for a selection from *Creative Society*, by John Macmurray, copyright, 1938, John Macmurray; and for a selection from *The Cult of the Impersonal*, by John Macmurray, copyright, John Macmurray.

WILLIAM MORROW & COMPANY, INC., for a selection from *Black Elk Speaks*, by John Neihardt, copyright, 1932, John Neihardt.

THE NATIONAL COUNCIL OF CHURCHES OF CHRIST IN THE U.S.A., for a selection from the Revised Standard Version of *The Bible*, published by Thomas Nelson and Sons.

NEW DIRECTIONS, for selections from *Poems from the Book of Hours*, by Rainer Maria Rilke, translated by Babette Deutsch, copyright, 1941, New Directions.

THE NEWMAN PRESS, for selections from St. Francis De Sales, *Spiritual Conferences*, and St. Bernard of Clairvaux, *On the Love of God*.

THE OPEN COURT PUBLISHING COMPANY, for a selection from *Selections from the Rhymes of a German Mystic*, by Angelus Silesius, translated by Paul Carus, copyright, 1909 The Open Court Publishing Company.

THE ESTATE OF JAMES OPPENHEIM, for a selection from *My Father's House*, by James Oppenheim, copyright, 1919, James Oppenheim.

OXFORD UNIVERSITY PRESS, INC., for a selection from *Prayer*, by Friedrich Heiler, translated and edited by Samuel McComb and J. Edgar Park, copyright, 1932, Oxford University Press, Inc.

OXFORD UNIVERSITY PRESS, London, for a selection from *The Koran*, translated by E. H. Palmer, copyright, Oxford University Press; for selections from *Poems of Gerard Manley Hopkins*, copyright, Oxford University Press; for a selection from *Our Knowledge of God*, by John Baillie, copyright, 1939, Oxford University Press; for a selection from *Poems*, by Geoffrey Scott, copyright, Oxford University Press; for a selection from *The Thirteen Principal Upanishads*, edited and translated by Robert E. Hume, copyright, 1921, Oxford University Press; and for a selection from *Spinoza's Ethics*, Book I, translated by W. Hale White, copyright, 1930, Oxford University Press.

PANTHEON BOOKS, INC., for selections from *The Soul Afire*, edited by H. A. Reinhold, copyright, 1944, Pantheon Books, Inc.; for a selection from *Behold the Spirit*, by Alan W. Watts, copyright, 1947, Pantheon Books, Inc.; and for a selection from *Pilgrim of the Absolute*, by Leon Bloy, copyright, 1947, Pantheon Books, Inc.

PETER PAUPER PRESS, for selections from *The Wisdom of Aquinas*, copyright, 1951, Peter Pauper Press.

DOROTHY PHILLIPS, for a selection from *The Choice Is Always Ours*, edited by Dorothy Phillips, copyright, 1948, Richard R. Smith.

PHILOSOPHICAL LIBRARY, for a selection from *A Treasury of Kahlil Gibran*, translated by A. R. Ferris, copyright, 1951, Philosophical Library; for a selection from *Out of My Later Years*, by Albert Einstein, copyright, Philosophical Library;

and for a selection from *Perplexities and Paradoxes,* by Miguel Unamuno, copyright, Philosophical Library.

PRENTICE-HALL, INC., for "What Do We Mean by Religion?," by Harry Emerson Fosdick, reprinted with permission of publishers from *Religious Faith and World Culture,* edited by A. W. Loos, copyright, 1951, Prentice-Hall, Inc., New York. PRINCETON UNIVERSITY PRESS, for selections from *Works of Love,* by Soren Kierkegaard, translated by David and Lillian Swenson, copyright, Princeton University Press.

THE QUARTERLY BOOK DEPARTMENT, for a selection from *Bhagavad Gita,* translated by Charles Johnson, copyright, The Quarterly Book Department.

RANDOM HOUSE, INC., for selections from *For the Time Being,* by W. H. Auden, copyright, 1944, W. H. Auden.

ROCKLIFF PUBLISHING CORPORATION, LTD., for a selection from *Selected Mystical Writings of William Law,* edited by Stephen Hobhouse, copyright, 1948, Harper & Brothers.

ALFRED ROMER, for a selection by him which appeared in *The Choice Is Always Ours,* edited by Dorothy Phillips, copyright, 1948, Richard R. Smith. Reprinted by permission of the author and publisher, and with the special permission of Dorothy Phillips.

ROUTLEDGE AND KEGAN PAUL LTD., for a selection from *Essays on the Bases of Mystic Knowledge,* by E. Récéjac, translated by Sara Carr Upton, copyright, 1899, Routledge and Kegan Paul Ltd.

SANDS & CO. LTD., for selections from *Mysticism,* by A. B. Sharpe, copyright, 1911, 1917, Sands & Co. Ltd.

SCHOCKEN BOOKS, INC., for a selection from *The Language of Faith,* edited by N. N. Glatzer, translated by Olga Marx, copyright, 1947, Schocken Books, Inc.; for selections from *In Time and Eternity,* edited by N. N. Glatzer, translated by Olga Marx, copyright, 1946, Schocken Books, Inc.; for selections from *Ten Rungs,* by Martin Buber, translated by Olga Marx, copyright, 1947, Schocken Books, Inc.; and for selections from *Modern Hebrew Literature,* by Simon Halkin, copyright, 1950, Schocken Books, Inc.

CHARLES SCRIBNER'S SONS, for "O World," reprinted from *Poems,* by George Santayana, copyright, 1923, Charles Scribner's Sons, 1951, George Santayana, used by permission of the publishers; for "Who Is My Neighbor?," reprinted from *Ransoming the Time,* by Jacques Maritain, copyright, 1941, Charles Scribner's Sons, used by permission of the publishers; for a selection from *Platonism and the Spiritual Life,* by George Santayana, copyright, Charles Scribner's Sons; for selections from *The Plain Man Seeks for God,* by Henry P. Van Dusen, copyright, 1933, Charles Scribner's Sons; for a selection from *From Immigrant to Inventor,* by Michael Pupin, copyright, Charles Scribner's Sons; for selections from *The Interpretation of Religion,* by John Baillie, copyright, 1928, Charles Scribner's Sons; for a selection from *Reflections on the End of an Era,* by Reinhold Niebuhr, copyright, Charles Scribner's Sons; for a selection from *Discerning the Signs of the Times,* by Reinhold Niebuhr, copyright, Charles Scribner's Sons; for a selection from *Beyond Tragedy,* by Reinhold Niebuhr, copyright, Charles Scribner's Sons; for selections from *The Meaning and Truth of Religion,* by Eugene W. Lyman, copyright, Charles Scribner's Sons; for a selection from

Ramakrishna, by Max Muller, copyright, 1899, Charles Scribner's Sons; for a selection from "Mysterious and Miraculous," in *Life and Letters of John Galsworthy*, edited by H. V. Marrot, copyright, Charles Scribner's Sons; for a selection from "Image and Reality," in *The Courtier*, by Baldesar Castiglione, translated by Leonard E. Opdycke, copyright, 1902, Charles Scribner's Sons; for a selection from *Development of Religion and Thought in Ancient Egypt*, by James Henry Breasted, copyright, 1912, Charles Scribner's Sons; for a selection from *The Hasidic Anthology*, by Louis I. Newman, copyright, 1934, Charles Scribner's Sons; and for a selection from *Science and Religion*, by John Arthur Thomson, copyright, 1925, Charles Scribner's Sons.

SHEED AND WARD INC., for a selection from the *Confessions of St. Augustine*, translated by F. J. Sheed, copyright, 1943, Sheed and Ward Inc., New York; and for selections from *Religion and Culture*, by Christopher Dawson, copyright, 1950, Sheed and Ward Inc., New York.

THE SHELDON PRESS, for selections from *Studies in Early Mysticism in the Near and Middle East*, by Margaret Smith, copyright, The Sheldon Press.

SIMON AND SCHUSTER, INC., for a selection by Albert Einstein from *Living Philosophies*, copyright, 1931, by Simon and Schuster, Inc.; and for "The Snow Blind," by Josephine W. Johnson, from *Year's End*, copyright, 1937, by Simon and Schuster, Inc.

EDITH SITWELL, for "How Many Heavens . . . ," from *The Canticle of the Rose*, by Edith Sitwell, copyright, 1949, Edith Sitwell, published by Vanguard Press, Inc.

THE ESTATE OF JAN CHRISTIAN SMUTS and MACMILLAN & COMPANY OF LONDON, for selections from *Holism and Evolution*, by Jan Christian Smuts, copyright, Jan Christian Smuts.

STUDENT VOLUNTEER MOVEMENT, for a selection from *Letters of a Modern Mystic*, by Frank Laubach, copyright, Student Volunteer Movement.

THE UNIVERSITY OF CHICAGO, for selections from *Systematic Theology*, by Paul Tillich, copyright, 1951, The University of Chicago; and for selections from *The Bible, an American Translation*, copyright, 1936, The University of Chicago.

VEDANTA SOCIETY OF NEW YORK, for a selection from *The Sayings of Sri Ramakrishna*, compiled by Swami Abhedenanda, copyright, 1903, Vedanta Society of New York.

VEDANTA SOCIETY OF SOUTHERN CALIFORNIA, for a selection from *Mundaka Upanishad*, translated by Swami Prabhavananda, copyright, Vedanta Society of Southern California.

VISION PRESS, LTD., for a selection from *Purify Your Hearts*, by Sören Kierkegaard, translated by A. S. Olworth and W. S. Ferrie, copyright, Vision Press, Ltd.

GREGORY VLASTOS, for a selection from "The Religious Way," copyright, 1934, The Woman's Press.

VON OGDEN VOGT, for a selection from *Art and Religion*, by Von Ogden Vogt, published by The Beacon Press, copyright, Von Ogden Vogt; and for a selection for *Cult and Culture*, by Von Ogden Vogt, published by The Macmillan Company, copyright, Von Ogden Vogt.

JOHN M. WATKINS, for selections from *Works of Meister Eckhart*, translated by

C. de B. Evans, copyright, 1924, John M. Watkins; for a selection from *The Scale of Perfection,* by Walter Hilton, copyright, 1923, John M. Watkins; for a selection from *The Cloud of Unknowing,* edited by Evelyn Underhill, copyright, John M. Watkins; and for a selection from *Thrice Great Hermes,* translated by G. R. S. Mead, copyright, 1906, John M. Watkins.

THE ESTATE OF H. G. WELLS, for a selection from *Mr. Britling Sees It Through,* by H. G. Wells, copyright, 1916, H. G. Wells, and for a selection from *God the Invisible King,* by H. G. Wells, copyright, 1917, H. G. Wells.

YALE UNIVERSITY PRESS, for a selection from *Psychoanalysis and Religion,* by Erich Fromm, copyright, 1950, Yale University Press, for selections from *The Meaning of God in Human Experience,* by William Ernest Hocking, copyright, 1912, Yale University Press, for a selection from *A Common Faith,* by John Dewey, copyright, Yale University Press, and for "The Falconer of God," from *The Falconer of God and Other Poems,* by William Rose Benêt, copyright, Yale University Press.

To our daughter
CARLYN GROTE VOSS
and her generation

Many are the wand-bearers but few the God-possessed.

— PLATO

Table of Contents

Introduction

SEVERAL years ago, on a gray wintry morning, my wife and I set out on a new adventure. From our home in New York City we walked through slush and snow to the library of near-by Hunter College to begin a search for poetic and prose statements about man's quest for God. This was only the first of innumerable visits to many libraries to gather treasures for an interfaith anthology about mankind's search for the Universal God. But even on our first expedition, we knew we had traveled more than a city block. We had encompassed vast worlds of mind and spirit.

In the days, weeks and months that followed, we came to know a host of men and women who had sought the Meaning behind all other meanings. We met them in scores of lands through more than a hundred generations. Your own encounter with the men and women in the pages of this book will, I hope, yield no less fruit for you than it did for us: we found quietude of spirit and wholeness of heart amid the dis-ease of this, our age of anxiety.

As we assembled these selections, we made a discovery: we became increasingly aware that others had suffered the same spiritual malaise now afflicting us all in the second half of our frenetic twentieth century. What is our sickness of the spirit? It is this: the plight of our era seems to stem from a fatalistic resignation to a meaninglessness in life, an ennui born of emptiness. Despite the naïve, compulsive optimism which appears on the surface, American life is bitten deep with despair and dismay. We hear a cry for purpose, direction, and guidance. It becomes apparent that God cannot be grasped as an object or known by the intellect. But such a book as this may help to point the way each of us must go to experience intuitively the Ultimate Reality.

An inner anguish of my own served only to underscore this insight. As have millions before me, I felt the poignancy of the Psalmist's plaint: "Why art thou cast down, O my soul? And why art thou disquieted within?" And like these others whom we encountered in our research for this anthology, I, too, sought not only an answer within myself, but a suprahuman answer. The preparation of this book evoked courage to face my own dark night of the soul. Perhaps for you these pages will not give *the* answer, but many different answers from which to satisfy your spiritual need. Here are varied seekers after God, as disparate as Platonists and Aristotelians, Augustinians and Thomists, followers of Plotinus and Pascal, Kant and Kierkegaard; here are Jesuits and Jansenists, Calvinists and Lutherans, high churchmen and low churchmen, mystics and rationalists, sages of Judaism: Psalmist and Hasidic, Orthodox and Conservative, Reformed and Reconstructionist. Included as well are the religions of the East in quotations from such seekers after God as Mohammed and Lao-tse, Kabir and Jami, Kagawa and Gandhi, Tagore and Ramakrishna, Ikhnaton and Feisi.

Although I stand in the Protestant tradition, I realize anew that Roman Catholic, Protestant, and Jew are as one in their search for God. Striking differences in creed and dogma may seem to sever one from the other irremediably, but there is an underlying basic unity.

Orient is linked with Occident in this quest for Divine Reality. No matter how different may be the cultural tradition and climatic conditions, the symbols and sacraments, the liturgies, methods of worship, and national aspirations of the pilgrims along the way, we are all bent on the same objective.

No religion vouchsafes a certainty to be found at the end of the quest. It is rather the way that all religions affirm: the way of wonder and worship. Throughout the world men try to relate themselves creatively to the *mysterium tremendum,* the Wholly Other which opposes us and yet attracts us from the other side of the abyss of our existence. The walls of partition built by differences of doctrine or liturgy, denomination or hierarchy, are not easily razed. Nevertheless, each believer is aware, even if but vaguely, that individuals in search of God and the institutions that give them spiritual nurture are indissolubly united in a never ceasing search for knowledge and experience of the One God who unites mankind as a single brotherhood. Millions of Hindus pray each day: "As different streams having different sources and with wanderings crooked or straight, all reach the sea, so, Lord, the different paths which men take, guided by their different tendencies, all lead to Thee."

We often forget that no single religious persuasion has a monopoly on the truth by which we find meaning for our individual lives and direction for society as a whole. Every living religion is, as the Buddhist says, "a pointer to the Absolute." One of the three major

faiths of America—Protestantism, Roman Catholicism, or Judaism—
may claim our allegiance; but we should remind ourselves that other
faiths, as well, have given men clues to the nature of God. Daily we
find new light to illumine their darkness—and ours, too. "The foundation of all religion is one," says the Koran, "and God's is the East
and the West, and wherever ye turn, there is God's face."

The choice of prose and poetry for this anthology was therefore
as *catholic* as possible, that is, inclusive and universal. Two questions
were the criteria:

a) Are the selections of significance for Americans who stand
in the stream of thought which courses through the Judaic-
Christian ethos of our Western civilization?

b) Are the quotations distinctive in literary quality and artistic
value, in aesthetic beauty and spiritual content?

I do not intend this book as a capsule dose of theism to be swallowed on the run. Nor is it a reference work solely for students and
scholars, nor only a working manual for ministers, priests, and rabbis.
It makes no pretense at finality or totality. Here is no special plead-
ing for a single school of thought or sounding board for one particular ideology, no defense of one designated idea of God or devotion to a particular theological or philosophical point of view.

My hope is that uncertain confused people may find new courage
by reading a few pages at a time in the quiet hour before slumber at
night or in leisure moments during a crowded day. Here, I hope, is
a font of faith, a source of strength in troubled times.

These pages reflect man's response to God as the Father of all
humankind. They are designed to reaffirm the essential unity of us
all in our search for spiritual certitude. *The Universal God* will fulfill its purpose by bringing a new, fresh meaning to the age-old
Biblical truth that "God hath made of one blood all men for to
dwell on the face of the earth" and "to enjoy Him forever."

CARL HERMANN VOSS

Autumn 1953
New York City

PERSONAL ACKNOWLEDGMENTS

I shall always remember gratefully the members of many a library staff who helped with careful thought and patient kindness: Hunter College, The Church Peace Union, the Congregational House in Boston, Union Theological Seminary, the Crandall Library at Glens Falls, and the Hillview Library of Diamond Point, New York. In like fashion, a host of friends made their personal libraries available and gave invaluable counsel.

My wife, Dorothy Grote Voss, assisted me every step of the way. She aided in the selection of a large number of the passages in this book, subjected all of the myriad possibilities to her high literary standards and discriminating taste, and spent countless hours in helping me to collate and group the selections for the reader. It was she who encouraged me to undertake the task when its complexities seemed too intricate; the material, oceanic in enormity; and my own time and strength, inadequate. My debt to Dorothy is incalculable. She knows, as well as do I, the spiritual rewards of this joint quest. Without her at my side, I could never have brought this book to completion.

C. H. V.

The foundation of all foundations, the pillar supporting all wisdoms, is the recognition of the reality of God.

— MAIMONIDES, 1135-1204

COME NOW, little man! flee for awhile from your tasks, hide yourself for a little space from the turmoil of your thoughts. Come, cast aside your burdensome cares, and put aside your laborious pursuits. For a little while give your time to God, and rest in Him for a little while. Enter into the inner chamber of your mind, shut out all things save God and whatever may aid you in seeking God; and having barred the door of your chamber, seek Him.

—ST. ANSELM, 1033-1109

Let not the authority of the writer offend thee whether he be of great or small learning; but let the love of pure truth draw thee to read.

—THOMAS A KEMPIS, 1380-1471

Fishers of joy and pain
Grey words are we,
Who sift
Man's dream and drift;
Whose net
Under the moon is set
To drag the tidal secret of the world
Up from the shadowy sea.

— GEOFFREY SCOTT, 1885-1929

You say you buried God (weeping you say it)
And split the flesh to its essential parts,
But you have left us bodies bright with flame
And buried God no deeper than our hearts.

— PAUL ENGLE, 1908-

Know that, by nature, every creature seeks to become like God.
Nature's intent is neither food nor drink nor clothing, nor comfort,
nor anything else in which God is left out. Whether you like it or
not, whether you know it or not, secretly nature seeks, hunts, tries
to ferret out the track on which God may be found.

— MEISTER ECKHART, 1260?-?1327

Religion is the divinity within us reaching up to the divinity above.

— BAHAI SAYING

There is worse than oppression—there is inward stagnation of the
spiritual life.

— ISRAEL ZANGWILL, 1864-1926

Each interprets in his own way the music of heaven.

— CHINESE PROVERB

The ways of God are as the number of the souls of the sons of men.

— PERSIAN PROVERB

Different creeds are but different paths to reach the Almighty. As
with one gold various ornaments are made having different forms
and names, so one God is worshipped in different countries and ages,
has different forms and names.

— RAMAKRISHNA, 1834-1886

                    The very name of God
        Sounds like a juggler's charm; and, bold with joy,
        (Portentous sight!) the owlet Atheism,
        Sailing on obscene wings athwart the noon,
        Drops his blue-fringèd lids and holds them close,
        And hooting at the glorious sun in Heaven,
        Cries out, "Where is it?"

                    — SAMUEL TAYLOR COLERIDGE, 1772-1834

'Tis not the lack of links within the chain
From cause to cause, but that the chain exists;
That's the unfathomable mystery,
The one unquestioned miracle that we *know*,
Implying every attribute of God.

— ALFRED NOYES, 1880-

As rivers have their source in some far off fountain, so the human spirit has its source. To find his fountain of spirit is to learn the secret of heaven and earth.

— LAO-TSE, 604?-531 B.C.

Religion consisteth not in a patched coat, or a Yogi's staff, or in ashes smeared over the body; religion consisteth not in earrings worn or a shaven head, or in the blowing of horns. . . . Religion consisteth not in mere words; he who looketh on all men as equal is religious. Religion consisteth not in wandering to tombs . . . or in sitting in attitudes of contemplation; religion consisteth not in wandering in foreign countries, or in bathing at places of pilgrimage. Abide pure amid the impurities of the world; thus shalt thou find the way of religion.

— NANAK, 1469-1538

Ask that I may be forgiven if my pen
has gone astray or my foot has slipped,
for to plunge into the abyss of the Divine
mysteries is a perilous thing and no easy
task is it to seek to discover the Un-
clouded Glory which lies behind the veil.

— ABU-HAMID MUHAMMAD AL-GHAZZALI, 1058-1111

All that you speak of God is rather untrue than true, for God is unspeakable; and what you say of God is therefore always something else.

— DIONYSIUS THE AREOPAGITE, about 500 A.D.

Every lock has its key which fits into and opens it. But there are strong thieves who know how to open locks without keys. They break the lock. So every mystery in the world can be unriddled by the particular kind of meditation fitted to it. But God loves the thief who breaks the lock open: I mean, the man who breaks his heart for God.

— HASIDIC SAYING

The search for God is a game of love; the Lover and the beloved, God and the soul, seek each other in continuous dalliance, one seeming to resist while the other attacks, then attacking while the other resists. Because the end is certain and destructively ecstatic the reaching of it is made into a deliberately delayed, deliberately frustrating, quietly joyous combat, during which nothing whatever of any sort matters except the divine wrestlers themselves. The magic of it is that the soul, as it touches the arms of its Lover, finds it is touching the universe; and that God, as His grasp closes on the beloved, takes to Himself all that He has created.

— THOMAS SUGRUE, 1907-1953

CHAPTER ONE

In the Beginning

In a creative act of Spirit, in the creative act of knowing God and proving God, the birth of God takes place in vital fashion.

— Nicolas Aleksandrovich Berdyaev, 1874-1948

· I ·

All things come from one source, from that ruling Reason of the Universe, either under a primary impulse from it or by way of consequence. And therefore the gape of the lion's jaws and poison and all noxious things, such as thorns and mire, are but after results of the grand and the beautiful. Look not then on these as alien to that which thou doest reverence, but turn thy thoughts to the one source of all things.

— Marcus Aurelius, 121-180

I am the wind which breathes upon the sea,
I am the wave of the ocean,
I am the murmur of the billows,
I am the ox of the seven combats,
I am the vulture upon the rocks,
I am a beam of the sun,
I am the fairest of plants,
I am a wild boar in valour,

I

I am a salmon in the water,
I am a lake in the plain,
I am a word of science,
I am the point of the lance in battle,
I am the God who creates in the head the fire.
Who is it who throws light into the meeting on the mountain?
Who announces the ages of the moon?
Who teaches the place where couches the sun?

— ANONYMOUS

In the beginning was the Word, and the Word was with God, and the Word was God.

The same was in the beginning with God.

All things were made by Him; and without Him was not any thing made that was made.

In Him was life; and the life was the light of men.

And the light shineth in darkness; and the darkness comprehended it not.

— THE BIBLE, John 1:1-5

All mankinde is of one Author, and is one volume; when one Man dies, one Chapter is not torne out of the booke, but translated into a better language; and every Chapter must be so translated; God emploies several translators; some peeces are translated by age, some by sicknesse, some by warre, some by justice; but Gods hand is in every translation; and his hand shall binde up all our scattered leaves againe, for that Librarie where every booke shall lie open to one another. As therefore the Bell that rings to a Sermon, calls not upon the Preacher onely, but upon the Congregation to come; so this Bell calls us all: but how much more mee, who am brought so neere the doore by this sicknesse.

— JOHN DONNE, 1573-1631

In the beginning God created the world. Waste and void. Waste and
      void. And darkness was upon the face of the deep.
And when there were men, in their various ways, they struggled in
      torment towards God

Blindly and vainly, for man is a vain thing, and man without God is
a seed upon the wind: driven this way and that, and finding no
place of lodgement and germination.
They followed the light and the shadow, and the light led them forward to light and the shadow led them to darkness,
Worshipping snakes or trees, worshipping devils rather than nothing: crying for life beyond life, for ecstasy not of the flesh.
Waste and void. Waste and void. And darkness on the face of the
deep.

And the Spirit moved upon the face of the water.
And men who turned towards the light and were known of the light
Invented the Higher Religions; and the Higher Religions were good
And led men from light to light, to knowledge of Good and Evil.

— T. S. Eliot, 1888-

I had rather believe all the fables in the Legend, and the Talmud,
and the Alcoran, than that this universal frame is without a mind;
and, therefore, God never wrought miracles to convince atheism, because his ordinary works convince it. It is true, that a little philosophy inclineth Man's mind to atheism, but depth in philosophy
bringeth men's minds about to religion; for while the mind of Man
looketh upon second causes scattered, it may sometimes rest in them,
and go no farther; but when it beholdeth the chain of them con-
federate, and linked together, it must needs fly to Providence and
Deity.

Francis Bacon, 1561-1626

Such is the First Mover: a principle upon which depend the heavens
and the world of nature. Its life is such as the best which we enjoy:
waking, perceiving, and thinking; and its thought, which is thought
in the fullest sense, deals with that which is best in the fullest sense.
It is an active contemplation, in which it contemplates itself: thought
and its object being here identical. God's essential actuality is thus
life at its very best; and this state persists for ever. We say therefore
that God is a living being, eternal, and most good.

— Aristotle, 384-322 b.c.

The one God, the first and sole and universal Maker and Lord, had nothing coeval with him, not infinite chaos, not measureless water, or solid earth, or dense air, or warm fire, or subtle breath, nor the azure cope of the vast heaven: but He was one, alone by Himself, and by His will He made the things that are, that before were not, except so far as they existed in His foreknowledge.

— HIPPOLYTUS, third century

O Lord, who can comprehend Thy power?
For Thou hast created for the splendour of Thy glory a pure radiance
"Hewn from the rock of rocks and digged from the bottom of the pit."
Thou hast imparted to it the spirit of wisdom
And called it the Soul.
And of flames of intellectual fire hast Thou wrought its form,
And like a burning fire hast Thou wafted it,
And sent it to the body to serve and guard it,
And it is as fire in the midst thereof yet doth not consume it,
For it is from the fire of the soul that the body hath been created,
And goeth from Nothingness to Being,
"Because the Lord descended on him in fire."

— SOLOMON IBN-GABIROL, 1021?-?1058

· II ·

Then was not non-existent nor existent: there was no realm of air, no sky beyond it.
What covered in, and where? and what gave shelter? Was water there, unfathomed depth of water?

Death was not then, nor was there aught immortal: no sign was there, the day's and night's divider.
That One Thing, breathless, breathed by its own nature: apart from it was nothing whatsoever.

Darkness there was: at first concealed in darkness this All was undiscriminated chaos.
All that existed then was void and formless: by the great power of warmth was born that unit.

Thereafter rose desire in the beginning, desire, the primal seed and
   germ of spirit.
Sages who searched with their heart's thought discovered the existent's kinship in the non-existent.

Transversely was their severing line extended: what was above it
   then, and what below it?
There were begetters, there were mighty forces, free action here and
   energy up yonder.

Who verily knows and who can here declare it, whence it was born
   and whence comes this creation?
The gods are later than this world's production. Who knows then
   whence it first came into being?

He, the first origin of this creation, whether he formed it all or did
   not form it,
Whose eye controls this world in highest heaven, he verily knows it,
   or perhaps he knows not.

                                              — HINDU SCRIPTURES

Before this worlds great frame, in which all things
Are now contain, found any being place,
Ere flitting Time could wag his eyas wings
About that mightie bound which doth embrace
The rolling Spheres, and parts their houres by space,
That high eternall powre, which now doth move
In all these things, mov'd in it selfe by love.

                              — EDMUND SPENSER, 1552?-1599

Thee, self begotten, who, in ether rolled
Ceaselessly round, by mystic links dost blend
The nature of all things, whom veils enfold
Of light, of dark night flecked with gleams of gold,
Of star-hosts dancing round thee without end.

                              — EURIPIDES, fifth century B.C.

The Lord of the universe being Himself the substance of the whole, not yet having brought any creature into being, was alone: and since all power over both visible and invisible things was with Him, He Himself by the power of His word gave substance to all things with Himself.

— TATIAN, second century

Now must we hymn the Master of heaven,
The might of the Maker, the deeds of the Father,
The thought of His heart. He, Lord everlasting,
Established of old the source of all wonders:
Creator all-holy, He hung the bright heaven,
A roof high upreared, o'er the children of men;
The King of mankind then created for mortals
The world in its beauty, the earth spread beneath them,
He, Lord everlasting, omnipotent God.

— CAEDMON'S HYMN, seventh century

O how manifold are Thy works!
They are hidden from our face,
O Thou sole God, whose powers none other possesseth.
Thou didst create the earth at Thy will,
Thou existing alone,—
Men and women, cattle large and small,
All that go upon the earth,
All that fly on high.

Thou settest each man in his place,
Supplying his necessities, the portion allotted to him;
And his days are reckoned.
Their tongues are divers in speech,
Their forms likewise and the colour of their skins.

Thou dost create the seasons
To develop all things Thou hast made;
The winter season to bring them coolness,
The summer to bring them heat.

Thou dost fashion the beauty of form
Through Thyself alone.
For Thou art the Lord of the day at its zenith.
And Thou art in my heart.

— IKHNATON, fourteenth century B.C.

· III ·

I was here from the moment of the
Beginning, and here I am still. And
I shall remain here until the end
Of the world, for there is no
Ending to my grief-stricken being.

I roamed the infinite sky, and
Soared in the ideal world, and
Floated through the firmament. But
Here I am, prisoner of measurement.

I heard the teachings of Confucius;
I listened to Brahma's wisdom;
I sat by Buddha under the Tree of Knowledge.
Yet here am I, existing with ignorance
And heresy.

I was on Sinai when Jehovah approached Moses;
I saw the Nazarene's miracles at the Jordan;
I was in Medina when Mohammed visited.
Yet here I am, prisoner of bewilderment.

Then I witnessed the might of Babylon;
I learned of the glory of Egypt;
I viewed the warring greatness of Rome.
Yet my earlier teachings showed the
Weakness and sorrow of those achievements.

I conversed with the magicians of Ain Dour;
I debated with the priests of Assyria;
I gleaned depth from the prophets of Palestine.
Yet, I am still seeking the truth.

I gathered wisdom from quiet India;
I probed the antiquity of Arabia;
I heard all that can be heard.
Yet, my heart is deaf and blind.

I suffered at the hands of despotic rulers;
I suffered slavery under insane invaders;
I suffered hunger imposed by tyranny;
Yet, I still possess some inner power
With which I struggle to greet each day.

My mind is filled, but my heart is empty;
My body is old, but my heart is an infant.
Perhaps in youth my heart will grow, but I
Pray to grow old and reach the moment of
My return to God. Only then will my heart fill!

— KAHLIL GIBRAN, 1883-1931

The great fact for which all religion stands is the confrontation of the human soul with the transcendent holiness of God. When God reveals Himself to man, then a characteristic disturbance is set up in the human soul and in the life of our human society, and that disturbance is what we mean by religion. It is a disturbance of which we have all had some experience. Not one of us has been left alone by God. Not one of us has been allowed to live a purely human life with complete peace of mind. It is, indeed, our common sin and shame that we do our best to ignore God's gracious approach, shutting ourselves up within our human finitude, living unto ourselves alone, as if God were not there at all. Nevertheless, try as we may, we never quite succeed in shutting God out. We never quite attain the self-containedness we so impiously desire. We can live in forgetfulness of Him, but not with peace of mind.

— JOHN BAILLIE, 1886-

The Lord of all, himself through all diffus'd,
Sustains, and is the life of all that lives.
Nature is but a name for an effect,
Whose cause is God. He feeds the secret fire
By which the mighty process is maintain'd,

Who sleeps not, is not weary; in whose sight
Slow circling ages are as transient days;
Whose work is without labour; whose designs
No flaw deforms, no difficulty thwarts;
And whose beneficence no charge exhausts.
Him blind antiquity profan'd, not serv'd,
With self-taught rites, and under various names,
Female and male, Pomona, Pales, Pan,
And Flora, and Vertumnus; peopling earth
With tutelary goddesses and gods
That were not; and commending, as they would,
To each some province, garden, field, or grove.
But all are under one. One Spirit—His
Who wore the platted thorns with bleeding brows—
Rules universal nature. Not a flow'r
But shows some touch, in freckle, streak, or stain,
Of his unrivall'd pencil. He inspires
Their balmy odours, and imparts their hues,
And bathes their eyes with nectar, and includes,
In grains as countless as the sea-side sands,
The forms with which he sprinkles all the earth.
Happy who walks with him! whom what he finds
Of flavour or of scent in fruit or flow'r,
Or what he views of beautiful or grand
In nature, from the broad majestic oak
To the green blade that twinkles in the sun,
Prompts with remembrance of a present God!

— WILLIAM COWPER, 1731-1800

Particularly worthy of admiration is the degree of power which God has given even to the tiniest of His creatures. His might He seems to have willed to show forth in the larger creatures, but in the small, His wisdom. Who indeed would suspect the power latent in the grain of mustard-seed, which is the smallest of all seeds, so small that the eye can barely see it, and yet within that seed is hidden a tree so large that the birds of the air dwell in the branches thereof, as Truth Himself has said in the Gospel. This is not peculiar to the mustard-seed: it is the common property of all seeds, for in them are hidden virtually the roots, trunks, branches, leaves, flowers and fruit of the mightiest trees. If personal observation did not force this fact on us, it would surely be difficult to persuade anybody that so large an agglomeration of disparate objects could come forth from so tiny a seed. Who also would imagine that ants, gnats, fleas, and other minute insects have feet that move with lightning-like rapidity, a head, heart, internal and external senses, and even, in their own imperfect fashion, prudence and judgment? Who would dream that these insects, despite their infinitesimally tiny size, have the power to pierce and perforate living flesh? Gnats, for example, are not only a nuisance to men, but even terrify lions and elephants.

God, therefore, is great, and great is His wisdom in the greatest as in the smallest.

The "length" of God's practical wisdom is patent in the conservation of creatures, even as its "breadth" we have seen to be evident in the fact of creation. Hence in the conservation and duration of created things, especially the corruptible, we may see the great and admirable wisdom of God.

In the first place reflection on the manner in which God gives nourishment and growth to herbs, plants, animals and our own bodies for their maximum preservation can only leave one stupefied with amazement and admiration at the wisdom of God. For with earth and water He feeds the flowers and the trees, and makes the nourishing sap flow from the roots to the trunk, and from the trunk to the branches and the leaves until fruit is brought forth and the cycle is completed. And this fits admirably into a general and well thought out plan. For God uses fruit and vegetables and meat to feed the animals and man himself. And He has so arranged matters that the nourishment, which we take into our bodies, penetrates to every part, both internal and external, with almost incredible ease and agreeableness.

God acts like a learned and sympathetic doctor, who knows how to mix drugs in such a way that the medicine is not only easily absorbed but even to the patient's liking. For food is assuredly a medicine: if we mortals did not take it at frequent intervals we would die. But our most thoughtful and wise doctor, God Himself, has made food pleasant to eat. Why, He has afforded enough varieties of food for even the most fastidious. Then, by means of various reactions in mouth, stomach, liver and heart He changes our food into a juice thin and subtle enough to course painlessly and endlessly throughout every vein, capillary and pore of the body until it penetrates every part of our flesh and bones and nerves, and all this without our feeling anything of the process and even during our sleep.

When philosophers see these marvels they admire the ingenuity and artfulness of nature. But how can they speak of ingenuity in inanimate things that are bereft of sense and reason? They should admire not the ingenuity of nature but the wisdom of the Creator, for He made nature and discovered the way to accomplish all these wonders.

— ROBERT BELLARMINE, 1542-1621

Blessed art thou, O Lord our God, King of the universe, who formest light and createst darkness, who makest peace and createst all things:

Who in mercy givest light to the earth and to them that dwell thereon, and in thy goodness renewest the creation every day continually. How manifold are thy works, O Lord! In wisdom hast thou made them all: the earth is full of thy creatures. O King, who alone wast exalted from aforetime, praised, glorified and extolled from days of old; O everlasting God, in thine abundant mercies, have mercy upon us, Lord of our strength, Rock of our stronghold, Shield of our salvation, thou Stronghold of ours!

— THE SIDDUR

CHAPTER TWO

Can Man by Searching
Find Out God?

> *Canst thou by searching find out God? canst thou find out the Almighty unto perfection?*
> *It is as high as heaven; what canst thou do? deeper than hell; what canst thou know?*
> *The measure thereof is longer than the earth, and broader than the sea.*

— THE BIBLE, Job 11:7-9

· I ·

UN DIEU défini est un Dieu fini.

— OLD FRENCH PROVERB

Om, Amitaya! measure not with words
 Th' Immeasurable; nor sink the string of thought
Into the Fathomless. Who asks doth err,
 Who answers, errs. Say nought!

— SIR EDWIN ARNOLD, 1832-1904

He is incomprehensible: not even the whole universe, much less the human mind, can contain the conception of Him: we know *that* He

12

is, we cannot know *what* He is: we may see the manifestations of Him in His works, but it were monstrous folly to go behind His works and inquire into His essence. He is hence unnamed: for names are the symbols of created things, whereas His only attribute is to *be*.

— PHILO JUDAEUS, late first century B.C
and early first century A.D.

All those who seek Thee tempt Thee,
And those who find would bind Thee
To gesture and to form.

But I would comprehend Thee
As the wide Earth enfolds Thee.
Thou growest with my maturity,
Thou art in calm and storm.

I ask of Thee no vanity
To evidence and prove Thee.
Thou wert in aeons old.
Perform no miracles for me,
But justify Thy laws to me—
Which, as the years pass by me,
All soundlessly unfold.

— RAINER MARIA RILKE, 1875-1926

Dangerous it were for the feeble brain of man to wade far into the doings of the Most High; Whom although to know be life, and joy to make mention of His name, yet our soundest knowledge is to know that we know Him not indeed as He is, neither can know Him, and our safest eloquence concerning Him is our silence, when we confess without confession that His glory is inexplicable, His greatness above our capacity and reach. He is above and we upon earth; therefore it behoveth our words to be wary and few.

— RICHARD HOOKER, 1554?-1600

· II ·

We cannot reach any religious truth or conviction along scientific lines, but . . . a careful scientific description of Animate Nature is

not inconsistent with a spiritual . . . interpretation. . . . Science has
come to mean so much to man . . . that we cannot wonder at his desire to have it also as an aid to his faith. But this way lies disappoint-
ment. We cannot by scientific searching find out God. . . . It is not
by science that we can pass from nature to nature's God. The pathway is that of religious experience, just as the pathway of the vision
of beauty is that of æsthetic discipline.

—JOHN ARTHUR THOMSON, 1861-1933

O God, I know not Thy world, Thy world in its vastness—
Yea, what is man that he should know it?

    Everywhere hast Thou sown Thy glorious grace,
    And in every creature.

Day by day and hour by hour Thou renewest the work of creation.
And if Thou hast given me an understanding mind
To discern the inner meaning and reveal things hidden,
Yea, if even above myriads,
Thou hast favored me with the power of self-expression,
That I might give tone and color to my vision,
And thus hast made me partner in Thy work,
What am I even so, yea, what my life work?
How can I hope to glimpse one faint and fleeting ray of
Thine awe-inspiring splendor?

    And if I attempted to celebrate in song Thy manifest glory,
    Would my singing not sound like the murmur of the dumb?

Ah me! how I desire to stand in Thy presence all the days of my life,
A faithful witness to all Thy wonders!
Ah me! How I desire to view all that has been wrought,
And how exceedingly I long to stand at watch and to scan,
From the world's beginning even to its end,

    All motion and change, all mysteries and meanings,
    All things in their essence and in their relations!

Why then must I perish like a bird within a cage,
Going down into the grave with all my life's thirst unquenched?
And why must I molder in the dark cold pit, while all the suns
Whirl in the dance of life eternal and are ever renewed?
Why, God, O why dost Thou baffle me?

—JACOB COHEN, 1891-1949

It is the Heart, and never the Reason, which leads us to the Absolute.

— E. Récéjac, nineteenth century

Wit, seeking Truth, from cause to cause ascends,
  And never rests till it the First attain;
Will, seeking Good, finds many middle ends,
  But never stays till it the Last do gain.

Now God the Truth and First of causes is,
  God is the Last Good End which lasteth still,
Being Alpha and Omega nam'd for this,
  Alpha to wit, Omega to the will.

— Sir John Davies, 1569-1626

Once the noble Ibrahim, as he sat on his throne,
Heard a clamour and noise of cries on the roof,
Also heavy footsteps on the roof of his palace.
He said to himself, "Whose heavy feet are these?"
He shouted from the window, "Who goes there?"
The guards, filled with confusion, bowed their heads saying,
"It is we, going the rounds in search."
He said, "What seek ye?" They said, "Our camels."
He said, "Who ever searched for camels on a housetop?"
They said, "We follow thy example,
Who seekest union with God, while sitting on a throne."

— Jalal-ud-din Rumi, 1207-1273

He who seeks God under settled form lays hold of the form, while missing the God concealed in it.

— Meister Eckhart, 1260?-?1327

It is not by the practice of perpetual silence, nor by the adoption of a religious dress, nor by shaving the head, nor by wearing a wooden necklace, nor by twisting matted hair round the head that God is found.

— Sikh Teaching

· III ·

I asked the earth and it answered me, "I am not He." And whatsoever is in it confessed the same. I asked the sea and the deeps, and the living creeping things, and they answered, "We are not thy God; seek above us." I asked the moving air; and the whole air with his inhabitants spoke, "Anaximenes was deceived; I am not God." I asked the heavens, sun, moon, stars, "Nor," say they, "are we the God whom thou seekest." And I replied unto all the things that encompass the door of my flesh: "Ye have told me of my God, that ye are not He; tell me something of Him." And they cried out with a loud voice, "He made us." What then do I love when I love my God? By my soul will I ascend to Him. See, I am mounting up through my mind toward Thee. I will pass beyond this power of mind which is called memory, desirous to arrive at Thee, and to cleave unto Thee.

How then do I seek Thee, O Lord? For when I seek Thee, I seek a happy life. I will seek Thee that my soul may live. For my body liveth by my soul, and my soul by Thee. Nor is it I alone nor some few besides, but we all would fain be happy. Happy then will (the soul of man) be when, no distraction interposing, it shall joy in that only Truth, by whom all things are true.

Too late I loved Thee, O thou Beauty of Ancient Days, yet ever new! Behold, Thou wert within,—and I abroad, and there I searched for Thee. Thou wert with me, but I was not with Thee. When I shall with my whole self cleave to Thee, I shall nowhere have sorrow or labor, and my life shall wholly live as wholly full of Thee.

— St. Augustine, 354-430

I sought Thee round about, O Thou my God,
　　　To find Thy abode:
I said unto the Earth, "Speak, art thou He?"
　　　She answered me,
"I am not." I enquired of creatures all,
　　　In general,
Contained therein: they with one voice proclaim
That none amongst them challenged such a name.

I asked the seas, and all the deeps below,
　　　My God to know:

I asked the reptiles, and whatever is
    In the abyss:
Even from the shrimp to the leviathan
    My enquiry ran:
But in those deserts, which no line can sound,
The God I sought for was not to be found.

I asked the Air, if that were He, but know
    It told me, "No":
I from the towering eagle to the wren
    Demanded then,
If any feathered fowl 'mong them were such:
    But they, all much
Offended at my question, in full quire
Answered, to find my God I must look higher.

And now, my God, by Thy illumining grace,
    Thy glorious face
(So far forth as Thou wilt discovered be)
    Methinks I see:
And though invisible and infinite,
    To human sight
Thou in Thy Mercy, Justice, Truth, appearest,
In which to our frail senses Thou com'st nearest.

O, make us apt to seek and quick to find,
    Thou God most kind:
Give us Love, Hope, and Faith in Thee to trust,
    Thou God most just:
Remit all our offences, we entreat,
    Most Good, most Great:
Grant that our willing though unworthy quest
May, through Thy grace, admit us 'mongst the blest.

         — THOMAS HEYWOOD, 1574? - 1641

And do You, O Lord my God, do You teach my heart where and how it shall seek You, where and how it may find You. If You are not here, Lord, where, since You are absent, shall I seek You? But if You are everywhere, why then, since You are present, do I not see You? Surely it is *light inaccessible* that You inhabit (I Timothy vi: 16). And yet where is inaccessible light, and how shall I approach a light that cannot be approached? Or who shall lead and direct me

to it that I may see You in it? What is more, in what signs and
appearances shall I seek You? I have never seen You, O Lord my
God, nor have I knowledge of Your face. Most high God, what
shall he do, what shall he do, this exile who is so far away from You?
What shall this servant of Yours do, tormented as he is in his love of
You, yet cast far away from Your face (Psalms 1:13)? He longs to
see You, and Your face is too far away from him. He desires to
approach You, and Your dwelling place is unapproachable. He desires to find You and he does not know where You are. He strives to
seek You out, and he does not know Your appearance. Lord, You
are my God, and You are my Lord, and I have never seen You.
You have made me and You have remade me, and whatever I possess
You have given to me,—and yet I have still to see You. And finally
I have been made in order that I may see You, and I have still to do
that for which I was made.

— St. Anselm, 1033-1109

The end of being is to find out God!
And what is God? A vast almighty Power
Great and unlimited, whose potent will
Brings to achievement whatsoe'er He please.
He is all mind. His being infinite—
All that we see and all that we do not see.
The Lord of heaven and earth, the God of Gods
Without Him nothing is. Yet what He is
We know not! When we strive to comprehend
Our feeble guesses leave the most concealed.
To Him we owe all good we call our own.
To Him we live, to Him ourselves approve.
He is a friend forever at our side.
What cares He for the bleeding sacrifice?
O purge your hearts and lead the life of good!
Not in the pride of temples made with stone
His pleasure lies, but in the piety
Of consecrated hearts and lives devout.

— Lucius Annaeus Seneca, 4 b.c.?-65 a.d.

· IV ·

I shall tell about two talks. One apparently came to a conclusion,
as only occasionally a talk can come, and yet in reality remained

unconcluded; the other was apparently broken off and yet found a completion such as rarely falls to the lot of discussions.

Both times it was a dispute about God, about the concept and the name of God, but each time of a very different nature.

On three successive evenings I spoke at the adult folk-school of a German industrial city on the subject "Religion as Reality." What I meant by that was the simple thesis that "faith" is not a feeling in the soul of man but an entrance into reality, an entrance into the *whole* reality without reduction and curtailment. This thesis is simple but it contradicts the usual way of thinking. And so three evenings were necessary to make it clear, and not merely three lectures but also three discussions which followed the lectures. At these discussions I was struck by something which bothered me. A large part of the audience was evidently made up of workers but none of them spoke up. Those who spoke and raised questions, doubts, and reflections were for the most part students (for the city had a famous old university). But all kinds of other circles were also represented; the workers alone remained silent. Only at the conclusion of the third evening was this silence, which had by now become painful to me, explained. A young worker came up to me and said: "Do you know, we can't speak in here, but if you would meet with us to-morrow, we could talk together the whole time." Of course I agreed.

The next day was a Sunday. After dinner I came to the agreed place and now we talked together well into the evening. Among the workers was one, a man no longer young, whom I was drawn to look at again and again because he listened as one who really wished to hear. Real listening has become rare in our time. It is found most often among workers, who are not indeed concerned about the person speaking, as is so often the case with the *bourgeois* public, but about what he has to say. This man had a curious face. In an old Flemish altar picture representing the adoration of the shepherds one of them, who stretches out his arms toward the manger, has such a face. The man in front of me did not look as if he might have any desire to do the same; moreover, his face was not open like that in the picture. What was notable about him was that he heard and pondered, in a manner as slow as it was impressive. Finally, he opened his lips as well. "I have had the experience," he explained slowly and impressively, repeating a saying which the astronomer Laplace is supposed to have used in conversation with Napoleon, "that I do not need this hypothesis 'God' in order to be quite at home in the world." He pronounced the word "hypothesis" as if he had attended the lectures of the distinguished natural scientist who had taught in that industrial and university city and had died shortly before. Although he did not reject the designation "God" for his idea of nature, that naturalist spoke in a similar manner whether he pursued zoology or *Weltanschauung*.

The brief speech of the man struck me; I felt myself more deeply challenged than by the others. Up till then we had certainly debated very seriously, but in a somewhat relaxed way; now everything had suddenly become severe and hard. How should I reply to the man? I pondered awhile in the now severe atmosphere. It came to me that I must shatter the security of his *Weltanschauung*, through which he thought of a "world" in which one "felt at home." What sort of a world was it? What we were accustomed to call world was the "world of the senses," the world in which there exists vermilion and grass green, C major and B minor, the taste of apple and of worm-wood. Was this world anything other than the meeting of our own senses with those unapproachable events about whose essential definition physics always troubles itself in vain? The red that we saw was neither there in the "things," nor here in the "soul." It at times flamed up and glowed just so long as a red-perceiving eye and a red-engendering "oscillation" found themselves over against each other. Where then was the world and its security? The unknown "objects" there, the apparently so well-known and yet not graspable "subjects" here, and the actual and still so evanescent meeting of both, the "phenomena"—was that not already three worlds which could no longer be comprehended from one alone? How could we in our thinking place together these worlds so divorced from one another? What was the being that gave this "world," which had become so questionable, its foundation?

When I was through a stern silence ruled in the now twilit room. Then the man with the shepherd's face raised his heavy lids, which had been lowered the whole time, and said slowly and impressively, "You are right."

I sat in front of him dismayed. What had I done? I had led the man to the threshold beyond which there sat enthroned the majestic image which the great physicist, the great man of faith, Pascal, called the God of the Philosophers. Had I wished for that? Had I not rather wished to lead him to the other, Him whom Pascal called the God of Abraham, Isaac, and Jacob, Him to whom one can say Thou?

It grew dusk, it was late. On the next day I had to depart. I could not remain, as I now ought to do; I could not enter into the factory where the man worked, become his comrade, live with him, win his trust through real life-relationship, help him to walk with me the way of the creature who *accepts* the creation. I could only return his gaze.

Some time later I was the guest of a noble old thinker. I had once made his acquaintance at a conference where he gave a lecture on elementary folk-schools and I gave one on adult folk-schools. That brought us together, for we were united by the fact that the word "folk" has to be understood in both cases in the same all-embracing sense. At that time I was happily surprised at how the man with the steel-grey locks asked us at the beginning of his talk to forget all that we believed we knew about his philosophy from his books. In the last years, which had been war years, reality had been brought so close to him that he saw everything with new eyes and had to think in a new way. To be old is a glorious thing when one has not unlearned what it means to *begin;* this old man had even perhaps first learned it thoroughly in old age. He was not at all young, but he was old in a young way, knowing how to begin.

He lived in another university city situated in the west. When the theology students of that university invited me to speak about prophecy, I stayed with the old man. There was a good spirit in his house, the spirit that wills to enter life and does not prescribe to life where it shall let it in.

One morning I got up early in order to read proofs. The evening before I had received galley proof of the preface of a book of mine, and since this preface was a statement of faith, I wished to read it once again quite carefully before it was printed. Now I took it into the study below that had been offered to me in case I should need it. But here the old man already sat at his writing-desk. Directly after greeting me he asked me what I had in my hand, and when I told him, he asked whether I would not read it aloud to him. I did so gladly. He listened in a friendly manner but clearly astonished, indeed with growing amazement. When I was through, he spoke hesitatingly, then, carried away by the importance of his subject, ever more passionately. "How can you bring yourself to say 'God' time after time? How can you expect that your readers will take the word in the sense in which you wish it to be taken? What you mean by the name of God is something above all human grasp and comprehension, but in speaking about it you have lowered it to human conceptualization. What word of human speech is so mis-

used, so defiled, so desecrated as this! All the innocent blood that
has been shed for it has robbed it of its radiance. All the injustice
that it has been used to cover has effaced its features. When I hear
the highest called 'God,' it sometimes seems almost blasphemous."

The kindly clear eyes flamed. The voice itself flamed. Then we sat
silent for awhile facing each other. The room lay in the flowing
brightness of early morning. It seemed to me as if a power from the
light entered into me. What I now answered, I cannot to-day repro-
duce but only indicate.

"Yes," I said, "it is the most heavy-laden of all human words.
None has become so soiled, so mutilated. Just for this reason I may
not abandon it. Generations of men have laid the burden of their
anxious lives upon this word and weighed it to the ground; it lies in
the dust and bears their whole burden. The races of men with their
religious factions have torn the word to pieces; they have killed for
it and died for it, and it bears their finger-marks and their blood.
Where might I find a word like it to describe the highest! If I took
the purest, most sparkling concept from the inner treasure-chamber
of the philosophers, I could only capture thereby an unbinding
product of thought. I could not capture the presence of Him whom
the generations of men have honoured and degraded with their awe-
some living and dying. I do indeed mean Him whom the hell-
tormented and heaven-storming generations of men mean. Certainly,
they draw caricatures and write 'God' underneath; they murder one
another and say 'in God's name.' But when all madness and delusion
fall to dust, when they stand over against Him in the loneliest darkness and no longer say 'He, He' but rather sigh 'Thou,' shout
'Thou,' all of them the one word, and when they then add 'God,' is
it not the real God whom they all implore, the One Living God, the
God of the children of man? Is it not He who *hears* them? And just
for this reason is not the word 'God,' the word of appeal, the word
which has become a *name*, consecrated in all human tongues for all
times? We must esteem those who interdict it because they rebel
against the injustice and wrong which are so readily referred to
'God' for authorization. But we may not give it up. How understandable it is that some suggest we should remain silent about the
'last things' for a time in order that the misused words may be redeemed! But they are not to be redeemed *thus*. We cannot cleanse
the word 'God' and we cannot make it whole; but, defiled and mutilated as it is, we can raise it from the ground and set it over an hour
of great care."

It had become very light in the room. It was no longer dawning, it was light. The old man stood up, came over to me, laid his hand on my shoulder and spoke: "Let us be friends." The conversation was completed. For where two or three are truly together, they are together in the name of God.

— MARTIN BUBER, 1878 -

Out of the depths have I cried unto Thee, O LORD.

Lord, hear my voice: let Thine ears be attentive to the voice of my supplications.

If Thou, LORD, shouldest mark iniquities, O Lord, who shall stand?

But there is forgiveness with Thee, that Thou mayest be feared.

I wait for the LORD, my soul doth wait, and in His word do I hope.

My soul waiteth for the Lord more than they that watch for the morning: I say, more than they that watch for the morning.

Let Israel hope in the LORD: for with the LORD there is mercy, and with Him is plenteous redemption.

And He shall redeem Israel from all his iniquities.

— THE BIBLE, Psalm 130

Why do we say: "Our God and the God of our father?" There are two sorts of persons who believe in God. The one believes because his faith has been handed down to him by his fathers; and his faith is strong. The other has arrived at faith by dint of searching thought. And this is the difference between the two: The first has the advantage that his faith cannot be shaken, no matter how many objections are raised to it, for his faith is firm because he has taken it over from his fathers. But there is a flaw in it: it is a commandment given by man, and it has been learned without thought or reasoning. The advantage of the second man is that he has reached faith through his own power, through much searching and thinking. But his faith too has a flaw: it is easy to shake it by offering contrary evidence. But he who combines both kinds of faith is invulnerable. That is why we say: "Our God," because of our searching, and "the God of our fathers," because of our tradition.

And a like interpretation holds when we say, "The God of Abraham, the God of Isaac, and the God of Jacob," for this means: Isaac and Jacob did not merely take over the tradition of Abraham, but sought out the divine for themselves.

— BAAL SHEM-TOB, 1700? - 1760

Like to the arctic needle, that doth guide
    The wand'ring shade by his magnetic pow'r,
And leaves his silken gnomon to decide
    The question of the controverted hour,
First frantics up and down from side to side,
        And restless beats his crystal'd iv'ry case,
        With vain impatience jets from place to place,
And seeks the bosom of his frozen bride;
        At length he slacks his motion, and doth rest
His trembling point at his bright pole's beloved breast,

E'en so my soul, being hurried here and there,
    By ev'ry object that presents delight,
Fain would be settled, but she knows not where;
    She likes at morning what she loathes at night:
She bows to honour; then she lends an ear
        To that sweet swan-like voice of dying pleasure,
        Then tumbles in the scatter'd heaps of treasure;
Now flatter'd with false hope; now foil'd with fear:
        Thus finding all the world's delight to be
But empty toys, good God, she points alone to Thee.

But hath the virtued steel a power to move?
    Or can the untouch'd needle point aright?
Or can my wand'ring thoughts forbear to rove,
    Unguided by the virtue of Thy sprite?
O hath my leaden soul the art t'improve
        Her wasted talent, and, unrais'd, aspire
        In this sad moulting time of her desire?
Not first belov'd, have I the power to love;
    I cannot stir, but as Thou please to move me,
Nor can my heart return Thee love, until Thou love me.

The still commandress of the silent night
    Borrows her beams from her bright brother's eye;
His fair aspect fills her sharp horns with light,
    If he withdraw, her flames are quench'd and die:
E'en so the beams of Thy enlight'ning sprite,
        Infus'd and shot into my dark desire,
        Inflame my thoughts, and fill my soul with fire,
That I am ravish'd with a new delight;
        But if Thou shroud Thy face, my glory fades,
And I remain a nothing, all compos'd of shades.

Eternal God! O Thou that only art
   The sacred fountain of eternal light,
And blessed loadstone of my better part,
   O Thou, my heart's desire, my soul's delight!
Reflect upon my soul, and touch my heart,
      And then my heart shall prize no good above Thee;
      And then my soul shall know Thee; knowing, love Thee;
And then my trembling thoughts shall never start
      From Thy commands, or swerve the least degree,
Or once presume to move, but as they move in Thee.

—FRANCIS QUARLES, 1592-1644

You will ask me questions how a man can give himself to that which
he has no feeling of, especially when it relates to an Object which
he does not see, nor never had acquaintance with? Sir, every day of
your life you love things you do not see. Do you see for instance the
wisdom of your friend? Do you see his sincerity, his disinterested-
ness, his virtue? You cannot see those objects with the eyes of the
body, yet you prize and value them, and love them in that degree
that you prefer them in your friend to riches, and outward beauty,
and to everything that strikes the eye. Love then the wisdom and
supreme goodness of God, as you love the wisdom and imperfect
goodness of your friend.

—FRANÇOIS FÉNELON, 1651-1715

Blessed are the pure in heart: for they shall see God.
Blessed are the peace-makers: for they shall be called the children of God.

—THE BIBLE, Matthew 5:8-9

Longing, I sought Thy presence;
Lord, with my whole heart did I call and pray,
   And going out toward Thee,
I found Thee coming to me on the way,
      Yea, in Thy wonders' might as clear to see
      As when, within the shrine, I looked for Thee.

—YEHUDAH HALEVI, 1085?-?1140

God, having placed good and evil in our power, has given us full freedom of choice; he does not keep back the unwilling, but embraces the willing.

— St. John Chrysostom, 345?-407

· v ·

I have wander'd through eternal space
Seeking your spirit, Love;
Through the dark oceans of the sky,
Through the blue silences
Where no life breathes;—
Where Time like a wind
Stills and stirs the dust
Of annihilated forms
Only to create new wholes.
As the lonely pilgrim
Seeks his "Grail"
Have I sought mine own,
And by some law divine
Has my exiled spirit
Grown to strength
Through many an anguished past;—
Until at last
In Truth's quest
I found you, Love
One with earth's core
And the living stars above!

— Anonymous

For silence is not God, nor speaking is not God; fasting is not God, nor eating is not God; loneliness is not God, nor company is not God; nor yet any of all the other two such contraries. He is hid between them, and may not be found by any work of thy soul, but all only by love of thine heart. He may not be known by reason, He may not be gotten by thought, nor concluded by understanding; but He may be loved and chosen with the true lovely will of thine heart.

— Anonymous

The very difficulties of nature make it likely that a revelation should be made; the very mysteries of creation call for some act on the part of the Creator, by which those mysteries shall be alleviated to you or compensated. One of the greatest of the perplexities of nature is this very one, that the Creator should have left you to yourselves. You know there is a God, yet you know your own ignorance of Him, of His will, of your duties, of your prospects. A revelation would be the greatest of possible boons which could be vouchsafed to you. After all, you do not know, you only conclude that there is a God; you see Him not, you but hear of Him. He acts under a veil; He is on the point of manifesting himself to you at every turn, yet He does not. He has impressed on your hearts anticipations of His majesty; in every part of creation has He left traces of His presence and given glimpses of His glory; you come up to the spot, He has been there, but He is gone. He has taught you His law, un-equivocally indeed, but by deduction and by suggestion, not by direct command. He has always addressed you circuitously, by your inward sense, by the received opinion, by the events of life, by vague traditions, by dim histories; but as if of set purpose, and by an evi-dent law, He never actually appears to your longing eyes or your weary heart, He never confronts you with Himself. What can be meant by all this? a spiritual being abandoned by its Creator! there must doubtless be some awful and all-wise reason for it; still a sore trial it is; so sore, surely, that you must gladly hail the news of His interference to remove or diminish it.

The news then of a revelation, far from suspicious, is borne in upon our hearts by the strongest presumptions of reason in its behalf. It is hard to believe that it has not been given, as indeed the conduct of mankind has ever shown. You cannot help expecting it from the hands of the All-merciful, unworthy as you feel yourselves of it. It is not that you can claim it, but that He inspires hope of it; it is not you that are worthy of the gift, but it is the gift which is worthy of your Creator. It is so urgently probable, that little evi-dence is required for it, even though but little were given. . . . The very fact, I say, that there is a Creator, and a hidden one, powerfully bears you on and sets you down at the very threshold of revelation, and leaves you there looking up earnestly for Divine tokens that a revelation has been made.

— Cardinal John Henry Newman, 1801 - 1890

In all faces is shown the Face of faces, veiled and in a riddle. Howbeit, unveiled it is not seen, until, above all faces, a man enter into a certain secret and mystic silence, where there is no knowing or concept of a face. This mist, cloud, darkness or ignorance, into which he that seeketh thy Face entereth, when he goeth beyond all knowledge or concept, is the state below which thy Face cannot be found, except veiled; but that very darkness revealeth thy Face to be there beyond all veils. Hence I observe how needful it is for me to enter into the darkness and to admit the coincidence of opposites, beyond all the grasp of reason, and there to seek the Truth, where impossibility meeteth us.

—Nicholas of Cusa, 1401-1464

In this world God is neither entirely immanent nor entirely transcendent. He is both; but on the psychic plane neither His immanence nor His transcendence is fully known. In the spiritual world He is fully known as the supreme Reality; but this Reality, in order to be knowable, must contain some inner differentiations. In perfect knowledge, subject and object correspond perfectly to each other; they do not annihilate each other. It is precisely this recognition of a unity in duality as the condition of all existence which has led metaphysicians to postulate an absolute unity beyond existence. This Plotinus calls the One, Eckhart the Godhead. In considering cosmological problems I do not think we need speculate on the nature of this ineffable Being, of whom nothing positive can be predicated without contradiction. . . .

God is both in us and out of us; He is both immanent and transcendent. There can be no fundamental contradiction between God as known to philosophic thought and God as known to personal devotion. In philosophy we seek to know God and to honour Him through our intelligence; in devotion we approach Him through love and adoration. We have ample warrant for confidence that neither quest is in vain.

— W. R. Inge, 1860-1952

The more we understand individual things, the more we understand God.

— Baruch Spinoza, 1632-1677

My home
The shimmery-bounded glare,
The gazing fire-hung dome
Of scorching air.

My rest
To wander trembling-weak,
On vague hunger-quest
New hope to seek.

For friend
The dazzling breathing dream,
The strength at last to find
Of Glory Supreme.

— ANONYMOUS

CHAPTER THREE

The Heart Doth Need a Language

In the tablet of the universe there is no letter save Thy Name,
By what name, then, shall we invoke Thee?

— JAMI, 1414-1492

· I ·

GOD IS above the sphere of our esteem,
And is the best known, not defining Him.

— ROBERT HERRICK, 1591-1674

He cannot be seen: for He is too bright to look upon: nor comprehended: for He is too pure to be touched: nor measured: for He is wholly beyond the reach of the senses, infinite, immense, measurable by Himself alone. Our hearts are too small for any understanding of Him, and therefore we measure Him only when we say He is immeasurable. He who believes he has knowledge of God's greatness only diminishes it; he who would not diminish it, knows it not.

Seek no name for God: God is His name. When we attempt to

distinguish people from the mass, then we need vocabularies and titles, marks of distinction; but God, who alone is, is wholly summed in the name of God. If we should call Him "Father," then we introduce ideas of the flesh; and if we call Him "King" we reduce Him to the level of this world; and should we call Him "Lord," then we might believe He was mortal. But put away the list of names, and then you will see Him in His brightness.

— MARCUS MINUCIUS FELIX, third century

Why dost thou prate of God? Whatever thou sayest of Him is untrue.

— MEISTER ECKHART, 1260? - ? 1327

With the people, and especially with the clergymen, who have Him daily upon their tongues, God becomes a phrase, a mere name, which they utter without any accompanying idea. But if they were penetrated with His greatness, they would rather be dumb, and for very reverence would not dare to name Him.

— JOHANN WOLFGANG VON GOETHE, 1749-1832

Thinking about God begins at the mind's rugged shore, where the murmur breaks off abruptly, where we do not know any more how to yearn, how to be in awe. Only those who know how to live spiritually on edge will be able to go beyond the shore without longing for the certainties established on the artificial rock of our speculation.

Not theoretical speculation but the sense of the ineffable precipitates the problem of all problems. Not the apparent but the hidden in the apparent; not the wisdom but the mystery of the design of the universe; the questions we do not know how to ask have always poured oil on the flames of man's anxiety. Religion begins with the sense of the ineffable, with the awareness of a reality that discredits our wisdom, that shatters our concepts. . . .

The awareness of the ineffable is that with which our search must begin. Philosophy, enticed by the promise of the known, has often surrendered the treasures of higher incomprehension to poets and mystics, although without the sense of the ineffable there are no metaphysical problems, no awareness of being as being, of value as value.

The search of reason ends at the shore of the known; on the immense expanse beyond it only the sense of the ineffable can glide. It alone knows the route to that which is remote from experience and understanding. Neither of them is amphibious: reason cannot go beyond the shore, and the sense of the ineffable is out of place where we measure, where we weigh.

We do not leave the shore of the known in search of adventure or suspense or because of the failure of reason to answer our questions. We sail because our mind is like a fantastic sea shell, and when applying our ear to its lips we hear a perpetual murmur from the waves beyond the shore.

Citizens of two realms, we all must sustain a dual allegiance: we sense the ineffable in one realm, we name and exploit reality in another. Between the two we set up a system of references, but we can never fill the gap. They are as far and as close to each other as time and calendar, as violin and melody, as life and what lies beyond the last breath.

The tangible phenomena we scrutinize with our reason, the sacred and indemonstrable we overhear with the sense of the ineffable. The force that inspires readiness for self-sacrifice, the thoughts that breed humility within and behind the mind, are not identical with the logician's craftsmanship. The purity of which we never cease to dream, the untold things we insatiably love, the vision of the good for which we either die or perish alive—no reason can bound. It is the ineffable from which we draw the taste of the sacred, the joy of the imperishable. . . .

It is the sense of the sublime that we have to regard as the root of man's creative activities in art, thought and noble living. Just as no flora has ever fully displayed the hidden vitality of the earth, so has no work of art ever brought to expression the depth of the unutterable, in the sight of which the souls of saints, poets and philosophers live. The attempt to convey what we see and cannot say is the everlasting theme of mankind's unfinished symphony, a venture in which adequacy is never achieved. Only those who live on borrowed words believe in their gift of expression. A sensitive person knows that the intrinsic, the most essential, is never expressed. Most—and often the best—of what goes on in us is our own secret; we have to wrestle with it ourselves. The stirring in our hearts when watching the star-studded sky is something no language can declare.

What smites us with unquenchable amazement is not that which we grasp and are able to convey but that which lies within our reach but beyond our grasp; not the quantitative aspect of nature but something qualitative; not what is beyond our range in time and space but the true meaning, source and end of being, in other words, the ineffable. . . .

The ineffable inhabits the magnificent and the common, the grandiose and the tiny facts of reality alike. Some people sense this quality at distant intervals in extraordinary events; others sense it in the ordinary events, in every fold, in every nook; day after day, hour after hour. To them things are bereft of triteness; to them being does not mate with non-sense. They hear the stillness that crowds the world in spite of our noise, in spite of our greed. Slight and simple as things may be—a piece of paper, a morsel of bread, a word, a sigh—they hide and guard a never-ending secret: A glimpse of God? Kinship with the spirit of being? An eternal flash of a will?

Part company with preconceived notions, suppress your leaning to reiterate and to know in advance of your seeing, try to see the world for the first time with eyes not dimmed by memory or volition, and you will detect that you and the things that surround you —trees, birds, chairs—are like parallel lines that run close and never meet. Your pretense of being acquainted with the world is quickly abandoned.

How do we seek to apprehend the world? Intelligence inquires into the nature of reality, and, since it cannot work without its tools, takes those phenomena that appear to fit its categories as answers to its inquiry. Yet, when trying to hold an interview with reality face to face, without the aid of either words or concepts, we realize that what is intelligible to our mind is but a thin surface of the profoundly undisclosed, a ripple of inveterate silence that remains immune to curiosity and inquisitiveness like distant foliage in the dusk.

— ABRAHAM JOSHUA HESCHEL, 1907-

In many forms we try
To utter God's infinity,
But the boundless hath no form,
And the Universal Friend
Doth as far transcend
An angel as a worm.

The great Idea baffles wit,
Language falters under it,
It leaves the learned in the lurch;
No art, nor power, nor toil can find
The measure of the eternal Mind,
Nor hymn, nor prayer, nor church.

— RALPH WALDO EMERSON, 1803-1882

Those who live in God do not care to define. They have a peculiar confidence in the universe, a profound and peaceful acceptance of life in all its sides. Their response to ultimate Reality is not capable of a clear-cut, easily intelligible formulation. The mystery of God's being cannot be rationally determined. It remains outside the scope of logical concepts. Its form does not lie in the field of vision, none can see it with the eye. There is no equal to it. An austere silence is more adequate to the experience of God than elaborate descriptions.

— SIR SARVEPALLI RADHAKRISHNAN, 1888-

The statement that God is being-itself is a nonsymbolic statement. It does not point beyond itself. It means what it says directly and properly, . . . namely, that God is being-itself or the absolute.

However, after this has been said, nothing else can be said about God as God which is not symbolic. . . . God as being-itself is the ground of the ontological structure of being without being subject to this structure himself. He *is* the structure; that is, He has the power of determining the structure of everything that has being. Therefore, if anything beyond this bare assertion is said about God, it no longer is a direct and proper statement, no longer a concept. It is indirect, and it points to something beyond itself. In a word, it is symbolic. . . .

Special emphasis must be laid on the insight that symbol and sign are different; that, while the sign bears no necessary relation to that to which it points, the symbol participates in the reality of that for which it stands. The sign can be changed arbitrarily according to the demands of expediency, but the symbol grows and dies according to the correlation between that which is symbolized and the persons who receive it as a symbol. Therefore, the religious symbol, the symbol which points to the divine, can be a true symbol only if it participates in the power of the divine to which it points. . . .

The crucial question must now be faced. Can a segment of finite reality become the basis for an assertion about that which is infinite? The answer is that it can, because that which is infinite is being-itself and because everything participates in being-itself. . . .

Religious symbols are double-edged. They are directed toward the infinite which they symbolize *and* toward the finite through which they symbolize it. They force the infinite down to finitude and the finite up to infinity. They open the divine for the human and the human for the divine. For instance, if God is symbolized as "Father," he is brought down to the human relationship of father and child. But at the same time this human relationship is consecrated into a pattern for the divine-human relationship. If "Father" is employed as a symbol for God, fatherhood is seen in its theonomous, sacramental depth. One cannot arbitrarily "make" a religious symbol out of a segment of secular reality. Not even the collective unconscious, the great symbol-creating source, can do this. If a segment of reality is used as a symbol for God, the realm of reality from which it is taken is, so to speak, elevated into the realm of the holy. It no longer is secular. It is theonomous. If God is called the "king," something is said not only about God but also about the holy character of kinghood. If God's work is called "making whole" or "healing," this not only says something about God but also emphasizes the theonomous character of all healing. If God's self-manifestation is called "the word," this not only symbolizes God's relation to man but also emphasizes the holiness of all words as an expression of the spirit.

The truth of a religious symbol has nothing to do with the truth of the empirical assertions involved in it, be they physical, psychological, or historical. A religious symbol possesses some truth if it adequately expresses the correlation of revelation in which some person stands. A religious symbol *is* true if it adequately expresses the correlation of some person with final revelation. A religious symbol can die only if the correlation of which it is an adequate expression dies. This occurs whenever the revelatory situation changes and former symbols become obsolete. The history of religion, right up to our own time, is full of dead symbols which have been killed not by a scientific criticism of assumed superstitions but by a religious criticism of religion. The judgment that a religious symbol *is* true is identical with the judgment that the revelation of

which it is the adequate expression is true. This double meaning of
the truth of a symbol must be kept in mind. A symbol *has* truth: it is
adequate to the revelation it expresses. A symbol *is* true: it is the
expression of a true revelation.

—PAUL TILLICH, 1886-

Though we speak many words, still we shall not exhaust it. He is
the essence of all thoughts, the All.

— SIRACH

Any effort to visualize God reveals a surprising childishness. We
can no more conceive Him than we can conceive an electron. We
forget that this incapacity is not, in itself, a proof of non-existence.
We are in the habit of juggling nowadays with electrons, protons,
neutrons, etc. Individually, they are rigorously inconceivable and
physicists, who inspire as much confidence today as did the priests in
the past, affirm that without these particles our material objects, the
forces we employ—in other words, our whole inorganic universe—
become incoherent and unintelligible. (Let us not forget that these
particles move in a world where time and space do not have the same
value as in ours.) Nobody questions the reality of these now familiar
though elusive and strange elements.

The agnostic and the atheist do not seem to be in the least disturbed by the fact that our entire organized, living universe becomes
incomprehensible without the hypothesis of God. Their belief in
some physical elements, of which they know very little, has all the
earmarks of an irrational faith, but they are not aware of it. Some of
them have remained slaves to a naïve verbalism. I had the proof of
this in a letter received after the publication of one of my books and
in which the writer bitterly reproached me for having substituted
the word "God" for the word "anti-chance." Now, the word "anti-
chance" cannot be entirely satisfactory to a cultivated, scientific
mind, for it simply signifies that the whole intellectual pattern which
we call our science is basically wrong and, at best, but a set of artificial rules which, by a lucky chance, enables us to foresee a certain
number of events. Indeed, as we have seen, modern science rests ultimately on statistical concepts and the calculus of probabilities. These
laws postulate the completely disordered distribution of the con-
stitutive elements of our universe. If we admit the possibility of an

anti-chance in a part of this universe (the living world which has led to thought), the whole edifice crumbles unless we concede that Life obeys different laws. In either case, this is tantamount to accepting an irrational influence, foreign to our physical universe, as the determining factor in living and evolutive phenomena.

It matters little what name we give this influence. Today the study of life and evolution forces us to recognize that its action is logically required and has apparently always manifested itself in a "forbidden," ascensional direction finally to end in the thought and conscience of man. We, therefore, see no reason for not giving this cause, which perturbs our intellectual pastimes and our ideas, the name men have given since time immemorial to all the causes which escaped them, causes exacted, but not explained, by our intelligence.

The idea of God is a pure idea, like the idea of force, or of energy, and does not need to be visualized; nor can it be. It develops either spontaneously through intuition, unworded and irrational, and is then called revelation; or else it emerges rationally from the contradictions observed between the homogeneous but tentative pattern proposed by science and objective reality which made the construction of this scheme possible.

—PIERRE LECOMTE DU NOÜY, 1883-1947

· II ·

It is the heart that senses God, and not the reason. That is what faith is, God perceptible to the heart and not to reason.

—BLAISE PASCAL, 1623-1662

That which we dare invoke to bless;
 Our dearest faith; our ghastliest doubt;
 He, They, One, All; within, without;
The Power in darkness Whom we guess.

I found Him not in world or sun,
 Or eagle's wing, or insect's eye;
 Nor through the questions men may try,
The petty cobwebs we have spun.

If e'er when faith had fallen asleep,
 I heard a voice "Believe no more"
 And heard an ever-breaking shore
That tumbled in the Godless deep;

A warmth within the breast would melt
The freezing reason's colder part,
And like a man in wrath the heart
Stood up and answer'd "I have felt."

— ALFRED, LORD TENNYSON, 1809-1892

With partridges, it often occurs that some steal the eggs of others, in order to brood . . . and it is a strange but nevertheless well-attested fact that when the chick hatched and nourished under the wing of the thievish partridge first hears the cry of the true mother . . . it forthwith quits its thievish partridge, and hurries to meet and follow its own parent, drawn by its correspondence with her, which had remained hidden and as though sleeping in the depths of its nature, until the encounter of each with each . . . Thus it is with our heart, for although hatched, nourished, and brought up among things temporal, low and transitory, and, so to speak, under the wings of nature, yet at the first look it casts towards God, at the first consciousness inspired by Him, the natural inborn inclination to love Him, slumbering and imperceptible till now, awakes in an instant unawares, as a spark among ashes, and affecting the will, gives it an impulse of the supreme love due to the Sovereign and First Principle of all things.

— ST. FRANCIS OF SALES, 1567-1622

What can man accomplish that is worth speaking of, either in life or in art, that does not arise in his own self from the influence of this sense for the infinite? Without it, how can anyone wish to comprehend the world scientifically, or if, in some distinct talent, the knowledge is thrust upon him, how should he wish to exercise it? What is all science, if not the existence of things in you, in your reason? What is all art and culture if not your existence in the things to which you give measure, form, and order? And how can both come to life in you except in so far as there lives immediately in you the eternal unity of Reason and Nature, the universal existence of all finite things in the Infinite?

— FRIEDRICH SCHLEIERMACHER, 1768-1834

Ah woe is me!
What have I dared? where am I lifted? how
Shall I descend, and perish not? I know
That love makes all things equal: I have heard
By mine own heart this joyous truth averred,—
The spirit of the worm beneath the sod,
In love and worship, blends itself with God.

—PERCY BYSSHE SHELLEY, 1792-1822

Religion is an experience of kinship with the Deepest Reality in the Universe and hence of membership in an infinitely meaningful world and of sharing in an ever unfolding life. . . .

Religion, in one of its chief aspects, is the enhancement of life. It is enthusiasm, the heightening of the vital energies. It is vision, in which larger realities swing into view and new and abiding truths are discovered. It is freedom, through which dormant powers are awakened, deadlocked energies are released, and mind and heart expand to a fuller functioning. It is community-building, making men members one of another or lifting a merely natural solidarity upward toward a more articulate and spiritual community life. Religion can bring men into warm, living relation with a cosmic creative Spirit and so can infuse with poetry and passion the pursuit of the most distant ideals and can inspire men with unswerving purpose for their achievement. . . .

Religion is more than a single mood, or a simple reaction, or an attitude controlled by a single idea. It is, rather, a fusion of certain persistent traits of human experience. It is blended out of experiences of kinship, of inner power, of gaining insight and integrity, and of wonder. This blending is itself variable, different traits being at different times either dominant or recessive. . . . Religion is by no means bound to result in a single world-view, or a single attitude toward man's inner experience or social life. But the fusion or blending is real nevertheless, for it yields a distinctive form of human experience—that of kinship with Ultimate Reality and hence of membership and participation in an infinitely meaningful world. And in this form of experience all the traits which have been pointed out are, explicitly or implicitly, present. Without inner power, insight, and integrity no real participation in a meaningful world is possible, and without kinship and a vista of meaning stimulative of wonder the traits which make for individual participation will not be developed. . . .

Religion supplies the supreme interests which give direction to the interpretive quest—the interests concerning the Ground, the Goal, and the Way of life. Religion affords a wealth of data relevant to these interests through its history, its great personalities, and its classic literatures. And religion, in its worship, its meditation, and its communion, secures the brooding upon the meaning of experience from which fresh and significant intuitions may come. . . .

Religion fosters that functioning of the total self from which alone come synthetic intuitions that may prove to be genuine discernings of the deeper reality and meaning of the universe. Religion . . . is an experience which makes for inner integrity. It summons men to singleness of mind and of heart. It calls upon them to seek first the kingdom of God and His righteousness. And as it grows, it gathers around the central thought, motive, and purpose already achieved all the other interests and experiences of a person's life. Thus religion makes for wholeness of life, for peace, and for power. And these fruits of religion condition also its capacity to gain insight. The more the whole self enters into the mental quest, so much the more are we able to transcend partial and specific knowings and valuings and find a deeper and more meaningful wholeness in cosmic reality.

— EUGENE WILLIAM LYMAN, 1872-1948

Two went to pray? O rather say,
One went to brag, th' other to pray:

One stands up close and treads on high,
Where th' other dares not lend his eye.

One nearer to God's altar trod,
The other to the altar's God.

— RICHARD CRASHAW, 1613?-1649

In one salutation to Thee, my God, let all my senses spread out and touch this world at Thy feet.

Like a rain-cloud of July hung low with its burden of unshed showers let all my mind bend down at Thy door in one salutation to Thee.

Let all my songs gather together their diverse strains into a single current and flow to a sea of silence in one salutation to Thee.

Like a flock of homesick cranes flying night and day back to their mountain nests let all my life take its voyage to its eternal home in one salutation to Thee.

— Sir Rabindranath Tagore, 1861-1941

In proportion as you talk to Him He will talk to you; and often you should be silent and let Him speak, so that you may listen in the stillness of your heart.

— François Fénelon, 1651-1715

The heavens, the earth, the plant, the human frame, now that they are explored by science, speak of God as they never did before. His handwriting is brought out where former ages saw but a blank. Our nature is perpetually developing new senses for the perception and enjoyment of God. The human race, as it advances, does not leave religion behind it, as it leaves the shelter of caves and forests; does not outgrow faith, does not see it fading like the mist before its rising intelligence. On the contrary, religion opens before the improved mind in new grandeur. The soul, in proportion as it enlarges its faculties and refines its affections, possesses and discerns within itself a more and more glorious type of the Divinity, learns his spirituality in its own spiritual powers, and offers him a profounder and more inward worship.

Thus deep is the foundation of worship in human nature. Men may assail it, may reason against it; but sooner can the laws of the outward universe be repealed by human will, sooner can the sun be plucked from his sphere, than the idea of God can be erased from the human spirit, and His worship banished from the earth. All other wants of man are superficial. His animal wants are but for a day, and are to cease with the body. The profoundest of all human wants is the want of God.

— William Ellery Channing, 1780-1842

Man makes God in his own image. It is indeed because he is in part divine that he knows there is a God at all. To know it is to know something that is true, and therefore it is rightly said that there is "truth in all religions."

As we move upward in the scale, our idea of God is proportionately exalted. We learn to know him better. Still, we know him only as we are capable of knowing him and still, inevitably, make him in our own image. Herbert Spencer, the Positivist, observed with something of a sneer that, if a triangle could think, it would think that God was triangular. Undoubtedly—but the sneer is gratuitous. If God exists and triangles exist, then triangularity must be included in the Godhead which created them. So, when man believes that God is Personal, he believes rightly. How could Personality exist if God had not created it? And how could God create what he had not in himself? To say that God is "a Person" is no doubt an error; to say that his Being includes Personality must be true.

In the temples of Shintoism there are no images of God. High up on the wall, but tilted so that the worshiper, looking upward, sees himself reflected in it, there is a looking glass. A Shinto priest explained this to me by saying that no believer can see more of the Godhead than is already in his heart; the mirror in which he sees only himself reminds him of this. Is it not the counterpart of our Master's teaching, when he said, "Blessed are the pure in heart: for they shall see God"?

— MAUDE ROYDEN, 1876-

· III ·

Religion is an intercourse, a conscious and voluntary relation, entered into by a soul in distress with the mysterious power upon which it feels itself to depend, and upon which its fate is contingent. This intercourse with God is realized by prayer. Prayer is religion in act; that is, prayer is real religion. It is prayer that distinguishes the religious phenomena from such similar or neighboring phenomena as purely moral or æsthetic sentiment. Religion is nothing if it be not the vital act by which the entire mind seeks to save itself by clinging to the principle from which it draws its life. This act is prayer, by which term I understand no vain exercise of words, no mere repetition of certain sacred formulæ, but the very movement itself of the soul, putting itself in a personal relation of contact with the mysterious power of which it feels the presence,—it may be even before it has a name by which to call it. Wherever this interior prayer is lacking, there is no religion; wherever, on the other hand, this prayer rises and stirs the soul, even in the absence of forms or of doctrines, we have living religion. One sees from this why "natural religion," so-called, is not properly a religion. It cuts man off from prayer. It leaves him and God in mutual remoteness, with no intimate commerce, no interior dialogue, no interchange, no action of God in man, no return of man to God. At bottom this pretended religion is only a philosophy. Born at epochs of rationalism, of critical investigations, it never was anything but an abstraction. An artificial and dead creation, it reveals to its examiner hardly one of the characters proper to religion.

— AUGUSTE SABATIER, 1839-1901

Jesus . . . taught them, saying:
"And when thou prayest, thou shalt not be as the hypocrites are:
For they love to pray standing in the synagogues and in the corners of the streets, that they may be seen of men.
Verily I say unto you, They have their reward.
But thou, when thou prayest, enter into thy closet, and when thou hast shut thy door, pray to thy Father which is in secret;
And thy Father which seeth in secret shall reward thee openly.
But when ye pray, use not vain repetitions, as the heathen do:
For they think that they shall be heard for their much speaking.
Be not ye therefore like unto them:
For your Father knoweth what things ye have need of, before ye ask Him."

— THE BIBLE, Matthew 6:5-8

He who prays must address God as though he were in His presence; inasmuch as the Lord is everywhere, in every place, in every man, and especially in the soul of the just. Therefore let us not seek God on earth, nor in heaven, nor elsewhere; rather let us seek Him in our own heart, like unto the prophet that sayeth, "I will hearken unto that which the Lord shall say in me." In prayer a man may take heed to his words, and this is a wholly material thing; he may take heed to the sense of his words, and this is rather study than prayer; finally, he may fix his thoughts on God, and this is the only true prayer. We must consider neither the words nor the sentences, but lift our soul above our self, and almost lose self in the thought of God. This state once attained, the believer forgets the world and worldly desires, and has, as it were, a foreshadowing of heavenly bliss. To this height it is as easy for the ignorant as for the learned to rise. Words, in fact, are not essential to prayer; on the contrary,

when man is truly rapt in the spirit of devotion, speech is an impedi-
ment, and should be replaced by mental prayer. Thus it is seen how
great is the error of those that prescribe a fixed number of orations.
The Lord taketh not joy in a multitude of words, but rather in a
fervent spirit.

— GIROLAMO SAVONAROLA, 1452-1498

*Prayer is, therefore, a living communion of the religious man with
God, conceived as personal and present in experience, a communion
which reflects the forms of the social relations of humanity.* This is
prayer in essence. It is only imperfectly realized in the subordinate
types of prayer. In ritual prayer, cultual hymn, in liturgical prayer,
as in prayer regulated by law and deemed a thing in itself meritorious,
the experience of the Divine presence is, for the most part, weak and
shadowy. Here we have prayer as a more or less external action, not
as an inner contact of the heart with God. But also in the philosophical ideal of prayer and in certain forms of mystical communion,
we can discern but faintly the essence of prayer. If we are to distinguish clearly between the religious experiences and states of mind
related to prayer, which play an important part in the religion of
philosophers and mystics, and prayer itself considered simply from
the point of view which makes it to be prayer, some elucidation of
what we mean by "adoration" and "devotion" is necessary.

Adoration (or reverent contemplation) and devotion are absolutely necessary elements in religious experience. Both terms stand
for conceptions much wider than that of prayer; both denote religious experiences and states, the nature of which is obviously different from that of prayer; nay, we may go further and say that
they comprehend psychical events and experiences which belong to
the "secular," not to the strictly religious realm, or are on the
borderland of both.

Adoration is the solemn contemplation of the "Holy One" as the
highest Good, unreserved surrender to Him, a mingling of one's
being with His. We see this even in the religious life of primitive
peoples. The awe which primitive man evinces by speech and gesture as he stands in the presence of a "holy object," that is, an object
filled with supernatural and magical power, is "adoration," although
in a crude and imperfect fashion. The "holy" object has for him
ideal worth: yes, even supreme value in the moment when, overcome by awe and wonder, he sinks in the dust before it. But it is in

the personal experience of the poet and the mystic that we find adoration in its absolute purity and perfection. It is the soul-satisfying contemplation of the highest good, the very climax of mystical prayer: it is the unreserved losing of one's self in the glory of Nature as seen in the sacred poetry of ancient peoples and in the aesthetic mysticism of modern poets. Compared with it primitive ceremonial adoration is but a preliminary form. Now, a personal God can be the object of this adoration, just as He is the object of prayer. The God whom primitive man worships is an anthropomorphic being; the *summum bonum* of a mysticism centering in a personal God shows the traits of a spiritual personality. But the note of personality is by no means essential to the object of adoration. Primitive cults knew not only spiritual being made after man's image, but also lifeless objects which being "holy," that is, as *mana* and *tabu*, lay claim to worship. Moreover, the object in which the poetic spirit sinks in an ecstasy of adoration, is not personal: it is the life-giving sun, creative and nurturing Mother Nature, the Alone and the Infinite as revealed in the beautiful. There is, nevertheless, something that is beyond experience, something which shines through Nature as through a translucent medium. Just as the God whom the worshipper invokes, is felt to be palpably near and immediately present, so also the object of adoration which the pious spirit regards with awe is felt to be equally near and present. The relation to God into which he who prays enters, resembles in its intimacy the relation which subsists between the adoring person and the object of his adoration.

Religious persons and students of religion agree in testifying that prayer is the centre of religion, the soul of all piety. The definition of the essence of prayer explains this testimony; prayer is a living communion of man with God. Prayer brings man into direct touch with God, into a personal relation with Him. Without prayer faith remains a theoretical conviction; worship is only an external and formal act; moral action is without spiritual depth; man remains at a distance from God; an abyss yawns between the finite and the Infinite. "God is in heaven and thou art on the earth." "We cannot come to God," says Luther, "except through prayer alone, for He is too high above us." In prayer man rises to heaven, heaven sinks to earth, the veil between the visible and the invisible is torn asunder, man comes before God to speak with Him about his soul's welfare and salvation. "Prayer," says Mechthild of Magdeburg, "draws the great God down into a small heart; it drives the hungry soul up to God in His fullness." Similarly Johann Arndt says: "In prayer the highest and the lowest come together, the lowliest heart and the most exalted God."

As the mysterious linking of man with the Eternal, prayer is an incomprehensible wonder, a miracle of miracles which is daily brought to pass in the devout soul. The historian and psychologist of religion can only be a spectator and interpreter of that deep and powerful life which is unveiled in prayer: only the religious man can penetrate the mystery. But in the final analysis scientific inquiry stands under the same overwhelming impression as living religion. It is compelled to agree with the confession of Chrysostom: "There is nothing more powerful than prayer and there is nothing to be compared with it."

Every prayer is a turning of man to another Being to whom he inwardly opens his heart; it is the speech of an "I" to a "Thou."

— FRIEDRICH HEILER, 1892-

· IV ·

It will be the glory of our generation if we shall succeed in founding a human religion, a pure faith, a pure religious spirit, born of thought, but of a thought embodying life and fertile of new life.

At the present time we are witnessing the travail that presages the birth of such a religion; and in those painful throes we all are having our share. The old mythologies vigorously reassert themselves from time to time; and they provoke anew the negative, irreligious criticism which fulfilled so necessary a function in the past. Against the sterility and the violence and the prejudice of the mythologies rise the sterility, the violence, and the prejudice of the improvised anti-religions of a rationalistic, intellectualistic, or utilitarian character. But in spite of everything, man will have his God again, the God that is worthy of man's new estate. For without religion, that is to say, without poetry, without heroism, without a consciousness of universality, without harmony, without the aristocratic spirit, no society can endure. And human society is determined to endure.

— BENEDETTO CROCE, 1866-1952

Now, even though the realms of religion and science in themselves are clearly marked off from each other, nevertheless there exist between the two strong reciprocal relationships and dependencies. Though religion may be that which determines the goal, it has, nevertheless, learned from science, in the broadest sense, what means will contribute to the attainment of the goals it has set up. But science can only be created by those who are thoroughly imbued with the aspiration towards truth and understanding. This source of feeling, however, springs from the sphere of religion. To this there also belongs the faith in the possibility that the regulations valid for the world of existence are rational, that is, comprehensible to reason. I cannot conceive of a genuine scientist without that profound faith. The situation may be expressed by an image: Science without religion is lame, religion without science is blind.

Though I have asserted above that in truth a legitimate conflict between religion and science cannot exist I must nevertheless qualify this assertion once again on an essential point, with reference to the actual content of historical religions. This qualification has to do with the concept of God. During the youthful period of mankind's spiritual evolution human fantasy created gods in man's own image, who, by the operations of their will were supposed to determine, or at any rate to influence the phenomenal world. Man sought to alter the disposition of these gods in his own favor by means of magic and prayer. The idea of God in the religions taught at present is a sublimation of that old conception of the gods. Its anthropomorphic character is shown, for instance, by the fact that men appeal to the Divine Being in prayers and plead for the fulfilment of their wishes.

Nobody, certainly, will deny that the idea of the existence of an omnipotent, just and omnibeneficent personal God is able to accord man solace, help, and guidance; also, by virtue of its simplicity it is accessible to the most undeveloped mind. But, on the other hand, there are decisive weaknesses attached to this idea in itself, which have been painfully felt since the beginning of history. That is, if this being is omnipotent then every occurrence, including every human action, every human thought, and every human feeling and aspiration is also His work; how is it possible to think of holding men responsible for their deeds and thoughts before such an almighty Being? In giving out punishment and rewards He would to a certain extent be passing judgment on Himself. How can this be combined with the goodness and righteousness ascribed to Him?

The main source of the present-day conflicts between the spheres of religion and of science lies in this concept of a personal God. It is the aim of science to establish general rules which determine the reciprocal connection of objects and events in time and space. For these rules, or laws of nature, absolutely general validity is required

—not proven. It is mainly a program, and faith in the possibility of its accomplishment in principle is only founded on partial successes. But hardly anyone could be found who would deny these partial successes and ascribe them to human self-deception. The fact that on the basis of such laws we are able to predict the temporal behavior of phenomena in certain domains with great precision and certainty is deeply embedded in the consciousness of the modern man, even though he may have grasped very little of the contents of those laws. He need only consider that planetary courses within the solar system may be calculated in advance with great exactitude on the basis of a limited number of simple laws. In a similar way, though not with the same precision, it is possible to calculate in advance the mode of operation of an electric motor, a transmission system, or of a wireless apparatus, even when dealing with a novel development.

To be sure, when the number of factors coming into play in a phenomenological complex is too large scientific method in most cases fails us. One need only think of the weather, in which case prediction even for a few days ahead is impossible. Nevertheless no one doubts that we are confronted with a causal connection whose causal components are in the main known to us. Occurrences in this domain are beyond the reach of exact prediction because of the variety of factors in operation, not because of any lack of order in nature.

We have penetrated far less deeply into the regularities obtaining within the realm of living things, but deeply enough nevertheless to sense at least the rule of fixed necessity. One need only think of the systematic order in heredity, and in the effect of poisons, as for instance alcohol, on the behavior of organic beings. What is still lacking here is a grasp of connections of profound generality, but not a knowledge of order in itself.

The more a man is imbued with the ordered regularity of all events the firmer becomes his conviction that there is no room left by the side of this ordered regularity for causes of a different nature. For him neither the rule of human nor the rule of divine will exists as an independent cause of natural events. To be sure, the doctrine of a personal God interfering with natural events could never be *refuted,* in the real sense, by science, for this doctrine can always take refuge in those domains in which scientific knowledge has not yet been able to set foot.

But I am persuaded that such behavior on the part of the representatives of religion would not only be unworthy but also fatal.

For a doctrine which is able to maintain itself not in clear light but only in the dark, will of necessity lose its effect on mankind, with incalculable harm to human progress. In their struggle for the ethical good, teachers of religion must have the stature to give up the doctrine of a personal God, that is, give up that source of fear and hope which in the past placed such vast power in the hands of priests. In their labors they will have to avail themselves of those forces which are capable of cultivating the Good, the True, and the Beautiful in humanity itself. This is, to be sure, a more difficult but an incomparably more worthy task. After religious teachers accomplish the refining process indicated they will surely recognize with joy that true religion has been ennobled and made more profound by scientific knowledge.

If it is one of the goals of religion to liberate mankind as far as possible from the bondage of egocentric cravings, desires, and fears, scientific reasoning can aid religion in yet another sense. Although it is true that it is the goal of science to discover rules which permit the association and foretelling of facts, this is not its only aim. It also seeks to reduce the connections discovered to the smallest possible number of mutually independent conceptual elements. It is in this striving after the rational unification of the manifold that it encounters its greatest successes, even though it is precisely this attempt which causes it to run the greatest risk of falling a prey to illusions. But whoever has undergone the intense experience of successful advances made in this domain, is moved by profound reverence for the rationality made manifest in existence. By way of the understanding he achieves a far-reaching emancipation from the shackles of personal hopes and desires, and thereby attains that humble attitude of mind towards the grandeur of reason incarnate in existence, and which, in its profoundest depths, is inaccessible to man. This attitude, however, appears to me to be religious, in the highest sense of the word. And so it seems to me that science not only purifies the religious impulse of the dross of its anthropomorphism but also contributes to a religious spiritualization of our understanding of life.

— ALBERT EINSTEIN, 1880-

Religion, as I shall here define it, is a body of intuitions and working beliefs that issue out of that part of man's nature and experience which science, deliberately seeking piecemeal knowledge of an immediately verifiable nature, rejects. For the questions that religion asks are not concerned with particulars but with the whole: not specific questions as to What and How? but questions of the widest generality and the most teasing elusiveness: Why? Wherefore? For what purpose? Toward what end? Religion seeks, in other words, not a detailed causal explanation of this or that aspect of life, but a reasonable account of the entire sum of things.

All the transient phenomena of life and civilization and the human personality religion sets against the cosmic perspectives of time and space. The concepts of infinity and eternity, which are not verifiable by piecemeal observation, have been the very core of the higher religious consciousness: so at a period in culture when the scientific mind was still bogged in the materialism of the four elements, earth, air, fire, and water, a Pythagoras or a Plato sought to deduce from harmonic mathematical relationships a clue to a deeper pattern of order. In its widest reaches, religion concerns itself with the impenetrable substratum of reality; with what, from the standpoint of science, is unknowable: the *mysterium tremendum*.

In terms of positive science, most of the questions religion puts are unanswerable questions; and for the conventional scientist, still imprisoned in a partial, mechanistic ideology, they represent illusory problems. The very vocabulary of religion is regarded by many scientists as nonsense, because it cannot be turned into the Basic English of operationalism. So much the worse, then, for the limitations of the scientific method: primitive tribes and little children, who dare ask the same unanswerable questions, are in practice wiser, for they are not inhibited in their concern with the whole, and are not embarrassed in the free utterance of their bafflements, their forebodings, their hopes. . . .

We shall never get to the bottom of man's nature and his present dilemmas, unless we realize that he is, to begin with, the kind of creature who has persistently asked such ultimate questions about himself and the universe: indeed he is so thirsty for this order of truth that he will swallow it in almost any degree of dilution or adulteration. And so far, let us confess, those questions are wiser than all the answers. From the beginning man views life, above all his own life, with a mixture of curiosity, humility, and wonder: he claims the Unknown as his province and the Unknowable as his object, for the reason that he realizes that the true condition of man is "beyond him," and that the fate of man is not entirely in his own hands.

Man's answers to these mysteries were bound by the very terms of his own finite nature to be inadequate. However penetrating his vision, whatever man finds out about the all-enveloping world must be only so much of it as he can encompass within his person and culture: an infinitesimal sample in space and time. Almost certainly, his sense of the whole came forth at only a late date in his evolution and is plainly one of his most fragile and imperfect achievements. Yet each one of us, in some degree, resonates to the world as a whole, and picks up and transforms waves that come from distant transmitting stations: we hear their noise in our receivers, perhaps, long before we have learned the code or are able to spell out any part of the message. But because man has sought to project himself beyond the here and now, because he has been willing to traffic with the inactual, the unknown, the mysterious, he has had a better grasp of cosmic processes than a more limited, down-to-earth attitude would have given him. The little questions, for which there are definite answers, have an important practical function: yet it is only within the larger frame that they are fully significant. Nothing can be settled until everything is settled. The first step in the re-education of man is for him to come to terms with his ultimate destiny.

Each culture has developed its own way of putting these ultimate questions about man's nature and fate; and has assigned special values to the experiences symbolized as God, eternity, immortality, being and non-being. The answers to these questions differ in innumerable details; yet they all point to a common substratum of human experience which is none the less real because language is so inept and ineffectual in coping with it. Most of the more naïve conceits of theology are, to a great degree, impatient attempts to picture, in familiar terms, more obvious forms of continuity between the known and the unknown, between the immediate and the whole, the manifest and the mysterious, than the facts warrant. Yet without some recognition of the whole, the part played by earthly life would be almost as meaningless as the severed hand, in Aristotle's famous illustration, if one did not know its normal connections with the human body: the organ, by its very existence, implies the organism it serves.

Just as the anatomist, given the fragment of a human skull, can reconstruct with reasonable certainty many other characteristics of the head and even the rest of the human body, so the religious mind, repeatedly plumbing the depths of human experience, may have a faint twilight perception of the constitution of the universe itself; though no finite mind will ever grasp it fully or exhaust all its possibilities till the end of time: for time, in all its organic and human implications, is part of what must be revealed. Man's deepest needs prompt him to this exploration: the very concept of the stellar universe, as enveloping man's lifetime and persisting beyond it, came from man's deliberate attempt to give a rational account of his own appearance and acts, his birth, his ordeals, his triumphs, his frustrations, and his final dissolution.

—Lewis Mumford, 1895-

When the storms and fevers of this era are passed and modern civilization has achieved a social system which provides some basic justice compatible with the necessities of a technical age the perennial problems of humanity will emerge once more. Religious insights which seem for the moment to be inimical to moral progress and moral vigor will come into their own again. There will be unjust men in this new society of justice; and good men will feel that they are not as just as they ought to be. The perils of nature and the inhumanities of man will continue to take their toll in human life. Men's hopes will be shattered by untoward fortune; family circles will be invaded by death and widows and orphans will seek not only security from society but some faith in the meaning of life which will make the chaos of the moment bearable; good will still be turned into evil when the devotion of naïvely virtuous men is sluiced by the design of knaves and the ignorance of fools into ignoble causes and dangerous channels; men will continue in short to find the promptings of the spirit frustrated by the forces of nature within them and the hopes of the spirit shattered by the forces of nature about them. They will suffer both at the hands of nature and at the hands of man and they will find the semi-conscious cruelties of conscious men more difficult to bear than "the trampling march of unconscious power."

When these problems of man in nature and man in society are seen again as perennial problems of the human spirit, and not merely as injustices of an era, men will have to learn once more that though evil must be resisted there are limits to the possibility of resistance and some evil must be borne. The weak will cry out against the injustices of the strong and they will confront the eternal problem of how to prevent bitterness from corroding their spirit and spoiling the purity of their testimonies. Men will learn that Nature can never be completely tamed to do man's will. Her blind caprices, her storms and tempests will continue, on occasion, to brush aside man's handiwork as a housewife destroys a cobweb; and her inexorable processes will run counter to men's hopes and designs. Then men will see again the importance of accommodating the vision of perfection to an imperfect world without losing the urge to perfect the world. In order to do that they must find suggestions of meaning in chaos and glimpses of ultimate perfection within imperfection.

The inevitable imperfections of life and history will be borne with the greater serenity if the ego recognizes that the blind forces of nature which frustrate the spirit are in the self as well as outside it. . . .

Every effort to state the idea of the grace and forgiveness of God in purely rational terms suffers from the same difficulties encountered in stating the conception of the relation of God to the world. The idea of grace can be stated adequately only in mythical terms. In the mythos of Jesus the holy God reveals his holiness in terms of mercy and this mercy redeems the sinner. This redemption means that the sinner knows himself to be in the embrace of divine love in spite of his sin. The holiness of God thus creates both the consciousness of sin and the consolation which makes the consciousness of sin bearable. . . .

In classical Christianity it is suggested again and again that repentance is the beginning of redemption, even that it is synonymous with redemption. This is a profound insight; for the evils and frustrations of life and history would be, in fact, unbearable if contrition did not reduce the presumptions and pretensions of the self and reveal the fact that some of the confusions from which the spirit suffers have their direct source in the chaos of the self and that others may be regarded as punishment for the sins of the self even if they have not been obviously caused by them. The consciousness of sin in classical religion is closely related to the cynic's interpretation of human nature; but it is never purely pessimistic. Classical religious faith is always saved from despair because it knows that sin is discovered by the very faith through which men catch a glimpse of the reality of spirit. Both the heights and the depths of the world of spirit are known. The knowledge of the depths within the self saves from pride, prevents a bitter criticism of the sins of others and makes a sullen rebellion against the imperfections of nature and history impossible; the knowledge of the heights keeps profound self-knowledge from degenerating into bitter disillusionment.

These religious insights guarantee the ethically striving soul a measure of serenity and provide the spiritual relaxation without which all moral striving generates a stinking sweat of self-righteousness and an alternation of fanatic illusions and fretful disillusionments. Naturally it is not easy to preserve a decent balance between the ethical urge to realize perfection in history and the religious need of reconciliation with imperfection. In particular periods of history the one will devour the other. Sometimes the ethical urge will degenerate into an illusion-crammed ethical utopianism; at other times religious insights will betray the soul into a premature peace with and transcendence over the world's imperfections. But the human spirit will always discover in time that sanity and wholesomeness are possible only when two partially incompatible and partially supplementary attitudes toward life are both embraced and espoused. Then it will find its way back to the profound mythologies which do justice to both; and it will disavow not only the moribund religion which solves the problem of the spirit in nature by magic but also the superficial rational moralism which dreams of gaining a quick and easy victory of the spirit over nature.

— REINHOLD NIEBUHR, 1892-

It is by looking into our own nature that we first discover the failure of the physical universe to be co-extensive with our experience of reality. The "something to which truth matters" must surely have a place in reality whatever definition of reality we may adopt. In our own nature, or through the contact of our consciousness with a nature transcending ours, there are other things that claim the same kind of recognition—a sense of beauty, of morality, and finally at the root of all spiritual religion an experience which we describe as the presence of God. In suggesting that these things constitute a spiritual world I am not trying to substantialise them or objectivise them—to make them out other than we find them to be in our experience of them. But I would say that when from the human heart, perplexed with the mystery of existence, the cry goes up, "What is it all about?" it is no true answer to look only at that part of experience which comes to us through certain sensory organs and reply: "It is about atoms and chaos; it is about a universe of fiery globes rolling on to impending doom; it is about tensors and non-commutative algebra." Rather it is about a spirit in which truth has its shrine, with potentialities of self-fulfilment in its response to beauty and right. Shall I not also add that even as light and colour and sound come into our minds at the prompting of a world beyond, so these other stirrings of consciousness come from something which, whether we describe it as beyond or deep within ourselves, is greater than our own personality?

—SIR ARTHUR EDDINGTON, 1882-1944

CHAPTER FOUR

To the God Unknown

No man can succeed in life alone, and he cannot get the help he needs from men.

— An Indian Hunter

· I ·

So PAUL, standing in the middle of the Areopagus, said: "Men of Athens, I perceive that in every way you are very religious. For as I passed along, and observed the objects of your worship, I found also an altar with this inscription, 'To an unknown god.' What therefore you worship as unknown, this I proclaim to you. The God who made the world and everything in it, being Lord of heaven and earth, does not live in shrines made by man, nor is He served by human hands, as though He needed anything, since He Himself gives to all men life and breath and everything. And He made from one every nation of men to live on all the face of the earth, having determined allotted periods and the boundaries of their habitation, that they should seek God, in the hope that they might feel after Him and find Him. Yet He is not far from each one of us, for

'In him we live and move and have our being'; as even some of your poets have said,

'For we are indeed his offspring.'

Being then God's offspring, we ought not to think that the Deity is like gold, or silver, or stone, a representation by the art and imagination of man."

— The Bible, Acts 17:22-29

The revival of interest in religion derives from . . . the spiritual unease of modern man, which countless thinkers and writers have eloquently portrayed. The extraordinary development of modern theoretical science and its flowering in a many-sided technological advance, have brought men the breath-taking vision of a control of nature far greater than anything they have dared to imagine, bearing the possibility of physical well-being and ease beyond men's fondest dreams. Whoever has seen the ravages that disease, insecurity, and want have wrought upon the soul no less than upon the body of man these many centuries will not dismiss these achievements lightly as merely "material" and hence superficial. The fact is, however, that even this promise of physical welfare has not been fulfilled; it has been obscured and all but blotted out by the far more immediate peril of total annihilation inherent in the new engines of mass-destruction of the atomic age.

For with the detachment and objectivity which is essential to the scientific temper, the modern scientist has been as skilful and energetic in forging instruments for human destruction as he has been zealous in seeking a cure for poliomyelitis or cancer, and with rather greater success. This implies no criticism of science, merely of the peril involved in exalting a method into a goal, a technique into a philosophy. It is undeniable that science is man's most valuable tool for discovering all the ascertainable data which must be utilized in formulating a coherent picture of the universe. For it is clear that an acceptable philosophy of life for modern men cannot deny or ignore the verifiable conclusions of scientific research. Yet science has three basic limitations when it presumes to do duty as a philosophy of life. There is much in the world that science does not yet know or knows only imperfectly, while a world-view must reckon with the whole of life, the unknown as well as the known, the immeasurable as well as the measurable. It must grapple with chaos as well as with cosmos and teach man to face suffering and death as well as to taste the joys of life without having them turn to gall and wormwood. A valid philosophy cannot do violence to the segment of experience already included in scientific discovery, but it cannot overlook the more significant elements which science has not mastered. Nor will it do to wait, as Spencer felt he could do, for the continued progress of research to annex more and more territory from the realm of the Unknown to the empire of the Known until the hegemony of science becomes all-embracing. The neatly packaged "scientific" universe of nineteenth-century materialism has disintegrated into countless worlds of dazzling complexities; each new discovery adds to our knowledge in arithmetic progression, but to our ignorance in geometric degree. The Unknown we shall always have with us. Finally, science can help man reach his destination, if he knows where he is going; it cannot, except perhaps in negative terms, tell him what his destination ought to be. It can rule out certain ends as running counter to the realities; it cannot indicate which of several alternatives, which do not contradict the fact, is to be accepted and followed. Scientists, being human, have often sought to do so; that is their human right and duty, but then it is the man, not the scientist, who speaks. For science is concerned with the data of experience, not with the values upon which life depends, and by which experience is to be judged.

Increasingly, the erstwhile worshiper of science is realizing that his religion does not give him a basis for ethical judgment or action, or a rationale of life which will make it possible for him to face the grave material and spiritual perils of our times. Less and less is he disposed to accept the dogmatic assertion of some "philosopher of science" that whatever is not experimentally verifiable or subject to measurement is non-existent or meaningless. The thrill of technological invention having been worn thin, if only because of its frequent repetition, modern man is turning again to the quest for a worldview on the issues that are timeless—the meaning of life, the challenge of death, the purpose of suffering, the significance of the individual, his relation to society, and the goal of history.

— ROBERT GORDIS, 1908-

Hitherto God, if it means anything, has been accepted as the highest, remotest, most infinite, and final—*not* idea or conception *but*—emotional speculation of which man is capable; and to reduce God to Nature is merely to shift words about. Our minds do and always will emotionally speculate on the Unknowable, on what lies behind Nature, the Mysterious and Miraculous Adjustment conditioning all things. We shall never know, never find out, and this it is which constitutes the "glory and poetry of God," just as the poetry and glory of our lives is that we do not know from moment to moment what is coming.

— JOHN GALSWORTHY, 1867-1933

There is an indefinable mysterious Power that pervades everything. I feel it though I do not see it. It is this unseen Power which makes itself felt and yet defies all proof, because it is so unlike all that I perceive through my senses. It transcends the senses. But it is possible to reason out the existence of God to a limited extent.

I do dimly perceive that whilst everything around me is ever-changing, ever-dying, there is underlying all that change a Living Power that is changeless, that holds all together, that creates, dissolves, and re-creates. That informing Power or Spirit is God. And since nothing else I see merely through the senses can or will persist, He alone is.

And is this Power benevolent or malevolent? I see it as purely benevolent. For I can see that in the midst of death life persists, in the midst of untruth truth persists, in the midst of darkness light persists. Hence I gather that God is Life, Truth, Light. He is Love, He is the Supreme Good.

— MOHANDAS GANDHI, 1869-1948

There is an ocean—cold water without motion. In this ocean, however, is the Gulf Stream, hot water flowing from the Equator towards the Pole. Inquire of all scientists how it is physically imaginable that a stream of hot water flows between the waters of the ocean, which, so to speak, form its banks, the moving within the motionless, the hot within the cold, no scientist can explain it. Similarly, there is the God of love within the God of the forces of the universe—one with Him, and yet so totally different. We let ourselves be seized and carried away by that vital stream.

— ALBERT SCHWEITZER, 1875-

God himself, the father and fashioner of all that is, older than the sun or the sky, greater than time and eternity and all the flow of being, is unnameable by any lawgiver, unutterable by any voice, not to be seen by any eye. But we, being unable to apprehend his essence, use the help of sounds and names and pictures, of beaten gold and ivory and silver, of plants and rivers, mountain-peaks and torrents, yearning for the knowledge of him, and in our weakness naming all that is beautiful in this world after his nature—just as happens to earthly lovers. To them the most beautiful sight will be the actual lineaments of the beloved, but for remembrance' sake they will be happy in the sight of a lyre, a little spear, a chair, perhaps, or a running-ground, or anything in the world that wakens the memory of the beloved.

Why should I further examine and pass judgment about images? Let men know what is divine; let them know: that is all. If a Greek is stirred to the remembrance of God by the art of Phidias, an Egyptian by paying worship to animals, another man by a river, another by fire—I have no anger for their divergences; only let them know, let them love, let them remember.

— MAXIMUS OF TYRE, second century

O how may I ever express that secret word?
O how can I say He is not like this, and He is like that?
If I say that He is within me, the universe is ashamed:
If I say that He is without me, it is falsehood.
He makes the inner and the outer worlds to be indivisibly one;
The conscious and the unconscious, both are His footstools.
He is neither manifest nor hidden, He is neither revealed nor un-
                                                              revealed:
There are no words to tell that which He is.

— KABIR, 1450? - 1518

Think'st thou in temporal speech God's
        Name may uttered be?
It is unspeakable to all eternity.

— ANGELUS SILESIUS, 1624 - 1677

· II ·

He cannot be sculptured in stone. He cannot be seen. Service cannot be rendered to Him. Gifts cannot be presented to Him. He is not to be approached in the sanctuaries. Where He is is not known. He is not to be found in inscribed shrines. No habitation can contain Him.

— ANONYMOUS EGYPTIAN SCRIBE

Now mark! God is nameless, for no one can know or say anything of Him. Anent which a heathen philosopher observes that what we know or predicate about the First Cause is what we ourselves are rather than what the First is, seeing that this transcends speech and knowledge. If I say God is good, it is not true: I am good, God is not good. I say more: I am better than God is, for what is good can be better, and what is better can be best. Now since God is not good therefore He cannot be better: and since He cannot be better therefore He cannot be best. These three: good, better, best, are remote from God for He is above all.

Again, if I say, God is wise, it is not true: I am wiser than He is. And if I say, God is a being, it is not true: He is a transcendental, a super-essential nothingness. Anent which St. Augustine says: the finest thing a man can say of God is that He is silent from consciousness of interior fulness. Therefore hold thy peace and prate not of God, for prating of Him thou liest, committing sin. An thou wilt be without sin and perfect, babble not of God. Neither know anything of God for God is beyond knowing. One philosopher says: had I a God that could know I would have Him for my God no longer. Know'st thou of Him anything? He is no such thing, and in that thou knowest of him anything at all thou dost lapse into ignorance, and from ignorance to the condition of a brute. For that which is ignorant in creatures is brutish. Art thou minded, therefore, not to become brutish, know nothing of the unuttered God.

—What then shall I do?

Thou shalt lose thy *thyness* and dissolve in His *hisness;* thy *thine* shall be His *mine,* so utterly one *mine* that thou in Him shalt know eternalwise His *isness,* free from becoming: His nameless nothingness.

—MEISTER ECKHART, 1260? -? 1327

The being of God is being-itself. The being of God cannot be understood as the existence of a being alongside others or above others. If God is *a* being, He is subject to the categories of finitude, especially to space and substance. Even if He is called the "highest being" in the sense of the "most perfect" and the "most powerful" being, this situation is not changed. When applied to God, superlatives become diminutives. They place him on the level of other beings while elevating him above all of them. . . . Whenever infinite or unconditional power and meaning are attributed to the highest being, it has ceased to be *a* being and has become being-itself. Many confusions in the doctrine of God and many apologetic weaknesses could be avoided if God were understood first of all as being-itself or as the ground of being. The power of being is another way of expressing the same thing in a circumscribing phrase. Ever since the time of Plato it has been known—although it often has been disregarded, especially by the nominalists and their modern followers—that the concept of being as being, or being-itself, points to the power inherent in everything, the power of resisting nonbeing. Therefore, instead of saying that God is first of all being-itself, it is possible to say that He is the power of being in everything and above everything, the infinite power of being. . . .

As being-itself God is beyond the contrast of essential and existential being. We have spoken of the transition of being into existence, which involves the possibility that being will contradict and lose itself. This transition is excluded from being-itself . . . for being-itself does not participate in nonbeing. In this it stands in contrast to every being. As classical theology has emphasized, God is beyond essence and existence. Logically, being-itself is "before," "prior to," the split which characterizes finite being.

For this reason it is as wrong to speak of God as the universal essence as it is to speak of Him as existing. If God is understood as universal essence, as the form of all forms, He is identified with the unity and totality of finite potentialities; but He has ceased to be the power of the ground in all of them, and therefore He has ceased to transcend them. He has poured all His creative power into a system of forms, and He is bound to these forms. This is what pantheism means.

On the other hand, grave difficulties attend the attempt to speak of God as existing. In order to maintain the truth that God is beyond essence and existence while simultaneously arguing for the existence of God, Thomas Aquinas is forced to distinguish between two kinds of divine existence: that which is identical with essence and that which is not. But an existence of God which is not united with its essence is a contradiction in terms. It makes God a being whose existence does not fulfil His essential potentialities; being and not-yet-being are "mixed" in Him, as they are in everything finite. God ceases to be God, the ground of being and meaning. What really has happened is that Thomas has had to unite two different traditions: the Augustinian, in which the divine existence is included in His essence, and the Aristotelian, which derives the existence of God from the existence of the world and which then asserts, in a second step, that His existence is identical with His Essence. Thus the question of the existence of God can be neither asked nor answered. If asked, it is a question about that which by its very nature is above existence, and therefore the answer—whether negative or affirmative—implicitly denies the nature of God. It is as atheistic to affirm the existence of God as it is to deny it. God is being-itself, not *a* being. On this basis a first step can be taken toward the solution of the problem which usually is discussed as the immanence and the transcendence of God. As the power of being, God transcends every being and also the totality of beings—the world. Being-itself is beyond finitude and infinity; otherwise it would be conditioned by something other than itself, and the real power of being would lie beyond both it and that which conditioned it. Being-itself infinitely transcends every finite being. There is no proportion or gradation between the finite and the infinite. There is an absolute break, an infinite "jump." On the other hand, everything finite participates in being-itself and in its infinity. Otherwise it would not have the power of being. It would be swallowed by nonbeing, or it never would have emerged out of nonbeing. This double relation of all beings to being-itself gives being-itself a double characteristic. In calling it creative, we point to the fact that everything participates in the infinite power of being. In calling it abysmal, we point to the fact that everything participates in the power of being in a finite way, that all beings are infinitely transcended by their creative ground.

—PAUL TILLICH, 1886-

I am unknown to him who saith he knoweth Me, but to him who knoweth that he knoweth Me not, I am known.

— ANONYMOUS

God is neither sonship nor fatherhood nor anything else known to us or to any other beings, either of the things that are or of the things that are not; nor does anything that is, know Him as He is, nor does He know anything that is as it is; He has neither word nor name nor knowledge; He is neither darkness nor light nor truth nor error; He can be neither affirmed nor denied; nay, though we may affirm or deny the things that are beneath him, we can neither affirm nor deny Him; for the perfect and sole cause of all is above all affirmation, and that which transcends all is above all subtraction, absolutely separate, and beyond all that is.

—DIONYSIUS THE AREOPAGITE, about 500 A.D.

God cannot be given a name because He is above being named. His essence is above all that we can understand and signify in words.

— St. Thomas Aquinas, 1225?-1274

Wherefore, O Hermes, never think that aught of things above or things below is like to God, for thou wilt fall from truth. For naught is like to That which hath no like, and is Alone and One.

— Hermes Trismegistus

· III ·

Imagine a race of underground men living a civilized existence, provided with every necessity and luxury, but deprived of the light of day. And if one day the jaws of the earth were opened, and they beheld for the first time the earth and the seas and the shining sun and the changing moon and the unchanging order of the heavens, such men would surely confess that the gods exist and that these things are the works of God.

— Aristotle, 384-322 b.c.

We lay it down as a position not to be controverted, that the human mind, even by natural instinct, possesses some sense of a Deity. For that no man might shelter himself under the pretext of ignorance, God hath given to all some apprehension of his existence, the memory of which He frequently and insensibly renews; so that as men universally know that there is a God, and that He is their Maker, they must be condemned by their own testimony, for not having worshipped Him and consecrated their lives to His service. If we seek for ignorance of a Deity, it is nowhere more likely to be found than among tribes the most stupid and farthest from civilization. But, as (the celebrated) Cicero observes, there is no nation so barbarous, no race so savage, as not to be firmly persuaded of the being of a God. Even those who in other respects appear to differ but little from brutes, always retain some sense of religion, so fully are the minds of men possessed with this common principle, which is closely interwoven with their original composition. Now since there has never been a country or family, from the beginning of the world, totally destitute of religion, it is a tacit confession that some sense of the Divinity is inscribed on every heart.

— JOHN CALVIN, 1509-1564

I conclude, *there is a Mind which affects me every moment with all the sensible impressions I perceive.* And, from the variety, order, and manner of these, I conclude *the Author of them to be wise, powerful, and good beyond comprehension.* Mark it well; I do not say, I see things by perceiving that which represents them in the intelligible Substance of God. This I do not understand; but I say, the things by me perceived are known by the understanding, and produced by the will of an infinite Spirit. And is not all this most plain and evident?

To me it is evident that sensible things cannot exist otherwise than in a mind or spirit. Whence I conclude, not that they have no real existence, but that, seeing they depend not on my thought, and have an existence distinct from being perceived by me, *there must be some other Mind wherein they exist.* As sure, therefore, as the sensible world really exists, so sure is there an infinite omnipresent Spirit who contains and supports it. . . .

Did men but consider that the sun, moon, and stars, and every other object of the senses, are only so many sensations in their minds, which have no other existence but barely being perceived, doubtless they would never fall down and worship their own *ideas;* but rather address their homage to that ETERNAL INVISIBLE MIND which produces and sustains all things.

— GEORGE BERKELEY, 1685-1753

Two things fill the mind with ever new and increasing admiration and awe, the oftener and the more steadily we reflect on them: *the starry heavens above and the moral law within.* I have not to search for them and conjecture them as though they were veiled in darkness or were in the transcendent region beyond my horizon; I see them before me and connect them directly with the consciousness of my existence. The former begins from the place I occupy in the external world of sense, and enlarges my connexion therein to an unbounded extent with worlds upon worlds and systems of systems, and moreover into limitless times of their periodic motion, its beginning and continuance. The second begins from my invisible self, my personality, and exhibits me in a world which has true infinity, but which is traceable only by the understanding, and with which I discern that I am not in a merely contingent but in a universal and necessary connexion, as I am also thereby with all those visible worlds. The former view of a countless multitude of worlds annihilates, as it were, my importance as an *animal creature,* which after it has been for a short time provided with vital power, one knows not how, must again give back the matter of which it was formed to the planet it inhabits (a mere speck in the universe). The second, on the contrary, infinitely elevates my worth as an *intelligence* by my personality, in which the moral law reveals to me a life independent of animality and even of the whole sensible world—at least so far as may be inferred from the destination assigned to my existence by this law, a destination not restricted to conditions and limits of this life, but reaching into the infinite.

— IMMANUEL KANT, 1724-1804

As long as the pain-ridden race of Adam's children shall continue on this earth, there will be men hungry for the Beautiful and the Infinite, just as men hunger for bread. Their number will be small: that is most likely. They will be persecuted: that is wholly probable. Disconsolate wanderers of the great Dream, they will roam like Cains over the face of the earth and will perhaps be forced to make friends of the wild beasts so as not to remain without shelter. Hunted as are incendiaries or well poisoners, abhorred by women with fleshly eyes who will see them only as rugamuffins, screamed at by children and howled at by dogs, frightful flotsam of the Joy of sixty centuries, tossed about by the waves of all the filth in this last age, they will at last draw their final breath as comfortably as it will be given them to do—in burrows so stinking that even the centipedes and scarab beetles of death will not dare search out their corpses!

Yet despite everything they will continue to exist, in order to drive executioners to despair; and, since nature is indestructible and inviolable, it could very well happen that some day—through the agency of some astonishing kiss from the sun or the influence of some unknown heavenly body—an exceptionally large brood of these vagabonds, overflowing the earth, may forever drown out in waters of rapture this aborted society of blackguardly wiseacres who thought they had exterminated the aristocracy of our human species!

— LEON BLOY, 1846-1917

In the case of our human friends we take their existence for granted, not caring whether it is proven or not. Our relationship is such that we could read philosophical arguments designed to prove the non-existence of each other, and perhaps even be convinced by them— and then laugh together over so odd a conclusion. I think that it is something of the same kind of security we should seek in our relationship with God. The most flawless proof of the existence of God is no substitute for it; and if we have that relationship the most convincing disproof is turned harmlessly aside. If I may say it with reverence, the soul and God laugh together over so odd a conclusion.

— SIR ARTHUR EDDINGTON, 1882-1944

Under many names, names which are not that of God, in ways only known to God, the interior act of a soul's thought can be directed towards a reality which in fact truly may be God. For, as a result of our spiritual weakness, there can easily be a discordance between what in reality we believe and the ideas in which we express to ourselves what we believe, and take cognisance of our beliefs. To every soul, even to one ignorant of the name of God, even one reared in atheism, grace offers, at the moment when the soul deliberates with itself and chooses its final end, grace offers as an object, as something to be loved above all things, under whatever name the soul describes such an end to itself,—but it is then a case (and this is the whole question to which God alone knows the answer) of its thinking under that name of *something other* than it signifies, of going beyond the false name,—offers that Reality of absolute goodness, which merits all our love and is able to save our life.

And if this grace is not rejected, the soul in question, in its choice of that reality, believes obscurely in the true God and really chooses Him, even where in good faith it is in error and adheres, not by its own fault, but by that of the education it has received, to a philosophical system of atheism, and conceptualises this faith in the true God under formulas which deny Him. An atheist of good faith would thus, against his own apparent choice, really choose God as the true end of his life.

—JACQUES MARITAIN, 1882-

Abyssus invocat abyssum. Deep calls unto deep, say our mystics with the Psalmists. And they mean thereby that the depth of their own being cries out to the depth and abyss of the divine. But that saying also provides a good metaphor for the strange meeting, intertwining and running together of the "two ways" of mystical approach of which we have already spoken. Here also deep calls unto deep: the numinous depth of the eternal One in and behind all things (including the perceiver) calls to the numinous depth of the soul in its inmost being—where lies the marvel of God united with the soul. It was a meeting and mutual discovery of two primarily very different elements, when the old Ekam of the Vedas encountered the Ātman. The words of the Chhāndogya, "Sa ātmā," give expression to no self-evident experience and are no analytical judgment, but they reveal a most surprising synthesis. From that time onward in India, the two ways have been entangled with one another. Thus we find them in Śankara, and also in Eckhart, and in many another mystic of still other countries and races.

For those of us who are not mystics, this interpenetration of the two ways is always puzzling, and to those who misunderstand their fundamental difference it is very necessary to point out the enigma of their union, and to make clear the peculiarity of each in sharpest distinction. True, for the mystic himself there is here no riddle; to him the necessity of their combination is obvious. He knows nothing of the twofoldness of the ways, but from the peculiar quality of the objects he experiences both unfold clearly before him. He does not reflect on their difference. If he did so, he would probably not be able to explain in clear-cut conceptions the necessity of their combining. It is to him an immediately felt necessity, and he has no need to analyze intellectually what is given as a certainty in feeling.

We can neither recognize nor feel this necessity. The interlocking must always appear to us as an astonishing fact. It is particularly amazing when we view it from the starting point of the first way. We have nothing to do here with reflection upon outward things and their unity or non-unity. The root fact is quite other and is clearly presented to our gaze. It is obviously this: casting the self free from all outward events, in an inward gathering, there breaks upon the mystics from the inward depths an experience, secret and wonderful, a foreshadowing of greater things not to be comprehended by thought. That which he neither knew nor felt before becomes living within him as the inconceivably strange and great, which he himself bears. It overflows and quickens within him, it lays hold on him and is his being. Is it the wonder of the soul itself which is revealed to him in its immeasurability? What can the things of the world trouble him then with their unity or multiplicity, with the query as to what lies behind them or at their base? Or, is it an oversoul, penetrating the soul of man, welling up and flowing through him, absorbing and uniting him within it—the Godhead? Then it is also the Godhead of the soul, her essence and her being, her life and her blessedness. But as to whether this Godhead is at the same time "all things" and the unity and being of all things—what does that matter to the soul!

To discover in the inwardness of the self the divine miracle in the soul, or the indwelling Ātman, and on the other hand, behind and beyond the multiplicity of things to behold the One that is the essence of all things and of the self—these are, we say, two absolutely different experiences, and as non-mystics we cannot conceive how they can slip into one another and become indissolubly bound together. In India we see most clearly the entirely different starting points of each.

Here, the first is the discovery of the Ekam in and behind the world, which is recognized as the eternal Brahman. The discovery of the "inward ātman," of the āścharyam in the inner self, is the second, and is completely independent of the first.

But the realization that this Ekam-Brahman is the "inward ātman" —is the third discovery, and is again a new treasure trove in itself. How did it come to pass? Why do the Brahman and Ātman meet one another? Our religious history simply relates the fact—that Brahman and Ātman speculation "interpenetrate." But why did they do it? That it is "natural" is certainly not true and this is proven by the circumstance that ātman-speculation in Sānkhya and Yoga can arise not only without Brahman, but can definitely refuse to accept both Brahman mysticism and Advaitam. Did this happen by chance? and is it true that in certain directions Indian speculation forms a mere "syncretism" of the two and in others leaves them apart? Yet the doctrine of Śankara is certainly no syncretism, no chance flowing together and intermingling of previously existing streams. The inner uniting of these two ways and elements evidently takes place in Vedānta-mysticism under the compulsion of a strongly felt need.

Such an inward compulsion toward this type of synthesis may also be induced historically: for the fact remains that not only once in India, but to the same extent in many totally different places, a corresponding synthesis is achieved, from essentially different starting points and under widely differing conditions. We find the same synthesis of the two ways in Eckhart and Plotinus and Al-Hallāj. If this correspondence does not point to a hidden law of necessity, it at least indicates a powerfully constraining inward element.

The mystic himself would say: "Even that which was Eternal-One and is in all things, that is the ground of my soul—that is my soul. This I know. He who does not know this has not yet seen, or has only partially seen." But the non-mystic will look about him for definite elements of reciprocal attraction, which must exist in any affinities between these two mysticisms. What the mystic perceives as the cogent root of the matter, appears to our secular vision only as a question of "similarity" or "relationship" between the intuitions of the two different ways, which gives us a mere psychological guide. What is for the mystic an essential and necessary connection of the two seems to us only a reciprocal attraction following the laws of psychology; e.g. the rule that in certain circumstances different, in other circumstances like experiences can intermingle in the soul under the compulsion of their resemblance, and can not only mix together but in certain events can also arouse one another— abyssus invocat abyssum—can be the occasion of the wakening of each other, and in interpenetration can mutually enhance each other.

— RUDOLF OTTO, 1869-1938

MARGARET.   'Tis long since thou hast been to mass or to confession.
                 Believest thou in God?

FAUST.   My darling, who shall dare
                 "I believe in God!" to say?
                 Ask priest or sage the answer to declare,
                 And it will seem a mocking play,
                 A sarcasm on the asker.

MARGARET.   Then thou believest not!

FAUST.   Hear not falsely, sweetest countenance!
                 Who dare express Him?
                 And who profess Him,

Saying: I believe in Him!
Who, feeling, seeing,
Deny His being,
Saying: I believe Him not!
The All-enfolding,
The All-upholding,
Folds and upholds he not
Thee, me, Himself?
Arches not there the sky above us?
Lies not beneath us, firm, the earth?
And rise not, on us shining,
Friendly, the everlasting stars?
Look I not, eye to eye, on thee,
And feel'st not, thronging
To head and heart, the force,
Still weaving its eternal secret,
Invisible, visible, round thy life?
Vast as it is, fill with that force thy heart,
And when thou in the feeling wholly blessed art,
Call it, then, what thou wilt,—
Call it Bliss! Heart! Love! God!
I have no name to give it!
Feeling is all in all:
The Name is sound and smoke,
Obscuring Heaven's clear glow.

MARGARET.   All that is fine and good, to hear it so:
Much the same way the preacher spoke,
Only with slightly different phrases.

FAUST.   The same thing, in all places,
All hearts that beat beneath the heavenly day—
Each in its language—say;
Then why not I, in mine, as well?

— JOHANN WOLFGANG VON GOETHE, 1749-1832

· IV ·

I see clearly that God reserved for Himself those who serve in secret.
For He said to Elias: I love the unknown adorers in the world.

— BLAISE PASCAL, 1623-1662

Eternall God, (for whom who ever dare
Seeke new expressions, doe the Circle square,
And thrust into strait corners of poore wit
Thee, who art cornerlesse and infinite)
I would but blesse Thy Name, not name Thee now;
(And Thy gifts are as infinite as Thou:)
Fixe we our prayses therefore on this one,
That, as thy blessed Spirit fell upon
These Psalmes' first Author in a cloven tongue;
(For 'twas a double power by which he sung
The highest matter in the noblest forme;)
So Thou hast cleft that spirit, to performe
That worke againe, and shed it, here, upon
Two, by their bloods, and by Thy Spirit one;
A Brother and a Sister, made by Thee
The Organ, where Thou art the Harmony.

— JOHN DONNE, 1573-1631

Everything that is true, is God's word, whoever may have said it.

— ULRICH ZWINGLI, 1484-1531

From the uttermost depths of the fountains of my soul
To Thee, O Hidden God, I pray; hearken unto my
        prayer.

    O Hidden God, ask of me what Thou wilt. Here am I!
    But let me see Thy face,
    Thy face let me see.

Of what worth is the pride of life
That I gather from every side,
Of what worth is all the glory of nature which
        Thou hast put into my heart?

    They are but shadows—pale shadows
        of Thy hidden light;
    Blurred outlines are they of Thine image.

But I thirst to drink from the Source of all sources,

And I yearn to bathe in the light of the Sun of suns,
And I long to gaze on Thy luminous Presence.

— Jacob Cohen, 1891-1949

Great Spirit, You have been always, and before You no one has been. There is no other one to pray to but You. You Yourself, everything that You see, everything has been made by You. The star nations all over the universe You have finished. The four quarters of the earth You have finished. The day, and in that day, everything you have finished. Great Spirit, lean close to the earth that You may hear the voice I send. You towards where the sun goes down, behold me! You where the sun shines continually, whence come the day-break star and the day, behold me! You where the summer lives, behold me! You in the depths of the heavens, an eagle of power, behold! And you, Mother Earth, the only mother, you who have shown mercy to your children!

Hear me, four quarters of the world—a relative I am! Give me the strength to walk the soft earth, a relative to all that is! Give me the eyes to see and the strength to understand, that I may be like You. With your power only can I face the winds.

Great Spirit, Great Spirit, all over the earth the faces of living things are all alike. With tenderness have these come up out of the ground. Look upon these faces of children without number and those with children in their arms, that they may face the winds and walk the good road to the day of quiet.

This is my prayer; hear me! The voice I have sent is weak, yet with earnestness I have sent it. Hear me!

— Black Elk, nineteenth century

Soul of the Soul!
Neither thought nor reason comprehends Thy essence, and no one knows Thy attributes.
Souls have no idea of Thy being.
The prophets themselves sink in the dust of Thy road.
All intellect exists by Thee; has it ever yet found the path of Thy existence?
O Thou who art in the interior and in the exterior of the soul! Thou art and Thou art not what I say.

In Thy presence reason grows dizzy; it loses the thread that would direct it in Thy way.

I perceive clearly the universe in Thee, and yet discover Thee not in the world.

All beings are marked with Thy impress, but Thyself hast no impress visible;

Thou reservest the secret of Thy existence.

— Mohammedan Prayer of Adoration

Sublime and Living Will, named by no name, compassed by no thought! I may well raise my soul to Thee, for Thou and I are not divided. Thy voice sounds within me, mine resounds in Thee; and all my thoughts, if they be but good and true, live in Thee also. In Thee, the incomprehensible, I myself and the world in which I live become clearly comprehensible to me; all the secrets of my existence are laid open and perfect harmony arises in my soul. . . .

How Thou art and seemest to Thine own being, I can never know, any more than I can assume Thy nature. That which I conceive becomes finite through my very conception of it; I will not attempt that which the imperfection of my finite nature forbids. But let me be what I ought to be, and Thy relations to me, the mortal, and to all mortals, lie open before my eyes and surround me more clearly than the consciousness of my own existence. Thou workest in me the knowledge of my duty, of my vocation in the world of reasonable beings, how, I know not, nor need I to know. Thou knowest what I think and what I will: how Thou canst know, through what act thou bringest about that consciousness, I cannot understand. Thou willest that my free obedience shall bring with it eternal consequences: the act of Thy will I cannot comprehend.

In the contemplations of these Thy relations to me, the finite being, will I rest in calm blessedness. I remain tranquil amid all the events of this world, for they are in Thy world. Nothing can perplex or surprise or dishearten me, as surely as Thou livest and I can look upon Thy life. For in Thee, and through Thee, O Infinite One! do I behold even my present world in another light.

— Johann Gottlieb Fichte, 1762-1814

O bird of the morning! Learn love from the moth,
Because it burnt, lost its life, and found no voice.

These prattlers about God are ignorantly in search of Him,
Because he who obtained knowledge has not returned.
O Thou who art above all imaginations, conjectures, opinions and
    ideas,
Above anything people have said, or we have heard or read,
The assembly is finished, and life has reached its term,
And we are as at first, at the beginning in describing Thee.

                    —SAADI, 1184?-1291

I am all that was, and is, and is to be, and my veil no man hath lifted.

        —ANONYMOUS (from the shrine of Neith at Saïs)

CHAPTER FIVE

Across a Void of Mystery and Dread

> *Anxiety about meaninglessness is the characteristically human form of ontological anxiety. It is the form of anxiety which only a being can have in whose nature freedom and destiny are united. The threat of losing this unity drives man toward the question of an infinite, unthreatened ground of meaning; it drives him to the question of God.*
>
> — PAUL TILLICH, 1886 -

· I ·

FATHER MAPPLE rose, and in a mild voice of unassuming authority ordered the scattered people to condense. "Starboard gangway, there! side away to larboard—larboard gangway to starboard! Midships! midships!"

There was a low rumbling of heavy sea-boots among the benches, and a still slighter shuffling of women's shoes, and all was quiet again, and every eye on the preacher.

He paused a little; then kneeling in the pulpit's bows, folded his large brown hands across his chest, uplifted his closed eyes, and offered a prayer so deeply devout that he seemed kneeling and praying at the bottom of the sea.

This ended, in prolonged solemn tones, like the continual tolling of a bell in a ship that is foundering at sea in a fog—in such tones he

76

commenced reading the following hymn; but changing his manner
toward the concluding stanzas, burst forth with a pealing exultation
and joy—

> "The ribs and terrors in the whale,
> Arched over me a dismal gloom,
> While all God's sun-lit waves rolled by,
> And lift me deepening down to doom.
>
> "I saw the opening maw of hell,
> With endless pains and sorrows there;
> Which none but they that feel can tell—
> Oh, I was plunging to despair.
>
> "In black distress, I called my God,
> When I could scarce believe Him mine,
> He bowed His ear to my complaints—
> No more the whale did me confine.
>
> "With speed he flew to my relief,
> As on a radiant dolphin borne;
> Awful, yet bright, as lightning shone
> The face of my Deliverer God.
>
> "My song for ever shall record
> That terrible, that joyful hour;
> I give the glory to my God,
> His all the mercy and the power."

Nearly all joined in singing this hymn, which swelled high above
the howling of the storm. A brief pause ensued; the preacher slowly
turned over the leaves of the Bible, and at last, folding his hand
down upon the proper page, said: "Beloved shipmates, clinch the last
verse of the first chapter of Jonah—'And God had prepared a great
fish to swallow up Jonah.'

"Shipmates, this book, containing only four chapters—four yarns
—is one of the smallest strands in the mighty cable of the Scriptures.
Yet what depths of the soul Jonah's deep sealine sound! what a pregnant lesson to us is this prophet! What a noble thing is that canticle
in the fish's belly! How billow-like and boisterously grand! We feel
the floods surging over us, we sound with him to the kelpy bottom
of the waters; sea-weed and all the slime of the sea is about us! But
what is this lesson that the book of Jonah teaches? Shipmates, it is a
two-stranded lesson; a lesson to us all as sinful men, and a lesson to
me as a pilot of the living God. As sinful men, it is a lesson to us all,

because it is a story of the sin, hard-heartedness, suddenly awakened fears, the swift punishment, repentance, prayers, and finally the deliverance and joy of Jonah. As with all sinners among men, the sin of this son of Amittai was in his wilful disobedience of the command of God—never mind now what that command was, or how conveyed—which he found a hard command. But all the things that God would have us do are hard for us to do—remember that—and hence, He oftener commands us than endeavors to persuade. And if we obey God, we must disobey ourselves; and it is in this disobeying ourselves, wherein the hardness of obeying God consists.

"With this sin of disobedience in him, Jonah still further flouts at God, by seeking to flee from Him. He thinks that a ship made by men, will carry him into countries where God does not reign, but only the Captains of this earth. He skulks about the wharves of Joppa, and seeks a ship that's bound for Tarshish. There lurks, perhaps, a hitherto unheeded meaning here. By all accounts Tarshish could have been no other city than the modern Cadiz. That's the opinion of learned men. And where is Cadiz, shipmates? Cadiz is in Spain; as far by water, from Joppa, as Jonah could possibly have sailed in those ancient days, when the Atlantic was an almost unknown sea. Because Joppa, the modern Jaffa, shipmates, is on the most easterly coast of the Mediterranean, the Syrian; and Tarshish or Cadiz more than two thousand miles to the westward from that, just outside the Straits of Gibraltar. See ye not then, shipmates, that Jonah sought to flee worldwide from God? Miserable man! Oh! most contemptible and worthy of all scorn; with slouched hat and guilty eye, skulking from his God; prowling among the shipping like a vile burglar hastening to cross the seas. So disordered, self-condemning is his look, that had there been policemen in those days, Jonah, on the mere suspicion of something wrong, had been arrested ere he touched a deck. How plainly he's a fugitive! no baggage, not a hat-box, valise, or carpet-bag,—no friends accompany him to the wharf with their adieux. At last, after much dodging search, he finds the Tarshish ship receiving the last items of her cargo; and as he steps on board to see its Captain in the cabin, all the sailors for the moment desist from hoisting in the goods, to mark the stranger's evil eye. Jonah sees this; but in vain he tries to look all ease and confidence; in vain essays his wretched smile. Strong intuitions of the man assure the mariners he can be no innocent. In their gamesome but still serious way, one whispers to the other—"Jack, he's robbed a widow"; or, "Joe, do you mark him; he's a bigamist"; or, "Harry lad, I guess he's the adulterer that broke jail in old Gomorrah, or belike, one of the missing murderers from Sodom." Another runs to read the bill that's stuck against the spile upon the wharf to which the ship is moored, offering five hundred gold coins for the apprehension of a parricide, and containing a description of his person. He reads, and looks from Jonah to the bill, while all his sympathetic shipmates now crowd round Jonah, prepared to lay their hands upon him. Frighted Jonah trembles, and summoning all his boldness to his face, only looks so much the more a coward. He will not confess himself suspected; but that itself is strong suspicion. So he makes the best of it; and when the sailors find him not to be the man that is advertised, they let him pass, and he descends into the cabin.

" 'Who's there?' cries the Captain at his busy desk, hurriedly making out his papers for the Customs—'Who's there?' Oh! how that harmless question mangles Jonah! For the instant he almost turns to flee again. But he rallies. 'I seek a passage in this ship to Tarshish; how soon sail ye, sir?' Thus far the busy Captain had not looked up to Jonah, though the man now stands before him; but no sooner does he hear that hollow voice, than he darts a scrutinizing glance. 'We sail with the next coming tide,' at last he slowly answered, still intently eyeing him. 'No sooner, sir?'—'Soon enough for any honest man that goes a passenger.' Ha! Jonah, that's another stab. But he swiftly calls away the Captain from that scent. 'I'll sail with ye,'— he says,—'the passage money, how much is that?—I'll pay now.' For it is particularly written, shipmates, as if it were a thing not to be overlooked in this history, 'that he paid the fare thereof' ere the craft did sail. And taken with the context, this is full of meaning.

"Now Jonah's Captain, shipmates, was one whose discernment detects crime in any, but whose cupidity exposes it only in the penniless. In this world, shipmates, sin that pays its way can travel freely and without a passport; whereas Virtue, if a pauper, is stopped at all frontiers. So Jonah's Captain prepares to test the length of Jonah's purse, ere he judge him openly. He charges him thrice the usual sum; and it's assented to. Then the Captain knows that Jonah is a fugitive; but at the same time resolves to help a flight that paves its rear with gold. Yet when Jonah fairly takes out his purse, prudent suspicions still molest the Captain. He rings every coin to find a counterfeit. Not a forger, any way, he mutters; and Jonah is put down for his passage. 'Point out my state-room, Sir,' says Jonah now, 'I'm travel-weary; I need sleep.' 'Thou look'st like it,' says the Captain, 'there's thy room.' Jonah enters, and would lock the door, but the lock contains no key. Hearing him foolishly fumbling there, the Captain laughs lowly to himself, and mutters something about the doors of convicts' cells being never allowed to be locked within. All dressed and dusty as he is, Jonah throws himself into his berth, and finds the little state-room ceiling almost resting on his forehead. The air is close, and Jonah gasps. Then, in that contracted hole, sunk, too, beneath the ship's water-line, Jonah feels the heralding presentiment of that stifling hour, when the whale shall hold him in the smallest of his bowels' wards.

"Screwed at its axis against the side, a swinging lamp slightly oscillates in Jonah's room; and the ship, heeling over towards the wharf with the weight of the last bales received, the lamp, flame and all, though in slight motion, still maintains a permanent obliquity with reference to the room; though, in truth, infallibly straight itself, it but made obvious the false, lying levels among which it hung. The lamp alarms and frightens Jonah; as lying in his berth his tormented eyes roll round the place, and this thus far successful fugitive finds no refuge for his restless glance. But that contradiction in the lamp more and more appals him. The floor, the ceiling, and the side, are all awry. 'Oh! so my conscience hangs in me!' he groans, 'straight upward, so it burns; but the chambers of my soul are all in crookedness!'

"Like one who after a night of drunken revelry hies to his bed, still reeling, but with conscience yet pricking him, as the plungings of the Roman race-horse but so much the more strike his steel tags into him; as one who in that miserable plight still turns and turns in giddy anguish, praying God for annihilation until the fit be passed; and at last amid the whirl of woe he feels, a deep stupor steals over him, as over the man who bleeds to death, for conscience is the wound, and there's naught to staunch it; so, after sore wrestlings in his berth, Jonah's prodigy of ponderous misery drags him drowning down to sleep.

"And now the time of tide has come; the ship casts off her cables; and from the deserted wharf the uncheered ship for Tarshish, all careening, glides to sea. That ship, my friends, was the first of recorded smugglers! the contrabrand was Jonah. But the sea rebels; he will not bare the wicked burden. A dreadful storm comes on, the ship is like to break. But now when the boatswain calls all hands to lighten her; when boxes, bales, and jars are clattering overboard; when the wind is shrieking, and the men are yelling, and every plank thunders with trampling feet right over Jonah's head; in all this raging tumult, Jonah sleeps his hideous sleep. He sees no black sky and raging sea, feels not the reeling timbers, and little hears he or heeds he the far rush of the mighty whale, which even now with open mouth is cleaving the seas after him. Aye, shipmates, Jonah was gone down into the sides of the ship—a berth in the cabin as I have taken it, and was fast asleep. But the frightened master comes to him, and shrieks in his dead ear, 'What meanest thou, O sleeper! arise!' Startled from his lethargy by that direful cry, Jonah staggers to his feet, and stumbling to the deck, grasps a shroud, to look out upon the sea. But at that moment he is sprung upon by a panther billow leaping over the bulwarks. Wave after wave thus leaps into the ship, and finding no speedy vent runs roaring fore and aft, till the mariners come nigh to drowning while yet afloat. And ever, as the white moon shows her affrighted face from the steep gullies in the blackness overhead, aghast Jonah sees the rearing bowsprit pointing high upward, but soon beat downward again towards the tormented deep.

"Terrors upon terrors run shouting through his soul. In all his cringing attitudes, the God-fugitive is now too plainly known. The sailors mark him; more and more certain grow their suspicions of him, and at last, fully to test the truth, by referring the whole matter to high Heaven, they fall to casting lots, to see for whose cause this great tempest was upon them. The lot is Jonah's; that discovered, then how furiously they mob him with their questions. 'What is thine occupation? Whence comest thou? Thy country? What people?' But mark now, my shipmates, the behavior of poor Jonah. The eager mariners but ask him who he is, and where from; whereas, they not only receive an answer to those questions, but likewise another answer to a question not put by them, but the unsolicited answer is forced from Jonah by the hard hand of God that is upon him.

"'I am a Hebrew,' he cries—and then—'I fear the Lord the God of Heaven who hath made the sea and the dry land!' Fear him, O Jonah? Aye, well mightest thou fear the Lord God *then!* Straightway, he now goes on to make a full confession; whereupon the mariners became more and more appalled, but still are pitiful. For when Jonah, not yet supplicating God for mercy, since he but too well knew the darkness of his deserts,—when wretched Jonah cries out to them to take him and cast him forth into the sea, for he knew that for *his* sake this great tempest was upon them; they mercifully turn from him, and seek by other means to save the ship. But all in vain; the indignant gale howls louder; then, with one hand raised invokingly to God, with the other they not unreluctantly lay hold of Jonah.

"And now behold Jonah taken up as an anchor and dropped into the sea; when instantly an oily calmness floats out from the east, and the sea is still, as Jonah carries down the gale with him, leaving smooth water behind. He goes down in the whirling heart of such a masterless commotion that he scarce heeds the moment when he drops seething into the yawning jaws awaiting him; and the whale shoots-to all his ivory teeth, like so many white bolts, upon his prison. Then Jonah prayed unto the Lord out of the fish's belly. But observe his prayer, and learn a weighty lesson. For sinful as he is, Jonah does not weep and wail for direct deliverance. He feels that his dreadful punishment is just. He leaves all his deliverance to God, contenting himself with this, that spite of all his pains and pangs, he will still look towards His holy temple. And here, shipmates, is true and faithful repentance; not clamorous for pardon, but grateful for punishment. And how pleasing to God was this conduct in Jonah, is shown in the eventual deliverance of him from the sea and the whale. Shipmates, I do not place Jonah before you to be copied for his sin but I do place him before you as a model for repentance. Sin not; but if you do, take heed to repent of it like Jonah."

While he was speaking these words, the howling of the shrieking, slanting storm without seemed to add new power to the preacher, who, when describing Jonah's sea-storm, seemed tossed by a storm himself. His deep chest heaved as with a ground-swell; his tossed arms seemed the warring elements at work; and the thunders that rolled away from off his swarthy brow, and the light leaping from his eye, made all his simple hearers look on him with a quick fear that was strange to them.

There now came a lull in his look, as he silently turned over the leaves of the Book once more; and, at last, standing motionless, with closed eyes, for the moment, seemed communing with God and himself.

But again he leaned over towards the people, and bowing his head lowly, with an aspect of the deepest yet manliest humility, he spake these words:

"Shipmates, God has laid but one hand upon you; both his hands press upon me. I have read ye by what murky light may be mine the lesson that Jonah teaches to all sinners; and therefore to ye, and still more to me, for I am a greater sinner than ye. And now how gladly would I come down from this mast-head and sit on the hatches there where you sit, and listen as you listen, while some one of you reads *me* that other and more awful lesson which Jonah teaches to *me*, as a pilot of the living God. How being an anointed pilot-prophet, or speaker of true things, and bidden by the Lord to sound those

unwelcome truths in the ears of a wicked Nineveh, Jonah, appalled
at the hostility he should raise, fled from his mission, and sought to
escape his duty and his God by taking ship at Joppa. But God is
everywhere; Tarshish he never reached. As we have seen, God came
upon him in the whale, and swallowed him down to living gulfs of
doom, and with swift slantings tore him along 'into the midst of the
seas,' where the eddying depths sucked him ten thousand fathoms
down, and 'the weeds were wrapped about his head,' and all the
watery world of woe bowled over him. Yet even then beyond the
reach of any plummet—'out of the belly of hell'—when the whale
grounded upon the ocean's utmost bones, even then, God heard the
engulphed, repenting prophet when he cried. Then God spake unto
the fish; and from the shuddering cold and blackness of the sea, the
whale came breeching up towards the warm and pleasant sun, and all
the delights of air and earth; and 'vomited out Jonah upon the dry
land;' when the word of the Lord came a second time; and Jonah,
bruised and beaten—his ears, like two sea-shells, still multitudinously
murmuring of the ocean—Jonah did the Almighty's bidding. And
what was that, shipmates? To preach the Truth to the face of Falsehood! That was it!

"This, shipmates, this is that other lesson; and woe to that pilot
of the living God who slights it. Woe to him whom this world
charms from Gospel duty! Woe to him who seeks to pour oil upon
the waters when God has brewed them into a gale! Woe to him who
seeks to please rather than to appal! Woe to him whose good name
is more to him than goodness! Woe to him who, in this world,
courts not dishonor! Woe to him who would not be true, even
though to be false were salvation! Yea, woe to him who as the great
Pilot Paul has it, while preaching to others is himself a castaway!"

He drooped and fell away from himself for a moment; then lifting
his face to them again, showed a deep joy in his eyes, as he cried out
with a heavenly enthusiasm,—"But oh! shipmates! on the starboard
hand of every woe, there is a sure delight; and higher the top of that
delight, than the bottom of the woe is deep. Is not the main-truck
higher than the kelson is low? Delight is to him—a far, far upward,
and inward delight—who against the proud gods and commodores
of this earth, ever stands forth his own inexorable self. Delight is to
him whose strong arms yet support him, when the ship of this base
treacherous world has gone down beneath him. Delight is to him,
who gives no quarter in the truth, and kills, burns, and destroys all
sin though he pluck it out from under the robes of Senators and
Judges. Delight,—top-gallant delight is to him, who acknowledges no

law or lord, but the Lord his God, and is only a patriot to heaven.
Delight is to him, whom all the waves of the billows of the seas of
the boisterous mob can never shake from this sure Keel of the Ages.
And eternal delight and deliciousness will be his, who coming to lay
him down, can say with his final breath—O Father! chiefly known to
me by Thy rod—mortal or immortal, here I die. I have striven to be
Thine, more than to be this world's, or mine own. Yet this is nothing: I leave eternity to Thee; for what is man that he should live out
the lifetime of his God?"

He said no more, but slowly waving a benediction, covered his
face with his hands, and so remained kneeling, till all the people had
departed, and he was left alone in the place.

— HERMAN MELVILLE, 1819-1891

There has come to me an insight into the meaning of Darkness. The
reason one must face his darkness, and enter into that darkness is not
that he may return purified to face God. One must go into the darkness because that is where God is. The darkness is not sin, not evil.
Those are by-ways, side paths by which one can escape. The darkness is pure terror, and the last terror of all is to know as one turns
downward that there is no God. Then the darkness is upon you, and
there is God Himself, for God is the greatest destroyer of gods.

It seems as though we must each make himself a god of his own,
one not too big to carry. For some, the good will be God, or Nature,
or the Creative Idea, or the Indulgent Father. One must stay with
Him and in His universe, or go down into the darkness alone. It is
as though one had to take a hammer and smash his god to bits, only
to find that there on the instant stood God, God Himself, filling the
universe and personally near.

God is. That is so real, that to talk of His love, or of serving Him
is saying less, not more. He is, and He is with us, and there is no
need of promises.

— ALFRED ROMER, 1894-

In what torne ship soever I embarke,
That ship shall be my embleme of Thy Arke;
What sea soever swallow mee, that flood
Shall be to mee an embleme of Thy blood;

Though Thou with clouds of anger do disguise
Thy face; yet through that maske I know those eyes,
  Which, though they turne away sometimes,
    They never will despise.

I sacrifice this Iland unto Thee,
And all whom I lov'd there, and who lov'd mee;
When I have put our seas twixt them and mee,
Put thou Thy sea betwixt my sinnes and Thee.
As the trees' sap doth seeke the root below
In winter, in my winter now I goe,
  Where none but Thee, th'Eternall root
    Of true Love I may know.

Nor Thou nor Thy religion dost controule,
The amorousnesse of an harmonious Soule,
But Thou would'st have that love Thy selfe: As Thou
Art jealous, Lord, so I am jealous now,
That lov'st not, till from loving more, Thou free
My soule: Who ever gives, takes libertie:
  O, if Thou car'st not whom I love
    Alas, Thou lov'st not mee.

Seale then this bill of my Divorce to All,
On whom those fainter beames of love did fall;
Marry those loves, which in youth scattered bee
On Fame, Wit, Hopes (false mistresses) to Thee.
Churches are best for Prayer, that have least light:
To see God only, I goe out of sight:
  And to scape stormy dayes, I chuse
    An Everlasting night.

                — JOHN DONNE, 1573-1631

    How long, great GOD, how long must I
    Immured in this dark prison lie;
Where at the gates and avenues of sense,
My soul must watch to have intelligence;
Where but faint gleams of Thee salute my sight,
Like doubtful moonshine in a cloudy night:
    When shall I leave this magic sphere,
    And be all mind, all eye, all ear?

How cold this clime! And yet my sense
Perceives e'en here Thy influence.
E'en here Thy strong magnetic charms I feel,
And pant and tremble like the amorous steel.
To lower good, and beauties less divine,
Sometimes my erroneous needle does decline,
    But yet, so strong the sympathy,
    It turns, and points again to Thee.

I long to see this excellence
Which at such distance strikes my sense.
My impatient soul struggles to disengage
Her wings from the confinement of her cage.
Wouldst thou, great Love, this prisoner once set free,
How would she hasten to be link'd to Thee!
    She'd for no angels' conduct stay,
    But fly, and love-on, all the way.

        — JOHN NORRIS, 1657-1711

Many are the doors of the spirit that lead
    Into the inmost shrine:
And I count the gates of the temple divine,
    Since the god of the place is God indeed.
    And these are gates that God decreed
Should lead to his house: kisses and wine,
Cool depths of thought, youth without rest,
    And calm old age, prayer and desire,
The lover's and mother's breast,
    The fire of sense and the poet's fire.

But he that worships the gates alone,
    Forgetting the shrine beyond, shall see
    The great valves open suddenly,
Revealing, not God's radiant throne,
    But the fires of wrath and agony.

        — ALDOUS HUXLEY, 1894-

In every earnest life, there are weary flats to tread, with the heavens
out of sight,—no sun, no moon,—and not a tint of light upon the

path below; when the only guidance is the faith of brighter hours, and the secret Hand we are too numb and dark to feel. But to the meek and faithful it is not always so. Now and then, something touches the dull dream of sense and custom, and the desolation vanishes away: the spirit leaves its witness with us: the Divine realities come up from the past and straightway enter the present: the ear into which we poured our prayer is not deaf: the infinite eye to which we turned is not blind, but looks in with answering mercy on us. The mystery of life and the grievousness of death are gone: we know now the little from the great, the transient from the eternal: we can possess our souls in patience: and neither the waving palms and scattered flowers of triumph can elate us nor the weight of any cross appear too hard to bear. Tell me not that these undulations of the soul are the mere instability of enthusiasm and infirmity. . . . These intermittent movements of the soul are the sign of Divine gifts, not of human weakness. God has so arranged the chronometry of our spirits that there shall be thousands of silent moments between the striking hours.

— JAMES MARTINEAU, 1805-1900

The best prayers have often more groans than words.

—JOHN BUNYAN, 1628-1688

> You've never wept while tasting bread?
> Or lain awake for agonizing nights?
> You know them not, these Heavenly Powers!

— JOHANN WOLFGANG VON GOETHE, 1749-1832

As the hart panteth after the water brooks, so panteth my soul after Thee, O God.

My soul thirsteth for God, for the living God: when shall I come and appear before God?

My tears have been my meat day and night, while they continually say unto me, Where is thy God?

When I remember these things, I pour out my soul in me: for I had gone with the multitude, I went with them to the house of God, with the voice of joy and praise, with a multitude that kept holyday.

Why art thou cast down, O my soul? and why art thou disquieted in me? hope thou in God: for I shall yet praise Him for the help of His countenance.

O my God, my soul is cast down within me: therefore will I remember Thee from the land of Jordan, and of the Hermonites, from the hill Mizar.

Deep calleth unto deep at the noise of thy waterspouts: all Thy waves and Thy billows are gone over me.

Yet the Lord will command His lovingkindness in the daytime, and in the night His song shall be with me, and my prayer unto the God of my life.

I will say unto God my rock, Why hast thou forgotten me? why go I mourning because of the oppression of the enemy?

As with a sword in my bones, mine enemies reproach me; while they say daily unto me, Where is thy God?

Why art thou cast down, O my soul? and why art thou disquieted within me? hope thou in God: for I shall yet praise Him, who is the health of my countenance, and my God.

— THE BIBLE, Psalm 42

· II ·

D'ALCALA. Where this voyage started
we don't know, nor where it will end, nor whether
it has a meaning, nor whether there is good
or evil, whether man has a destiny
or happened here by chemical accident—
all this we never know. And that's our challenge—
to find ourselves in this desert of dead light-years,
blind, all of us, in a kingdom of the blind,
living by appetite in a fragile shell
of dust and water; yet to take this dust
and water and our range of appetites
and build them toward some vision of a god
of beauty and unselfishness and truth—
could we ask better of the mud we are
than to accept the challenge, and look up
and search for god-head? If it's true we came
from the sea-water—and children in the womb
wear gills a certain time in memory
of that first origin—we've come a long way;

so far there's no predicting what we'll be
before we end. It may be women help
this progress choosing out the men who seem
a fractional step beyond sheer appetite—
and it may be that's sacred, though my values
are hardly Biblical—and perhaps men help
by setting themselves forever, even to the death,
against cruelty and arbitrary power,
for that's the beast—the ancient, belly-foot beast
from which we came, which is strong within us yet,
and tries to drag us back down. Somehow or other,
in some obscure way, it's the love of woman
for man, and a certain freedom in her love
to choose tomorrow's men, and the leverage
in the interplay of choice between men and women,
that's brought us here—to this forking of the roads—
and may take us farther on.

KING. And where are we going?

D'ALCALA. To a conquest of all there is, whatever there is
among the suns and stars.

KING. And what if it's empty—
what if the whole thing's empty here in space
like a vast merry-go-round of eyeless gods
turning without resistance—Jupiter
and Mars and Venus, Saturn and Mercury,
carved out of rock and trailed with cloud and mist,
but nothing, and in all the constellations,
no meaning anywhere, nothing? Then if man gets up
and makes himself a god, and walks alone
among these limitless tensions of the sky,
and finds that he's eternally alone,
and can mean nothing, then what was the use of it,
why climb so high, and set ourselves apart
to look out on a place of skulls?

D'ALCALA. Now you want to know
what will come of us all, and I don't know that.
You should have asked the fish what would come of him
before the earth shrank and the land thrust up
between the oceans. You should have asked the fish
or asked me, or asked yourself, for at that time
we were the fish, you and I, or they were we—

and we, or they, would have known as much about it
as I know now—yet it somehow seems worth while
that the fish were not discouraged, and did keep on—
at least as far as we are.—For conditions
among the fish were quite the opposite
of what you'd call encouraging. They had
big teeth and no compunction. . . .
Over and over again the human race
climbs up out of the mud, and looks around,
and finds that it's alone here; and the knowledge
hits it like a blight—and down it goes
into the mud again.
Over and over again we have a hope
and make a religion of it—and follow it up
till we're out on the topmost limb of the tallest tree
alone with our stars—and we don't dare to be there,
and climb back down again.
It may be that the blight's on the race once more—
that they're all afraid—and fight their way to the ground.
But it won't end in the dark. Our destiny's
the other way. There'll be a race of men
who can face even the stars without despair,
and think without going mad.

KING. And a man who's lost
the very light from his sky, sits here in his sky
and can say this yet.

                              —MAXWELL ANDERSON, 1888-

In the midst of our bewilderments and near-despairs, we need a new
sure sense of what life requires of us. We need also to know what
we ourselves can depend upon in the universe and in man. The un-
nerving cruelties and appalling stupidities of our time have gone far
to shake our faith in both. Pessimism and cynicism abound, and their
correlate, a lack of confidence. Yet, when we look even at a small
part of the record of what men of sober mind are writing and of
what many of us are searching to understand, we seem to find that,
by and large, we are not surrendering before the problems of our
shaken world. Like Jacob of old, we wrestle through the darkness of
the world's night; and we refuse to let go until the great forces of
life give us their blessing.

Religion has always been an expression, varied throughout the ages and among the many peoples, of man's deep feeling about his relationship to a Reality immeasurably greater than himself. It is possible that out of the confusions of our present time of crisis this relationship will become both deepened and refined.

— Harry A. Overstreet, 1875-

I have gone through a number of stages in my own thoughts on God. . . . As a theological student, I lived through anguished months, when nothing in the external world could stifle the question, "Where is God?" Yet I know that these adolescent years of searching for God were invaluable in my own Odyssey. No religious leader can be of help to men and women who has not himself tasted the bitter cup of rejection, agnosticism, uncertainty. Then, there came a time when I thought that man was enough and that humanism was the answer. . . . Yet I have come to see over the span of years that the wider world just cannot be dismissed and that man considered independent of his cosmic setting can lead only to provincial pride or defiant despair. Man is not alone and neither his mind nor his conscience nor his creative powers can be truly understood if they are regarded as orphans without some universal Parent. I have come to feel that the whole human story, with all its tragedy and its triumph, is like a page torn from the middle of a book, without beginning or end—an undecipherable page, when cut out of its context.—The context of man is the Power greater than man. The human adventure is part of a universal sonnet—one line in a deathless poem.

— Joshua Loth Liebman, 1907-1948

It is a remarkable fact that for many centuries leading theologians and philosophers were almost equally divided between those who attacked and those who defended the arguments for the existence of God. Neither group prevailed over the other in a final way. This situation admits only one explanation: the one group did not attack what the other group defended. They were not divided by a conflict over the same matter. They fought over different matters which they expressed in the same terms. Those who attacked the arguments for the existence of God criticized their argumentative form; those who defended them accepted their implicit meaning.

There can be little doubt that the arguments are a failure. . . .
Both the concept of existence and the method of arguing to a conclusion are inadequate for the idea of God. However it is defined, the
"existence of God" contradicts the idea of a creative ground of
essence and existence. The ground of being cannot be found within
the totality of beings, nor can the ground of essence and existence
participate in the tensions and disruptions characteristic of the transition from essence to existence. The scholastics were right when they
asserted that in God there is no difference between essence and
existence. But they perverted their insight when in spite of this assertion they spoke of the existence of God and tried to argue in favor
of it. Actually they did not mean "existence." They meant the reality, the validity, the truth of the idea of God, an idea which did not
carry the connotation of some*thing* or some*one* who might or might
not exist. Yet this is the way in which the idea of God is understood
today in scholarly as well as in popular discussions about the "existence of God." It would be a great victory for Christian apologetics
if the words "God" and "existence" were very definitely separated
except in the paradox of God becoming manifest under the conditions of existence, that is, in the christological paradox. God does
not exist. He is being-itself beyond essence and existence. Therefore,
to argue that God exists is to deny Him. The arguments for the existence of God neither are arguments nor are they proof of the
existence of God. They are expressions of the *question* of God
which is implied in human finitude. This question is their truth;
every answer they give is untrue. . . .

The question of God is possible because an awareness of God is
present in the question of God. This awareness precedes the question. It is not the result of the argument but its presupposition. This
certainly means that the "argument" is no argument at all. The so-
called ontological argument points to the ontological structure of
finitude. It shows that an awareness of the infinite is included in
man's awareness of finitude. Man knows that he is finite, that he is
excluded from an infinity which nevertheless belongs to him. He is
aware of his potential infinity while being aware of his actual finitude. If he were what he essentially is, if his potentiality were identical with his actuality, the question of the infinite would not arise.
. . . Man must ask about the infinite from which he is estranged,
although it belongs to him; he must ask about that which gives him
the courage to take his anxiety upon himself. And he can ask this
double question because the awareness of his potential infinity is
included in his awareness of his finitude.

The question of God *can* be asked because there is an unconditional element in the very act of asking any question. The question
of God *must* be asked because the threat of nonbeing, which man
experiences as anxiety, drives him to the question of being conquering nonbeing and of courage conquering anxiety. This question is
the cosmological question of God. . . .

The cosmological question of God is the question about that
which ultimately makes courage possible, a courage which accepts
and overcomes the anxiety of categorical finitude: . . . the labile balance between anxiety and courage in relation to time, space, causal-
ity, and substance. In each case we finally have come face to face
with the question how the courage which resists the threat of nonbeing implied in these categories is possible. Finite being includes
courage, but it cannot maintain courage against the ultimate threat
of nonbeing. It needs a basis for ultimate courage. Finite being is a
question mark. It asks the question of the "eternal now" in which the
temporal and the spatial are simultaneously accepted and overcome.
It asks the question of the "ground of being" in which the causal
and the substantial are simultaneously confirmed and negated. The
cosmological approach cannot answer these questions, but it can and
it must analyze their roots in the structure of finitude.

The basis for the so-called teleological argument for the existence
of God is the threat against the finite structure of being, that is,
against the unity of its polar elements. The *telos*, from which this
argument has received its name, is the "inner aim," the meaningful,
understandable structure of reality. This structure is used as a spring-
board to the conclusion that finite *teloi* imply an infinite cause of
teleology, that finite and threatened meanings imply an infinite and
unthreatened cause of meaning. In terms of logical argument this
conclusion is as invalid as the other cosmological "arguments." As
the statement of a question it is not only valid but inescapable and,
as history shows, most impressive. Anxiety about meaninglessness
is the characteristically *human* form of ontological anxiety. It is the
form of anxiety which only a being can have in whose nature freedom and destiny are united. The threat of losing this unity drives
man toward the question of an infinite, unthreatened ground of
meaning; it drives him to the question of God.

—Paul Tillich, 1886-

When men have risen in revolt against God on the ground of the
evil and wrong of the world, they have, by the very fact of so doing,

presupposed the existence of a higher truth, that is to say in the last resort, of God. They rebel against God in the name of God; for the sake of purging men's understanding of God they revolt against a conception of Him which has been besmirched by the mire of this world. But as he treads this path of conflict and anguish man may pass through an experience which brings him moments not only of absolute Godforsakenness but even of the death of God.

— NICOLAS ALEKSANDROVICH BERDYAEV, 1874-1948

I wonder at the boldness with which these persons undertake to speak of God, in addressing their words to the irreligious. Their first chapter is to prove the Divinity by the works of nature. I should not be astonished at their undertaking if they addressed their discourse to believers, for it is certain that those who have faith alive in their hearts see at once that all that exists is nothing else than the work of the God whom they adore. But for those in whom this light is extinct, and in whom we desire to rekindle it, men destitute of faith and grace who, investigating with all their light whatever they see in nature which might lead them to this knowledge, find only clouds and darkness—to say to *them* that they need only look at the least of the things which surround them and they will see God plainly revealed, to give them as the sole proof of this great and important subject the course of the moon and of the planets, and to pretend that with such an argument we have completed the proof, is only to give them reason to suspect that the grounds of our faith are feeble indeed; and I know from reason and experience that nothing is better fitted to arouse in them contempt.

— BLAISE PASCAL, 1623-1662

A man's religious faith (whatever more special items of doctrine it may involve) means for me essentially his faith in the existence of an unseen order of some kind in which the riddles of the natural order may be found explained. The bare assurance that this natural order is not ultimate but a mere sign or vision, the external staging of a many storied universe, in which spiritual forces have the last word and are eternal,—this bare assurance is to such men enough to make life seem worth living in spite of every contrary presumption suggested by its circumstances on the natural plane. Destroy this inner assurance, however, vague as it is, and all the light and radiance of existence is extinguished for these persons at a stroke.

I confess that I do not see why the very existence of an invisible world may not in part depend on the personal response which any one of us may make to the religious appeal. God himself, in short, may draw vital strength and increase of very being from our fidelity. For my own part, I do not know what the sweat and blood and tragedy of this life mean, if they mean anything short of this. If this life be not a real fight, in which something is eternally gained for the universe by success, it is no better than a game of private theatricals from which one may withdraw at will. But it feels like a real fight,— as if there were something really wild in the universe which we, with all our idealities and faithfulnesses, are needed to redeem; and first of all to redeem our own hearts from atheisms and fears. For such a half-wild, half-saved universe our nature is adapted. The deepest thing in our nature is this dumb region of the heart in which we dwell alone with our willingnesses and unwillingnesses, our faiths and fears. As through the cracks and crannies of caverns those waters exude from the earth's bosom which then form the fountain-heads of springs, so in these crepuscular depths of personality the sources of all our outer deeds and decisions take their rise. Here is our deepest organ of communication with the nature of things; and compared with these concrete movements of our soul all abstract statements and scientific arguments—the veto, for example, which the strict positivist pronounces upon our faith—sound to us like mere chatterings of the teeth.

—WILLIAM JAMES, 1842-1910

To tear the will away from all finite aims and conditions . . . requires a painful effort and this effort's ceaseless repetition. And if, in addition to this, the soul has, in spite of all its striving, to be as though it simply were not, it becomes clear that the religious life signifies a dedication to suffering and to self-destruction. What wonder, then, that, for the Jew, death was the price of seeing God; or that, for the Gentile, the soul's entering into closer relations with the Deity meant the beginning of madness? . . . The soul's relation to God is a relation to a Being absolutely different from Man, who cannot confront him as his Superlative or Ideal, and who, nevertheless, is to rule in his inmost soul. Hence a necessary division, ever productive of new pains, is operative within man, as long as he perseveres in this

spiritual endeavour. . . . A finite being, he is to live in the Infinite and
Absolute: he is there like a fish upon dry land.

—SÖREN KIERKEGAARD, 1813-1855

· III ·

When we feel within ourselves that we desire God, then God has
touched the mainspring of power, and through this touch it swings
beyond itself and towards God.

—THEOLOGIA GERMANICA

I fled Him, down the nights and down the days;
   I fled Him down the arches of the years;
I fled Him down the labyrinthine ways
   Of my own mind; and in the midst of tears
I hid from Him and under running laughter.
      Up vistaed hopes I sped;
      And shot, precipitated
   Adown titanic glooms of chasmèd fears,
From those strong Feet that followed, followed after,
      But with unhurrying chase
      And unperturbèd pace,
   Deliberate speed, majestic instancy
     They beat—and a Voice beat
     More instant than the Feet—
"All things betray thee, who betrayest Me."

I pleaded, outlaw-wise,
By many a hearted casement, curtained red,
   Trellised with intertwining charities;
(For, though I knew His love Who followèd,
     Yet I was sore adread
Lest having Him I must have naught beside;)
But, if one little casement parted wide,
   The gust of His approach would clash it to.
Fear wist not to evade as Love wist to pursue.
Across the margent of the world I fled,
   And troubled the gold gateways of the stars,
   Smiting for shelter on their clangèd bars;
     Fretted to dulcet jars

And silvern chatter the pale ports o' the moon.
I said to dawn, Be sudden; to eve, Be soon;
  With thy young skyey blossoms heap me over
    From this tremendous Lover!
Float thy vague veil about me, lest He see!
  I tempted all His servitors, but to find
My own betrayal in their constancy,
In faith to Him their fickleness to me,
  Their traitorous trueness, and their loyal deceit.
To all swift things for swiftness did I sue;
  Clung to the whistling mane of every wind.
    But whether they swept, smoothly fleet,
  The long savannahs of the blue;
    Or, whether, thunder-driven,
  They clanged His chariot 'thwart a heaven
Plashy with flying lightnings round the spurn o' their feet;—
  Fear wist not to evade as Love wist to pursue.
    Still with unhurrying chase
    An unperturbèd pace,
  Deliberate speed, majestic instancy,
    Came on the following Feet,
    And a Voice above their beat—
"Naught shelters thee, who wilt not shelter Me."

I sought no more that after which I strayed,
  In face of man or maid;
But still within the little children's eyes
  Seems something, something that replies;
They are at least for me, surely for me!
I turned me to them very wistfully;
But just as their young eyes grew sudden fair
  With dawning answers there,
Their angel plucked them from me by the hair.
"Come, then, ye other children—Nature's—share
With me" (said I) "your delicate fellowship;
  Let me greet you, lip to lip,
  Let me twine you with caresses,
    Wantoning
  With our Lady Mother's vagrant tresses,
    Banqueting
  With her in her wind-walled palace,
  Underneath her azure dais.

Quaffing, as your taintless way is,
From a chalice
Lucent-weeping out of the dayspring."
So it was done:
I in their delicate fellowship was one—
Drew the bolt of nature's secrecies.
I knew all the swift importings
Of the wilful face of the skies,
I knew how the clouds arise
Spumèd of the wild sea snortings;
All that's born or dies
Rose and drooped with—made them shapers
Of mine own moods, or wailful or Divine—
With them joyed or was bereaven.
I was heavy with the even
When she lit her glimmering tapers
Round the day's dead sanctities.
I laughed in the morning's eyes.
I triumphed and I saddened with all weather,
Heaven and I wept together,
And its sweet tears were salt with mortal mine;
Against the red throb of its sunset-heart
I laid my own to beat,
And share commingling heat;
But not by that, by that, was eased my human smart.
In vain my tears were wet on Heaven's grey cheek.
For ah! we know not what each other says,
These things and I; in sound *I* speak—
Their sound is but their stir, they speak by silences.
Nature, poor stepdame, cannot slake my drouth;
Let her, if she would owe me,
Drop yon blue bosom-veil of sky, and show me
The breasts o' her tenderness:
Never did any milk of hers once bless
My thirsting mouth.
Nigh and nigh draws the chase
With unperturbèd pace,
Deliberate speed, majestic instancy;
And past those noisèd Feet
A voice comes yet more fleet—
"Lo, naught contents thee, who content'st not Me."

Naked I wait thy love's uplifted stroke.
My harness, piece by piece, thou hast hewn from me,
    And smitten me to my knee;
  I am defenseless utterly.
  I slept, methinks, and woke
And slowly gazing, find me stripped in sleep.
In the rash lustihood of my young powers,
  I stood the pillaring hours
And pulled my life upon me; grimed with smears
I stand amid the dust o' the mounded years—
My mangled youth lies dead beneath the heap.
My days have crackled and gone up in smoke,
Have puffed and burst as sun-starts on a stream.
  Yea, faileth now even dream
The dreamer, and the lute the lutanist;
Even the linked fantasies in whose blossomy twist
I swung the earth, a trinket at my wrist,
Are yielding; cords of all too weak account
For earth with heavy griefs so overplussed.
  Ah! is Thy love indeed
A weed, albeit an amaranthine weed,
Suffering no flowers except its own to mount?
  Ah! must—
  Designer Infinite!
Ah, must Thou char the wood ere Thou canst limn with it?
My freshness spent its wavering shower i' the dust:
And now my heart is as a broken fount,
Wherein tear-drippings stagnate, spilt down ever
  From the dank thoughts that shiver
Upon the sighful branches of my mind.
  Such is; what is to be?
The pulp so bitter, how shall taste the rind?
I dimly guess what Time in mists confounds:
Yet ever and anon a trumpet sounds
From the hid battlements of Eternity;
Those shaken mists a space unsettle, then
Round the half-glimpsèd turrets slowly wash again.
  But not ere him who summoneth
  I first have seen, enwound
With glooming robes purpureal, cypress-crowned;
His name I know and what his trumpet saith.

Whether man's heart or life it be which yields
  Thee harvest, must Thy harvest fields
  Be dunged with rotten death?

    Now of that long pursuit
    Comes on at hand the bruit;
  That Voice is round me like a bursting sea:
    "And is thy earth so marred,
    Shattered in shard on shard?
Lo, all things fly thee, for thou flyest Me!
  Strange, piteous, futile thing,
Wherefore should any set thee love apart?
Seeing none but I makes much of naught" (He said);
"And human love needs human meriting:
  How hast thou merited—
Of all man's clotted clay the dingiest clot?
  Alack, thou knowest not
How little worthy of any love thou art!
Whom wilt thou find to love ignoble thee
  Save Me, save only Me?
All which I took from thee, I did but take
  Not for thy harms,
But just that thou mightst seek it in My arms.
  All which thy child's mistake
Fancies as lost, I have stored for thee at home:
  Rise, clasp My hand and come!"
  Halts by me that footfall:
  Is my gloom, after all,
Shade of His hand, outstretched caressingly?
  "Ah, fondest, blindest, weakest,
  I am He Whom thou seekest!
Thou dravest love from thee, who dravest Me."

                    — FRANCIS THOMPSON, 1859-1907

Whoso draws near to God one step through doubtings dim
  God will advance a mile in blazing light to him.

                              — ANONYMOUS

O world, thou choosest not the better part!
It is not wisdom to be only wise,
And on the inward vision close the eyes,
But it is wisdom to believe the heart.
Columbus found a world and had no chart,
Save one that faith deciphered in the skies;
To trust the soul's invincible surmise
Was all his science and his only art.
Our knowledge is a torch of smoky pine
That lights the pathway but one step ahead
Across a void of mystery and dread.
Bid, then, the tender light of faith to shine
By which alone the mortal heart is led
Unto the thinking of the thought divine.

— GEORGE SANTAYANA, 1863-1952

I shall be asked, "What is your religion?" and I shall answer that my religion is to seek truth in life and life in truth, conscious that I shall not find them while I live; my religion is to struggle tirelessly and incessantly with the unknown; my religion is to struggle with God as they say Jacob did from earliest dawn until nightfall. I shall not admit the Unknowable and the Unrecognizable of which pedants write, nor any, "beyond this thou shalt not pass." I reject any eternal *ignorabimus*. In any event I wish to reach the inaccessible.

— MIGUEL DE UNAMUNO Y JUGO, 1864-1936

Not, I'll not, carrion comfort, Despair, not feast on thee;
Not untwist—slack they may be—these last strands of man
In me or, most weary, cry I can no more. I can;
Can something, hope, wish day come, not choose not to be.
But ah, but O thou terrible, why wouldst thou rude on me
Thy wring-world right foot rock? lay a lionlimb against me? scan
With darksome devouring eyes my bruisèd bones? and fan,
O in turns of tempest, me heaped there; me frantic to avoid thee
    and flee?
Why? That my chaff might fly; my grain lie, sheer and clear.
Nay in all that toil, that coil, since (seems) I kissed the rod,

Hand rather, my heart lo! lapped strength, stole joy, would laugh,
    cheer.
Cheer whom though? the hero whose heaven-handling flung me,
    foot trod
Me? or me that fought him? O which one? is it each one? That
    night, that year
Of now done darkness I wretch lay wrestling with (my God!)
    my God.

— GERARD MANLEY HOPKINS, 1844-1889

That everlasting spring, though hidden close,
Well do I know whither and whence it flows,
    Although it is the night.

— ST. JOHN OF THE CROSS, 1542-1591

Afar from mortals place the holy God,
Nor ever think that He, like to thyself,
In fleshly robes is clad; for all unknown
Is the great God to such a worm as thou.
Divers similitudes He bears; at times
He seems as a consuming fire that burns
Unsated; now like water, then again
In sable folds of darkness shrouds Himself.
Nay, even the very beasts of earth reflect
His sacred image; whilst the wind, clouds, rain,
The roll of thunder and the lightning flash,
Reveal to men their great and sovereign Lord.
Before Him sea and rocks, with every fount,
And all the water floods, in reverence bend;
And as they gaze upon His awful face,
Mountains and earth, with the profoundest depths
Of ocean, and the highest peaks of hills,
Tremble: for He is Lord Omnipotent;
And this the glory is of God Most High.

— AESCHYLUS, 525-456 B.C.

The plover, south of Capricorn, hears the call of the Labrador
Spring while yet white Winter reigns, and starts out on her twelve

thousand mile flight; the salmon in the sea is drawn to the breeding grounds of Maine and Scotland and Alaska; the compass-needle trembles at the influence of the distant pole; the moon draws the tides through two hundred and forty thousand miles of intervening space; light travels across the stellar universe; and through the power of gravity distant star greets distant star.

— JAMES BISSETT PRATT, 1875-1944

CHAPTER SIX

Yet a Long Way Off

Shall any gazer see with mortal eyes,
Or any searcher know by mortal mind?
Veil after veil will lift—but there must be
Veil upon veil behind.

— Sir Edwin Arnold, 1832-1904

· I ·

WHY IS it that people are so slow to look for God in earnest? When one is looking for a thing and finds no trace of its existence one hunts halfheartedly and in distress. But lighting on some vestige of the quarry, the chase grows lively, blithe and keen. The man in quest of fire, cheered when he feels the heat, looks for its source with eagerness and pleasure. And so it is with those in quest of God: feeling none of the sweetness of God they grow listless, but sensing the sweetness of divinity they blithely pursue their search for God.

— Meister Eckhart, 1260? - ? 1327

Progress is
The law of life, man is not Man as yet.
Nor shall I deem his object served, his end
Attained, his genuine strength put fairly forth,
While only here and there a star dispels

The darkness, here and there a towering mind
O'erlooks its prostrate fellows: when the host
Is out at once to the despair of night,
When all mankind alike is perfected,
Equal in full-blown powers—then, not till then,
I say, begins man's general infancy.
For wherefore make account of feverish starts
Of restless members of a dormant whole,
Impatient nerves which quiver while the body
Slumbers as in a grave? Oh, long ago
The brow was twitched, the tremulous lids astir,
The peaceful mouth disturbed; half uttered speech
Ruffled the lip, and then the teeth were set,
The breath drawn sharp, the strong right hand clenched stronger,
As it would pluck a lion by the jaw;
The glorious creature laughed out, even in sleep!
But when full roused, each giant-limb awake,
Each sinew strung, the great heart pulsing fast,
He shall start up and stand on his own earth,
Then shall his long triumphant march begin,
Thence shall his being date—thus wholly roused,
What he achieves shall be set down to him.
When all the race is perfected alike
As man, that is; all tended to mankind,
And, man produced, all has its end thus far;
But in completed man begins anew
A tendency to God. Prognostics told
Man's near approach; so in man's self arise
August anticipations, symbols, types
Of a dim splendor ever on before
In that eternal circle life pursues.
For men begin to pass their nature's bound,
And find new hopes and cares which fast supplant
Their proper joys and griefs; they grow too great
For narrow creeds of right and wrong, which fade
Before the unmeasured thirst for good; while peace
Rises within them ever more and more.
Such men are even now upon the earth,
Serene amid the half-formed creatures round
Who should be saved by them and joined with them.

— ROBERT BROWNING, 1812-1889

Men are children of this world,
Yet hath God set eternity in their hearts
As a firm possession, from the day that He created them.

The world is like a flowing brook,
They drink of it and are not sated;
    They would not be satisfied
    Were the sea emptied therein.

It is as though the water were strong brine,
And the craving of their hearts impelled them to drink thereof—
Like a torrent would it rush into their throats,
But their thirst would remain unquenched forever.

    —ABRAHAM BEN MEÏR IBN EZRA, 1092-1167

    Without, in power, we see Him everywhere;
    Within, we rest not, till we find Him there.

    —SIR FULKE GREVILLE, 1554-1628

We think we must climb to a certain height of goodness before we can reach God. But He says not "At the end of the end of the way you may find me"; He says "I am the Way; I am the road under your feet, the road that begins just as low down as you happen to be." If we are in a hole the Way begins in the hole. The moment we set our face in the same direction as His, we are walking with God.

    —HELEN WODEHOUSE, 1880-

    We know Thee, each in part—
        A portion small;
    But love Thee, as Thou art—
        The All in all:
    For Reason and the rays thereof
    Are starlight to the moon of Love.

    —JOHN BANISTER TABB, 1845-1909

And if any one, seeing God, knows what he sees, it is by no means God that he so sees, but something created and knowable. For God

abides above created intellect and existence, and is in such sense unknowable and non-existent that He exists above all existence and is
known above all power of knowledge. Thus the knowledge of Him
who is above all that can be known is for the most part ignorance.

— DIONYSIUS THE AREOPAGITE, about 500 A.D.

Grasp the Skirt of His Grace, for on a sudden He will flee away:
But draw Him not impatiently to thee, lest He fly as an arrow from
 the bow.
What shape will He not assume? What shifts He employeth!
If He be apprehended in Form, He will flee by way of the Spirit:
If thou seek Him in the sky, He will gleam in the water like the
 moon:
If thou go into the water, He fleeth to the sky:
If thou seek Him in the spaceless, He beckoneth to Space:
When thou seekest Him in Space, He fleeth to the spaceless . . .
His Name will flee, the while thou mouldest thy lips for speech:
Thou may'st not even say, Such an one will flee:
He will flee from thee, so that if thou paint His picture,
The picture will flee from the tablet, and His features from thy soul.

— JALAL-UD-DIN RUMI, 1207-1273

How far it is from the knowledge of God to a love of Him!

— BLAISE PASCAL, 1623-1662

The earth is the LORD's, and the fulness thereof; the world, and they
that dwell therein.
 For He hath founded it upon the seas, and established it upon the
floods.
 Who shall ascend into the hill of the LORD? or who shall stand in
His holy place?
 He that hath clean hands, and a pure heart; who hath not lifted
up his soul unto vanity, nor sworn deceitfully.
 He shall receive the blessing from the LORD, and righteousness
from the God of his salvation.
 This is the generation of them that seek Him, that seek thy face,
O Jacob.

Lift up your heads, O ye gates; and be ye lift up, ye everlasting doors; and the King of glory shall come in.

Who is this King of glory? The LORD strong and mighty, the LORD mighty in battle.

Lift up your heads, O ye gates; even lift them up, ye everlasting doors; and the King of glory shall come in.

Who is this King of glory? The LORD of hosts, He is the King of glory.

— THE BIBLE, Psalm 24

· II ·

I distrust all theology as soon as it becomes cocky and dogmatic. When in my senior year in college I returned from agnosticism to theism, I was a neo-Hegelian of sorts, strongly impressed by the type of argument offered in the philosophy of Josiah Royce of Harvard, and in the "Personalism" of Borden P. Bowne of the University of Boston. Then William James called in question my too great confidence in this kind of absolutism, and I became in general attitude a pragmatist. It was the study of theology itself, however, that finished the process. The theology of any generation cannot be understood, apart from the conditioning social matrix in which it is formulated. All systems of theology are as transient as the cultures they are patterned from. The Barthians today talk as though their neo-orthodoxy were the everlasting truth, and some of them, inveighing against pride as a cardinal sin, are giving an exhibition of it that is painful, but Barth illustrates primarily the effect on one's philosophy of life that can come from a psychological response to a powerful conditioning social situation. Living in Europe through one of the most humiliating and disillusioning epochs in history, he turned from anything remotely tinctured with humanistic hopes to God as the "absolutely Other," and his consequent theology, for all the true and valuably corrective insights in it, will prove as a whole as temporary as the situation that produced it.

One would suppose that intelligent human beings living on this wandering island in the sky, on the outskirts of a universe where the nearest fixed star is millions of light-years away, would in the nature of the case be humble when they try to formulate the truth about life as they see it. And one would suppose that such humility would be forced on them when they see their successive theologies shifting and changing as their social cultures alter, never absolute and final, but always relative to the current situation. This is as true for the radicals as for the conservatives, and such liberalism as I have achieved has sprung in part from the honest endeavor to take account of it. . . .

All these theological systems and all others that will follow them are partial, tentative, contemporary formulations of great matters. To take the best insights in them all, to see the incompleteness and falsity in them all, to trust none of them as a *whole*, to see always that the Thing to be explained is infinitely greater than our tentative conditioned explanation—this seems to me wisdom.

— HARRY EMERSON FOSDICK, 1878-

The Book of God is not closed. The coming generations are not disinherited; they who preceded Jesus were not accursed. Revelation, which is, as Lessing says, the education of the human race, descends continuously from God to man.

From epoch to epoch the pages of that eternal gospel are turned; each fresh page disclosed, by the ever-renovating Spirit of God, indicates a period of the progress marked out for us by the providential plan, and corresponds, historically, to a religion. Each religion sets before mankind a new educational idea as its aim; each is a fragment, enveloped in symbols, of eternal truth. So soon as that idea, comprehended by the intelligence and incarnated in the hearts of mankind, has become an inalienable part of the universal tradition, even as the mountain traveler on reaching one summit beholds another rising above him, so is a new idea or aim presented to the human mind, and a new conception of life, a faith, arises to consecrate that idea, and unite the powers and activity of mankind in the fulfilment of that aim. Having accomplished its mission, that religion disappears, leaving behind the portion of truth it contained, the unknown quantity disengaged by it from its symbol, a new immortal star in humanity's heaven.

Eternal God! Thy word is not finished; thy thought, the thought of the world, is not yet all revealed. It still creates, and will continue to create, for long ages beyond all human calculation. The ages that have run their course have revealed to us only a few fragments. Our mission is not ended. We scarcely know its origin; we know nothing of its final end: time and our discoveries do but extend its confines. It ascends from century to century, towards destinies unknown to us; it seeks its own law, of which we possess but the first few lines.

From initiative to initiative through the series of thy successive in-carnations it purifies and extends the formula of self-sacrifice, pur-sues its own path, learns thy ever-widening law. Forms are altered and dissolved. Religions die. The human spirit leaves them behind, as the wayfarer leaves the fires that warmed him in the night, and goes in search of other suns; but religion remains. Thought is im-mortal: it survives all forms and is born again from its own ashes. The idea frees itself from the shrunken symbol, escapes from the chrysalis which prisoned it, which criticism had eaten through. It shines forth pure and bright, a new star in the firmament of human-ity. How many has faith yet to add that the whole way of the future may be illumined? Who can say how many stars, thoughts of the ages, have yet to rise in cloudless splendor and shine in the firma-ment of mind that man may become a living epitome of the Word on the earth?

— GIUSEPPE MAZZINI, 1805-1872

I flung my soul to the air like a falcon flying.
I said, "Wait on, wait on, while I ride below!
    I shall start a heron soon
    In the marsh beneath the moon—
A strange white heron rising with silver on its wings,
        Rising and crying
    Wordless, wondrous things;
    The secret of the stars, of the world's heart-strings
        The answer to their woe.
Then stoop thou upon him, and grip and hold him so!"

My wild soul waited on as falcons hover.
I beat the reedy fens as I trampled past.
    I heard the mournful loon
    In the marsh beneath the moon.
And then, with feathery thunder, the bird of my desire
        Broke from the cover
    Flashing silver fire.
    High up among the stars I saw his pinions spire.
        The pale clouds gazed aghast
As my falcon stooped upon him, and gript and held him fast.

My soul dropped through the air—with heavenly plunder?—
Gripping the dazzling bird my dreaming knew?

Nay! but a piteous freight,
 A dark and heavy weight
Despoiled of silver plumage, its voice forever stilled,—
  All of the wonder
  Gone that ever filled
  Its guise with glory. O bird that I have killed,
   How brilliantly you flew
Across my rapturous vision when first I dreamed of you!

Yet I fling my soul on high with new endeavor,
And I ride the world below with a joyful mind.
 I shall start a heron soon
 In the marsh beneath the moon—
A wondrous silver heron its inner darkness pledges!
  I beat forever
  The fens and the sedges.
 The pledge is still the same—for all disastrous pledges,
  All hopes resigned!
My soul still flies above me for the quarry it shall find!

—William Rose Benét, 1886-1950

They are on the way to truth who apprehend God by means of the divine, Light by the light.

—Philo Judaeus, late first century B.C.
and early first century A.D.

· III ·

We do not understand, but somehow we are part of a creative destiny, reaching backward and forward to infinity—a destiny that reveals itself, though dimly, in our striving, in our love, our thought, our appreciation. We are the fruition of a process that stretches back to star-dust. We are material in the hands of the Genius of the universe for a still larger destiny that we cannot see in the everlasting rhythm of worlds. Nothing happens but what somehow counts in the creative architecture of things. We fail and fall by the way, yet redeeming grace fashions us anew and eliminates our failures in the larger pattern. The pangs of pain, of failure, in this mortal lot, are the birth-throes of transition to better things. We are separated for a time by the indifference of space and by our blindness which particularizes and isolates us. But in us is the longing for unity. We are impelled by a hidden instinct to reunion with the parts of the larger heart of the universe.

— JOHN ELOF BOODIN, 1869-1947

The wasting thistle whitens on my crest,
The barren grasses blow upon my spear,
A green pale pennon: blazon of my faith
And love of fruitless things: yea, of my love,
Among the golden loves of all the knights
Alone: most hopeless, sweet and blasphemous,
The love of God:

              I hear the crumbling creeds
Like cliffs, washed down by water, change and pass;
I hear a noise of words, age after age,
A new cold wind that blows across the plains,
And all the shrines stand empty; and to me
All these things are nothing: priests and schools may doubt
Who never have believed: but I have loved.
Ah, friends, I know it passing well, the love
Wherewith I love: it shall not bring to me
Return or hire or any pleasant thing—
Ay, I have tried it: Ay, I know its roots.
Earthquake and plague have burst on it in vain,
And rolled back shattered—

              Babbling neo-phytes!
Blind, startled fools—think you I know it not?
Think you to teach me? Know I not His ways?
Strange-visaged blunders—mystic cruelties;
All! all! I know Him for I love Him. Go!
So, with the wan waste grasses in my spear,
I ride forever, seeking after God.
My hair grows whiter than my thistle-plume,
And all my bones are loose; but in my eyes
The star of an unconquerable praise:
For in my soul one hope forever sings,
That at the next white corner of a road
My eyes may look on Him. . . .
              Hush—I shall know
The place where it is found: a twisted path

Under a twisted pear-tree—this I saw
In the first dream I had e'er I was born,

Wherein He spoke. . . .

But the grey clouds come down
In hail upon the icy plains: I ride
Burning forever in consuming fire.

— GILBERT K. CHESTERTON, 1874-1936

We have found reason to hold that all actually lived Religion is, in proportion to the depth and delicacy of its spirituality, always simultaneously conscious of two closely interconnected things: *the more than human reality of the Object of its experience,* which Object indeed Itself reveals Itself in, and makes real, this experience, AND *the abiding difference between even this its present experience and the great Reality thus experienced and revealed.* And, in this twin consciousness, living Religion is like every other truly live apprehension. No true scientist, artist, philosopher, no moral striver, but finds himself, at his best and deepest moments, with the double sense that some abiding, trans-subjective, other-than-human or even more-than-human reality, or force, or law, is manifesting itself in his experiences; and yet that these very experiences, and still more his reasoned abstracts of them, give but a very incomplete, ever imperfect, conception of those trans-subjective realities.

— BARON FRIEDRICH VON HÜGEL, 1852-1925

· IV ·

I would define religion as a mysterious and mystic impulse working within us to make us greater than we are, and the world through us better than it is; to lift us to levels above the low ranges of physical appetite and satisfaction; to drive us to goals beyond the prudential bounds of time and sense. Religion belongs distinctively to man not because he can think and speculate, build churches and rear altars, but rather because he can sense the whole of life, catch a vision of the ideal in things real, and is willing to give his life to fulfilling this vision among men. To be compelled to serve an ideal cause by a conviction of its enduring value not merely for ourselves but for humanity and its high destiny upon earth—this is religion.

— JOHN HAYNES HOLMES, 1879-

We can use as our own the inscription on the wall of an ancient temple in Egypt. On one of the walls a priest of the old religion had written for his divinity: "I am He who was and is and ever shall be, and my veil hath no man lifted." On the opposite wall, some one who had found his way into the later, richer faith, wrote this inscription: "Veil after veil have we lifted and ever the Face is more wonderful!"

It must be held, I think, as Emerson so well puts it, that there is "no bar or wall in the soul" separating God and man. We lie open on one side of our nature to God, who is the Oversoul of our souls, the Overmind of our minds, the Overperson of our personal selves. There are deeps in our consciousness which no private plumb line of our own can sound; there are heights in our moral conscience which no ladder of our human intelligence can scale; there are spiritual hungers, longings, yearnings, passions, which find no explanation in terms of our physical inheritance or of our outside world. We touch upon the coasts of a deeper universe, not yet explored or mapped, but no less real and certain than this one in which our mortal senses are at home. We cannot explain our normal selves or account for the best things we know—or even for our condemnation of our poorer, lower self—without an appeal to and acknowledgment of a divine Guest and Companion who is the real presence of our central being.

—Rufus M. Jones, 1863-1948

It is well said, in every sense, that a man's religion is the chief fact with regard to him. A man's, or a nation of men's. By religion I do not mean here the church-creed which he professes, the articles of faith which he will sign and, in words or otherwise, assert; not this wholly, in many cases not this at all. We see men of all kinds of professed creeds attain to almost all degrees of worth or worthlessness under each or any of them. This is not what I call religion, this profession and assertion, which is often only a profession and assertion from the outworks of the man, from the mere argumentative region of him, if even so deep as that. But the thing a man does practically believe (and this is often enough without asserting it even to himself, much less to others); the thing a man does practically lay to heart, and know for certain, concerning his vital relations to this mysterious universe, and his duty and destiny there, that is in all cases the primary thing for him, and creatively determines all the rest. That is his religion; or, it may be, his mere skepticism and no-religion: the manner it is in which he feels himself to be spiritually related to the Unseen World-or-No-World; and I say, if you tell me what that is, you tell me to a very great extent what the man is, what the kind of things he will do is.

— THOMAS CARLYLE, 1795-1881

Religion is the vision of something which stands beyond, behind, and within, the passing flux of immediate things; something which is real, and yet waiting to be realized; something which is a remote possibility, and yet the greatest of present facts; something which gives meaning to all that passes, and yet eludes apprehension; something whose possession is the final good, and yet is beyond all reach; something which is the ultimate ideal, and the hopeless quest.

The immediate reaction of human nature to the religious vision is worship. Religion has emerged into human experience mixed with the crudest fancies of barbaric imagination. Gradually, slowly, steadily, the vision recurs in history under nobler form and with clearer expression. It is the one element in human experience which persistently shows an upward trend. It fades and then recurs. But when it renews its force it recurs with an added richness and purity of content. The fact of the religious vision, and its history of persistent expansion, is our one ground for optimism. Apart from it, human life is a flash of occasional enjoyments lighting up a mass of pain and misery, a bagatelle of transient experience.

The vision claims nothing but worship; and worship is a surrender to the claim for assimilation, urged with the motive force of mutual love. The vision never overrules. It is always there, and it has the power of love presenting the one purpose whose fulfillment is eternal harmony. Such order as we find in nature is never force—it presents itself as the one harmonious adjustment of complex detail. Evil is the brute motive force of fragmentary purpose, disregarding the eternal vision. Evil is overruling, retarding, hurting. The power of God is the worship He inspires. That religion is strong which in its ritual and its modes of thought evokes an apprehension of the commanding vision. The worship of God is not a rule of safety—it is an adventure of the spirit, a flight after the unattainable. The death of religion comes with the repression of the high hope of adventure.

— ALFRED NORTH WHITEHEAD, 1861-1947

Now faith is the substance of things hoped for, the evidence of things not seen.

For by it the elders obtained a good report.

Through faith we understand that the worlds were framed by the word of God, so that things which are seen were not made of things which do appear.

By faith Abel offered unto God a more excellent sacrifice than Cain, by which he obtained witness that he was righteous, God testifying of his gifts: and by it he being dead yet speaketh.

By faith Enoch was translated that he should not see death; and was not found, because God had translated him: for before his translation he had this testimony, that he pleased God.

But without faith it is impossible to please Him: for he that cometh to God must believe that He is, and that He is a rewarder of them that diligently seek Him.

By faith Noah, being warned of God of things not seen as yet, moved with fear, prepared an ark to the saving of his house; by the which he condemned the world, and became heir of the righteousness which is by faith.

By faith Abraham, when he was called to go out into a place which he should after receive for an inheritance, obeyed; and he went out, not knowing whither he went.

By faith he sojourned in the land of promise, as in a strange country, dwelling in tabernacles with Isaac and Jacob, the heirs with him of the same promise:

For he looked for a city which hath foundations, whose builder and maker is God.

Through faith also Sara herself received strength to conceive seed, and was delivered a child when she was past age, because she judged him faithful who had promised.

Therefore sprang there even of one, and him as good as dead, so many as the stars of the sky in multitude, and as the sand which is by the sea shore innumerable.

These all died in faith, not having received the promises, but having seen them afar off, and were persuaded of them, and embraced them, and confessed that they were strangers and pilgrims on the earth.

For they that say such things declare plainly that they seek a country.

And truly, if they had been mindful of that country from whence they came out, they might have had opportunity to have returned.

But now they desire a better country, that is, an heavenly: wherefore God is not ashamed to be called their God: for He hath prepared for them a city. . . .

And what shall I more say? for the time would fail me to tell of Gedeon, and of Barak, and of Samson, and of Jephthah; of David also, and Samuel, and of the prophets:

Who through faith subdued kingdoms, wrought righteousness, obtained promises, stopped the mouths of lions,

Quenched the violence of fire, escaped the edge of the sword, out of weakness were made strong, waxed valiant in flight, turned to flight the armies of the aliens.

Women received their dead raised to life again: and others were tortured, not accepting deliverance; that they might obtain a better resurrection:

And others had trial of cruel mockings and scourgings, yea, moreover of bonds and imprisonment:

They were stoned, they were sawn asunder, were tempted, were slain with the sword: they wandered about in sheepskins and goatskins; being destitute, afflicted, tormented;

(Of whom the world was not worthy:) they wandered in deserts, and in mountains, and in dens and caves of the earth.

And these all, having obtained a good report through faith, received not the promise:

God having provided some better thing for us, that they without us should not be made perfect.

— THE BIBLE, Hebrews 11:1-16, 32-40

· v ·

I am a lamp on the water; at what ghat did'st Thou place me on the
    stream? Where is the ghat at which Thou sett'st me afloat?
In the dark night speaks but the garland of the waves, and under it
    ever flows the stream like a flowing, deep dark night;
My only companion is the little flame, and no bank and no end is
    near . . .
O Ocean, in which all rivers find their destination,
Friend, End of all endless movement, how many bends of the river
    are still before me?
And Thou, with what call wilt Thou reveal Thyself to me?

Thou wilt take me from the water, and there, under the protection
of Thy arm, near to Thy heart, wilt extinguish the burning
of the whole long journey.

— EAST BENGAL BOATMEN'S SONG

Batter my heart, three person'd God; for, You
As yet but knocke, breathe, shine, and seeke to mend:
That I may rise, and stand, o'erthrow mee, 'and bend
Your force, to breake, blowe, burn and make me new.
I, like an usurpt towne, to'another due,
Labour to'admit You, but Oh, to no end,
Reason Your viceroy in mee, mee should defend,
But is captiv'd, and proves weake or untrue.
Yet dearely'I love You,'and would be loved faine,
But am betroth'd unto your enemie:
Divorce mee,'untie, or breake that knot againe,
Take mee to You, imprison mee, for I
Except You'enthrall mee, never shall be free,
Nor ever chast, except You ravish mee.

— JOHN DONNE, 1573-1631

Whosoever walks towards God one cubit, God runs towards him
twain.

— HEBREW PROVERB

Burn, then, little lamp; glimmer straight and clear—
Hush! a rustling wing stirs, methinks the air:
He for whom I wait, thus ever comes to me;
Strange Power! I trust Thy might; trust Thou my constancy.

— EMILY BRONTË, 1818-1848

CHAPTER SEVEN

The Lord, Our God,

Is One God

Men have parabled of Thee in many figures;
Lo, through all their images, Thou art one.

— ANONYMOUS

·I·

WHEN Alexander, the son of Philip, was at Babylon, he sent for a priest from every country and nation which he had vanquished and assembled them in his palace. Then he sat down on his throne and asked them (and there was a great number of them), saying: "Tell me, do you acknowledge and worship a supreme invisible Being?"

Then all the priests bowed their heads and answered: "Yea, O king!"

And the king asked again, "By what name do you call this Being?"

Then the priest from India answered: "We call it Brahma, which signifieth the Great." The priest from Persia said: "We call it Ormus, that is, the Light." The priest from Judea said: "We call it Jehovah Adonai, the Lord which is, which was, and is to come."

Thus each priest had a peculiar word and particular name by which he designated the Supreme Being.

Then the king was wroth in his heart and said, "You have only one lord and king; henceforth you shall have only one God: Zeus is his name."

Then the priests were grieved at the saying of the king, and spake:
"Our people always called him by the name we have proclaimed,
from their youth up. How then may we change it?"

But the king was yet more wroth. Then an old sage stood forth, a
Brahmin, who had accompanied him to Babylon, and said, "Will it
please my lord the king that I speak unto this assembly?"

Then he turned to the priests and said: "Doth not the celestial
day-star, the source of earthly light, shine upon every one of you?"

Then all the priests bowed their heads and answered: "Yea!"

Then the Brahmin asked them one by one: "How do you call it?"

And each priest told him a different word and a peculiar name,
according to his own country and nation.

Then the Brahmin said to the king, "Shall they not henceforth call
the day-star by one name? Helios is his name."

At these words the king was ashamed and said, "Let them use each
his own word; for I perceive that the name and the image constitute
not the being."

—Friedrich Adolph Krummacher, 1767-1845

God's is the east and the west, and wherever ye turn, there is the
face of God. Verily, God comprehends and knows.

Your God is one God; there is no God but Him, the merciful, the
compassionate.

He is God, the creator, the maker, the fashioner, His are the excellent names. His praises, whatever are in the heavens and the earth
do celebrate; for God is the mighty, the wise.

O ye who believe! Remember God with frequent remembrance,
and celebrate His praises morning and evening.

—Mohammed, 570-632

There is one God, in truth there is but one,
Who made the heavens and the broad earth beneath,
The glancing waves of ocean, and the winds;
But many of us mortals err in heart,
And set up, for a solace in our woes,
Images of the gods in stone and brass,
Or figures carved in gold or ivory;

And, furnishing for these, our handiworks,
Both sacrifice and rite magnificent,
We think that thus we do a pious work.

— SOPHOCLES, 496?-406 B.C.

Hear, O Israel: the Lord is our God, the Lord is One.
Blessed be His name, whose glorious kingdom is for ever and ever.
And thou shalt love the Lord thy God with all thine heart, and with all thy soul, and with all thy might. And these words, which I command thee this day, shall be upon thine heart: and thou shalt teach them diligently unto thy children, and shalt talk of them when thou sittest in thine house, and when thou walkest by the way, and when thou liest down, and when thou risest up. And thou shalt bind them for a sign upon thine hand, and they shall be for frontlets between thine eyes. And thou shalt write them upon the door-posts of thy house, and upon thy gates.

— THE SIDDUR

There is one body, and one Spirit. . . .
One Lord, one faith, one baptism,
One God and Father of all, who is above all, and through all, and in you all.

— THE BIBLE, Ephesians 4:4-6

O Thou one God, who art spirit Power to the Animist, darkness-conquering Light to the Parsee, Soul of our soul to the Hindu, Peace to the Buddhist, heavenly Order to the Confucianist, universal Way to the Taoist, Ruler of the judgment day to the Moslem, Shepherd of His people to the Hebrew, and loving Father to the Christian, if it be true that we are ascending the same mountain of truth by different trails, then help us to be kind to our fellow-journeyers upon the ascent, and lead us on toward that single summit, where at last we shall clasp hands with one another in the light of Thy presence.

— JACK FINEGAN, 1908-

The only God whom man can worship without idolatry is the Unknown God—that Supreme Power who "is not a Mind, but something higher than a Mind; not a Force, but something higher than a Force; not a Being, but something higher than a Being; something for which we have no words, something for which we have no ideas."

The expression of the divine element, the glory in nature, as found in the Vedic and Egyptian Hymns, the stress which Buddha places on the inevitability of Cause and Effect, which Zoroaster lays on the conflict of the Good and Evil Powers; Confucius' calm insistence on decorous virtue, the impassioned pleadings of the inspired Prophet of Islam—all have met some inner need of man. Unto each and all of these seers appeared "tongues like as of fire . . . and they were all filled with the Holy Ghost." The paths by which men climb from the shadows of the mountain's base toward its towering summit, start from widely divergent points. As they mount, their ways converge. Once on the cloudless peak, they all see at last the selfsame God. St. Augustine quotes a heathen of his day as saying: "Under different names we adore the only Divinity whose eternal power animates all the elements of the world." Amon or Ormazd, Ishtar, Indra or Osiris, Jupiter or Jehovah, God or Goddess—the names do not greatly signify; the divinities they designate equally answer to the deep human need, as they all embody the most prized ideals of man. "Whensoever piety languisheth, and impiety doth prevail, I create Myself. I am born age after age for the preservation of the righteous, the destruction of evildoers, and the establishment of virtue. . . . Whatever god a worshipper may seek in earnest faith, that selfsame faith in his own god do I confirm. . . . However men may come to Me, thus even serve I them."

In the earliest existing documents there already comes to light the ceaseless searching after God if haply He might be found; and the unanimity of this quest all down the ages is the surest evidence of man's need of Deity. Whatever this straining after God may signify, whether He can be expressed in human terms or not, whether He is but the projection of our own highest ideals, no study is more uplifting than the tracing through the centuries of man's eager, often crude attempt to overtake His Creator and portray Him in all His blinding glory to our mortal eyes.

As far into the remote reaches of existence as we can penetrate, we find too the persistent idea of holiness and righteous living, however that ideal may vary from age to age. Strange, how this notion of holiness (*wholeness*) first entered human thought! Yet there it is, voicing itself in admonitions and aspirations very like our own, in prayers that might have been written yesterday, in lives that approach the Christian ideal if not that of Christ Himself!

If man's conception of God be but the projection of his own highest ideal, then he has cause for deepest humility in that this his ideal has not grown consistently in spiritual beauty throughout the ages. The ancient potters and builders of Egypt long before Isaiah's day conceived of the Highest as Xnum (Potter or Builder). His manifestation was through Thoth (the Word) ages before St. John saw that the "Word was God." Amon was the Ancient of Days who "wipeth away tears from all eyes" centuries before the God of Daniel was conceived or the God of Revelation. "Thy love is in the south, Thy grace is in the north, Thy beauty taketh possession of all hearts," sang the old Egyptian to his God hundreds of years before we learned that "God is Love." "Recompense evil with good," said Lao-Tzu six hundred years before Christ proclaimed the Golden Rule, and two hundred years before the Sermon on the Mount had been pronounced the Law of Manu had admonished man to bless when he is cursed.

Lessons of the beauty of love and self-sacrifice, and of the horror of war, as well as conceptions of the infinity of God and the grace of the life of the spirit fall with double force from the lips of pagan prophets, and we cannot but be touched by the sublimity of the ideals of these old philosophers, preachers and poets too far from Christ in time and place to have ever touched His garment or known the virtue that went out from Him.

— GRACE HILL TURNBULL, 1880-

One Life through all the immense creation runs,
One Spirit is the moon's, the sea's, the sun's;
All forms in the air that fly, on the earth that creep,
And the unknown nameless monsters of the deep,—
Each breathing thing obeys one Mind's control,
And in all substance is a single Soul.

— VERGIL, 70-19 B.C.

To Mercy, Pity, Peace, and Love
All pray in their distress;
And to these virtues of delight
Return their thankfulness,

For Mercy, Pity, Peace, and Love
Is God, our Father dear,
And Mercy, Pity, Peace, and Love
Is man, His child and care.

For Mercy has a human heart,
Pity a human face,
And Love, the human form divine,
And Peace, the human dress.

Then every man, of every clime,
That prays in his distress,
Prays to the human form divine,
Love, Mercy, Pity, Peace.

And all must love the human form,
In heathen, Turk, or Jew;
Where Mercy, Love, and Pity dwell
There God is dwelling too.

— WILLIAM BLAKE, 1757-1827

O God, in every temple I see people that see Thee, and in every
   language I hear spoken, people praise Thee.
Polytheism and Islam feel after Thee.
Each religion says, "Thou art one, without equal."
If it be a mosque, people murmur the holy prayer; and if it be a
   Christian Church, people ring the bell from love to Thee.
Sometimes I frequent the Christian cloister, and sometimes the
   mosque,
But it is Thou whom I seek from temple to temple.
Thy elect have no feelings with heresy or with orthodoxy: for
   neither of them stands behind the screen of thy truth.
Heresy to the heretic, and religion to the orthodox,
But the dust of the rose-petal belongs to the heart of the perfume-
   seller.

— FEISI, 1547-1595

· II ·

Beneath the canopy of the skies roam I night and day:
My home is in the desert by night and day.
    No sickness troubleth me nor silent pain tormenteth;
One thing I know, that I sorrow night and day.

Homeless am I, O Lord: whither shall I turn?
A wanderer in the desert, whither shall I turn?
    I come to Thee at last, driven from every threshold;
And if Thy door be closèd, whither shall I turn?

Blessèd are they who live in sight of Thee,
Who speak with Thee, O Lord, and dwell with Thee.
    Faint are my limbs, and my heart is fearful;
Humbly I sit with those who are dear to Thee.

Drunk tho' we be with pleasure, Thou art our Faith;
Helpless, without hand or foot, Thou art our Faith;
    Whether we be Nazarenes, Mussalmans or Gebres,
Whatsoe'er our creed, Thou art our Faith.

                   — TAHIR, died 1019?

After long study and experience I have come to these conclusions:
that (1) all religions are true, (2) all religions have some error in
them, (3) all religions are almost as dear to me as my own Hinduism. My veneration for other faiths is the same as for my own faith.
Consequently, the thought of conversion is impossible. . . . Our
prayer for others ought never to be: "God! give them the light
Thou hast given to me!" but: "Give them all the light and truth
they need for their highest development!"
    The Allah of Islam is the same as the God of the Christian and
Īśvara of the Hindus. Even as there are numerous names of God in
Hinduism, there are many names of God in Islam. The names do not
indicate individuality but attributes, and little man has tried in his
humble way to describe mighty God by giving Him attributes,
though He is above all attributes, Indescribable, Immeasureable.
Living faith in this God means equal respect for all religions. It
would be the height of intolerance—and intolerance is a species of
violence—to believe that your religion is superior to other religions

and that you would be justified in wanting others to change over to your faith.

I believe in the fundamental truth of all great religions of the world. I believe that they are all God-given and I believe that they were necessary for the people to whom these religions were revealed. And I believe that if only we could all of us read the scriptures of the different faiths from the standpoint of the followers of these faiths, we should find that they were at the bottom all one and were all helpful to one another.

Belief in one God is the corner-stone of all religions. But I do not foresee a time when there would be only one religion on earth in practice. In theory, since there is one God, there can be only one religion. But in practice, no two persons I have known have had the same identical conception of God. Therefore, there will perhaps always be different religions answering to different temperaments and climatic conditions.

— MOHANDAS GANDHI, 1869-1948

Religion has been beyond question one of the supreme attitudes and creative activities of man's spirit here on the earth through the ages. Nothing else has ministered so effectively in the life of the human race to increase the depth and scope of living. Sir Oliver Lodge was speaking wisely when he said that religion has been "the pillar of fire that has gone before the human race in its march through history." The only rival in this field has been the slow refinement, the purification of love in human relationships, and *that* has all along been moulded and influenced by religion. Art and philosophy and music have without doubt been major influences in the depth-culture of the race, but they have all three had their birth under the spur and guidance of religion and they have never attained the full measures of their range and power except under the spell of eternity, which is at the heart of religion.

We shall never really account for the origin of religion by theories of animism, or schemes of magic, or psychologies of fear, or by the long list of pseudo-psychological explanations. Ever since man was really and truly *man* his spirit has been and is self-transcendent. He carries a beyond within himself. There is in him an imaginative dominion over any given experience. He travels and sees beyond everything which his senses present. The moment he is conscious of a limit he is conscious of beyond limit. From time immemorial man of this build has been aware of a *More* breaking in on him. There have been moments of mutual and reciprocal correspondence with a Larger Life impinging on the margins of himself. Mystical communion of this sort is as old in the race as smiling and weeping, as primitive as gravedigging. There has been no great, no permanent, religion that has not come to birth, been fed and fostered by this sort of mutual and reciprocal communion.

It is true of course that religion can become, and often has become, a hindrance to culture and progress. Like everything else that is human religion sometimes goes static, plows ruts, becomes a back wash, loses its vital contact with its original Source and Ground, is used for self-seeking ends, no longer has true savor or dynamic life-building quality. But that is true of every other one of man's supreme traits of life. Here as everywhere we must *level up* to the essential quality and not *level down* to the degenerate forms.

The religions that are living forces in the world today are Buddhism, Christianity—alas, how many forms of it—Confucianism, Hebraism, Hinduism, Islam, Jainism, Shinto, Sikhism, Taoism, and Zoroastrianism. Every intelligent person who is interested in the deeper aspects of human life across the world, now a more or less united whole, ought to know something about these eleven religions, which form the inner life of vast multitudes of people.

It has been my privilege to have had personal contact, in some instances intimate contact, with representatives or groups of every one of these eleven religions, except Zoroastrianism which I know only through books. . . . I am assured that some light and truth have been shed on the pathway of life for vast numbers of people through these religions, only one of which is my religion. I think, we can say, as Saint Peter said to Cornelius: "Of a truth I perceive that God is no respecter of persons; but in every nation he that feareth God and worketh righteousness is acceptable to Him." (Acts 10:34-35.)

When I visited Mahatma Gandhi I was taken over the Ashram by one of Gandhi's most remarkable disciples. I said to him that I found it difficult to understand how Gandhi with his depth of spiritual insight and his purity of faith in the living God could nevertheless approve and share in certain crude and to my mind primitive religious practices. The disciple quietly said: "Yes, I understand your feeling, but Mahatma says that all rivers, even the little rills, carry precious water to the sea, as well as does the mighty sacred Ganges. So it is with these cruder forms of religion. They bear some light and some truth for people who know no other way to God, and we must respect what flows in that tiny stream, though it may lack the unique splendor of the one true fountain."

I still prefer what seems to me to be "the unique splendor of the one Fountain," but I have learned much from these other streams, and I have gained a profound respect for every sincere yearning of man's heart for what is highest and truest.

— RUFUS M. JONES, 1863-1948

The intuition of God is universal, yet there is hardly a universal form—with few possible exceptions—to express it. Indeed, the conceptions of the divine have differed widely and contradicted each other, often flourishing like noisome weeds, inflicting sting and discord. If uniformity and impeccability of expression were the mark of authenticity, such divergence and distortion would refute our assumption of the reality of the mystery. The fact, however, is that men's opinions about God throughout history do not show a greater variety than, for example, their opinions about the nature of the world.

— ABRAHAM JOSHUA HESCHEL, 1907-

You see many stars at night in the sky but find them not when the sun rises; can you say that there are no stars in the heaven of day? So, O man! because you behold not God in the days of your ignorance, say not that there is no God.

As one can ascend to the top of a house by means of a ladder or a bamboo or a staircase or a rope, so divers are the ways and means to approach God, and every religion in the world shows one of these ways.

Different creeds are but different paths to reach the Almighty. Various and different are the ways that lead to the temple of Mother Kali at Kalighat (Calcutta). Similarly, various are the ways that lead to the house of the Lord. Every religion is nothing but one of such paths that lead to God.

I have found that it is the same God toward whom all are directing their steps, though along different paths. You must try all beliefs and traverse all the different ways once. Wherever I look, I see men quarrelling in the name of religion—Hindus, Mohammedans, Brahmans, Vaishnavas, and the rest. But they never reflect that He who is called Krishna is also called Siva, and bears the name of the Primal Energy, Jesus and Allah as well—the same Rama with a thousand names. A lake has several ghats. At one the Hindus take water in pitchers and call it "jal"; at another the Mussalmans take water in leather bags and call it "pani." At a third the Christians call it "water." Can we imagine that it is not "jal" but only "pani" or "water"? How ridiculous! The substance is one under different names, and everyone is seeking the same substance; only climate, temperament, and name create differences. Let each man follow his own path. If he sincerely and ardently wishes to know God, peace be unto him! He will surely realize Him.

Bow down and worship where others kneel, for where so many have been paying the tribute of adoration the kind Lord must manifest Himself, for He is all mercy.

—RAMAKRISHNA, 1834-1886

Just as around our bodies there is a physical world, so around our souls there is a Spiritual Environment—all the major religions teach *that.* They vary widely in their descriptions of this surrounding numinous world; even monotheism, polytheism and pantheism do not exhaust their endeavors to picture it. Confucius had little use for the "gods" familiar in his land and time, but the Spiritual Environment which he called "Tien" (heaven) was central to him. His commission came from beyond himself—"Tien has appointed me to teach this doctrine"—and, as for creation itself, "All Things originate from Tien." Even Gautama Buddha, who least of all the founders of religion believed in a Supreme Being to be depended on and worshipped, was not an atheist, much less a materialist, in our sense of the words. He was imbedded in a realm of spiritual Law, and to discover that Law, meditate upon it, make it one's own and live by it, was to him salvation: "He who abideth in the Law falleth not from security." As for Buddhism in general, its personifications of this "Beyond that is within" are endless and the cry, "Create for the Great King of Glory a palace, which shall be called 'righteousness,'" is typical.

So all religions worship, and in prayer and meditation find inner peace and strength.

> We kneel, how weak; we rise, how
>   full of power!

is an affirmation familiar in every major faith.

As for ethical teaching, the agreement between the great religions is startling to one who for the first time reads the world's sacred scriptures. Lord Krishna, in the Gita, describes the Hindu ideal:

> . . . humbleness,
>   Uprightness, heed to injure naught which lives;
>   Truthfulness, slowness to wrath, a mind
>   That lightly letteth go what others prize,
>   Equanimity and charity
>   Which spieth no man's faults; and tenderness
>   Towards all that suffer; a contented heart,
>   Fluttered by no desires; a bearing mild,
>   Modest and grave; with manhood nobly mixed;
>   With patience, fortitude, and purity;
>   An unrevengeful spirit, never given
>   To rate itself too high—such be the signs
>   Of him whose feet are set on the fair path which
>   leads to heavenly birth.

If Jesus says we must become like little children, Lao Tse says, "The great man is he who does not lose his child's heart"; if the Sermon on the Mount teaches undiscourageable love even toward enemies, Buddhism says,

> Never does hatred cease by hating,
> But by non-hating it does cease.
> That is the eternal Law.

If the New Testament teaches that we cannot love God whom we have not seen without loving our brother whom we have seen, Confucius says, "He who loves best his fellow man is serving God in the holiest way he can." All the religions teach love as against hate, altruism as against selfishness, simplicity of life, freedom from avarice and greed, self-committal and dedication to the highest we know and, in one way or another, from the Christian heaven to the Buddhist Nirvana, hold out the hope of "something after death."

Such common areas, where mutual understanding is possible, do exist amid the infinite diversities of mankind's faiths. As different languages have various words for the same kind of experience, and thus can be translated the one into the other, so religions are not as utterly alien and estranged as they outwardly appear. Undoubtedly this common ground can be overstressed, just as the differentials of the various faiths can be, and dreamers of a universal religion can be tempted to undue optimism. Nevertheless, even if one has no hope of a universal faith, even if one lacks confidence in, or desire for religious unanimity, and most certainly sees that such harmonies as we have described constitute no denial of discords radical and deep, still one can feel the momentous importance of this common ground. . . .

Our sectarian peculiarities have their good uses. The separate churches have performed an important service in history, representing minority convictions which the majority was denying or neglecting, and often with creative vitality, playing the part of trail-blazers and pioneers. Today, however, that emphasis is not enough. We are living in one world—one world, not only for the nations, but for religion too. To have religion go on as one of the most divisive and alienating forces on earth, as it now is, so that religious prejudice and racial prejudice are commonly and correctly paired as major curses of mankind, will never do. "New occasions teach new duties," and our new era urgently calls for a kind of religion which will make for unity, mutual understanding and brotherhood.

This shift of emphasis, this change of mind, this refocusing of thought and care on the common ground where all deeply religious men and women can understand one another is not a utopian dream. Not only are we *pulled* toward it by our idealism, we are also *pushed* toward it by the momentous pressures of our generation; and repeatedly in history, when the pull of idealistic hopes has been backed by the push of practical necessity, something has happened.

— HARRY EMERSON FOSDICK, 1878-

All religion is based on the recognition of a superhuman Reality of which man is somehow conscious and towards which he must in some way orientate his life. The existence of the tremendous transcendent reality that we name GOD is the foundation of all religion in all ages and among all peoples.

— CHRISTOPHER DAWSON, 1889-

The four intuitive religions of the Far East—Brahmanism, Buddhism, Confucianism and Taoism—identify their idea of God with the indeterminate, immortal, intuitively given factor in the aesthetic component of nature and man; and that the three theistic religions of the West and Middle East—Judaism, Christianity and Mohammedanism—identify the idea of God with the determinate, relational, invariant or immortal factor in the theoretic component of nature and man. Since contemporary scientific knowledge embraces both the aesthetic and the theoretic components as ultimate, real and irreducible roots of nature and human nature, it appears that an idea of God which is abreast of contemporary knowledge must enlarge the traditional concepts of God in the two major civilizations of the world to include in the single, complete divine nature the intuitive, indeterminate, aesthetic component of the intuitive religions of the Far East and the theoretic, determinate component of the theistic religions of the West and the Middle East.

We are living in an atomic age in which the failure to bring international deeds under the control of a single world law may mean the death of civilization. There are reasons for believing that, before we can hope to obtain the agreement in the political acts of men necessary for the creation of an effective world law, there must be agreement in the basic beliefs from which these acts stem. Thus the way to a single world religion, richer in its idea of the divine nature than any of the many existent competing religions, may well be a necessary accompaniment of the achievement of world law and the preservation of the hard and slowly won cultural institutions and values of mankind.

If this enrichment of the many present religions of the world by their transformation into one world religion is to be achieved as prescribed by the light of modern knowledge, one additional advance is necessary. Intimations of a theoretic component in nature and man, which is ultimate and immortal and hence divine, came early in the history of the Western world. The importance of these early theistic premonitions, as recorded in the ancient bibles and sacred books, can hardly be overemphasized. Nonetheless, the content of this theoretic component of divinity as thus initially conceived was usually excessively tribal, provincial and anthropomorphic on the one hand, or extremely ambiguous on the other. Consequently, the story of Western religious thought is the story of the continuous reformulation of its content in the light of new and further knowledge. The present conception of this content is no exception to this rule; it, too, cannot be that of yesterday. Hence, an adequate idea of the theoretic component of divinity must fill that component in with content derived from today's rather than yesterday's empirically verified and theoretically formulated knowledge.

Furthermore, this contemporary reformulation, following the aforementioned extremely intellectual and theoretic character of contemporary scientific knowledge, will be much more intellectual and rationalistic in its emphasis than is the traditional, modern Western religious doctrine. In this respect it will be more like medieval Arabian Mohammedanism and Judaism and Augustinian Platonic—rather than Thomistic Aristotelian—Roman Catholicism. The contemporary content, however, will give expression to the reformatory spirit of contemporary Turkish Mohammedanism, early prophetic Judaism and the initial modern Protestantism.

It appears, therefore, that contemporary knowledge entails two enlargements and enrichments of the traditional idea of God. First, the Oriental intuition of the divine as all-embracing, indeterminate, immediate feeling must be combined with the Western theistic conception of the deity as a doctrinately designated, determinate being. Second, the Western theistic contribution to this more complete, richer, truly universal world religion must be re-expressed in more completely nonsensuous, intellectual form with contemporary content.

The result will be a religion which places a greater emphasis upon passion, feeling and intuitive aesthetic sensitivity on the one hand, and upon reason, doctrine and intellect on the other hand, than does any one of the many existing religions. It is to be emphasized especially that this is not the tepid, watered-down common denominator of the many existing religions of the world that is usually suggested as a world religion; instead, the existing, separate religions are each made more passionate and intense in their own particular genius. The emotional love of God and the intellectual love of God are each maximized and then merged.

—F. S. C. NORTHROP, 1893-

To enjoy the benefits of providence is wisdom; to enable others to enjoy them is virtue. He who is indifferent to the welfare of others does not deserve to be called a man.
The best way of worshipping God is to allay the distress of the times and to improve the conditions of mankind.
This is true religion: to cleanse oneself with pure thoughts,

words and deeds. He needs no other rosary whose life is strung with beads of loving thought.

Have the religions of mankind no common ground? Is there not everywhere the same enrapturing beauty, beaming forth from many thousand hidden places?

Broad indeed is the carpet which the All-loving One has spread, and beautiful the colors He has given it.

There is but one lamp in His house, in the rays of which, wherever we look, a bright assembly greets us.

Diversity of worship has divided the human race into countless nations; from all their dogmas we may select one:—Divine Love.

— Zoroastrian Scriptures

· III ·

God is creative power, immanent in the Soul.

God is Mind Essence, the all-inclusive Whole, containing all things in potentiality.

God is the binding element in the world.

God is creative energy, the spring of all renewal.

God is Truth, Goodness and Beauty.

— Anonymous

By *God*, I mean a being absolutely infinite—that is, a substance consisting in infinite attributes, of which each expresses eternal and infinite essentiality.

— Baruch Spinoza, 1632 - 1677

He that dwelleth in the secret place of the most High shall abide under the shadow of the Almighty.

I will say of the Lord, He is my refuge and my fortress: my God; in Him will I trust.

Surely He shall deliver thee from the snare of the fowler, and from the noisome pestilence.

He shall cover thee with his feathers, and under His wings shalt thou trust: His truth shall be thy shield and buckler.

Thou shalt not be afraid for the terror by night; nor for the arrow that flieth by day;

Nor for the pestilence that walketh in darkness; nor for the destruction that wasteth at noonday.

A thousand shall fall at thy side, and ten thousand at thy right hand; but it shall not come nigh thee.

Only with thine eyes shalt thou behold and see the reward of the wicked.

Because thou hast made the LORD, which is my refuge, even the most High, thy habitation;

There shall no evil befall thee, neither shall any plague come nigh thy dwelling.

For He shall give His angels charge over thee, to keep thee in all thy ways.

They shall bear thee up in their hands, lest thou dash thy foot against a stone.

Thou shalt tread upon the lion and adder: the young lion and the dragon shalt thou trample under feet.

Because He hath set his love upon me, therefore will I deliver Him: I will set Him on high, because He hath known my name.

He shall call upon me, and I will answer Him: I will be with Him in trouble; I will deliver Him, and honour Him.

With long life will I satisfy Him, and show Him my salvation.

— THE BIBLE, Psalm 91

We worship the One God who fashioned the whole fabric with the instrument of elements, bodies, spirits, and who by His word commanded it, by the reason with which He ordered it, by the power wherewith He formed it, making it out of nothing as an ornament of His own majesty: whence it came about that the Greeks also gave the universe the name of *kosmos*. Invisible He is, though He is seen. Incomprehensible He is, though He is by grace revealed. Inconceivable He is, though our human senses may conceive Him. He is true, and He is great. But what in the ordinary sense may be seen, comprehended, conceived, is less than the eye that grasps it, the hands that soil it, the senses that discover it: for the infinite is known only to itself. So it is that we may conceive of God, though He is beyond our reckoning. The power of His greatness makes Him known to man, but He is yet unknown. And this is the sum total of their sin who will not recognize Him even when they cannot fail not to know Him. Would you have us prove Him to you from the vast variety of His works, those works which contain, sustain, delight and terrify us? Would you have us prove Him to you by the testimony of the human soul itself? The poor imprisoned soul, confined by its own depravity, exhausted by lusts and desires, enslaved to false gods, nevertheless after recovering its senses, having spewed out the evil within it, or as though awakening from sleep or from illness, when it comes to its proper health, why then, it utters the name of God, for no other reason except that it recognizes Him as the only true god.

— TERTULLIAN, 160?-?230

I am grateful to Nature, not so much when I see her on the side that is open to the world, as when I am permitted to enter her shrine. Then one may seek to know of what stuff the universe is made, who is its author and guardian, what is the nature of God.

Here at last the soul comes to learn what it has long sought, it begins to know God. But what is God? The universal Intelligence. What is God? did I say? All that you see and all that you cannot see.

His greatness exceeds the bounds of thought. He is all in all, He is at once within and without His works. In us the better part is spirit, in Him there is nothing except spirit.

He is wholly Reason: though the eyes of mortals are so sealed by error that they believe this frame of things to be but a fortuitous concourse of atoms, the sport of chance. Yet than this universe could aught be fairer, more carefully adjusted, more consistent in plan? . . .

The ancient sages recognized the same Jupiter as we do, the Guardian and Ruler of the universe, its soul and breath, the Maker and Lord of this earthly frame of things, to whom every name of power is appropriate.

If you prefer to call Him Fate, you will not be wrong. He it is on whom depend all things, the Cause of causes.

If you prefer to call Him Providence, you will still be right; for He it is by whose counsel provision is made for the world that it may pursue its orderly course and unfold the drama of its being.

If you prefer to call Him Nature, you will make no mistake; for He it is from whom all things derive being, and by whose breath we live.

If you prefer to call Him the World, you will not err, for He is everything that you can see. He is wholly infused in all His parts, self-sustained through inherent power.

— LUCIUS ANNAEUS SENECA, 4 B.C.? -65 A.D.

God is the Oneness
That spans the fathomless deeps of space
And the measureless eons of time,
Binding them together in act,
As we do in thought.

He is the sameness
In the elemental substance of stars and planets,
Of this our earthly abode
And of all that it holds.

He is the unity
Of all that is,
The uniformity of all that moves,
The rhythm of all things
And the nature of their interaction.

God is the mystery of life,
Enkindling inert matter
With inner drive and purpose.

He is the creative flame
That transfigures lifeless substance,
Leaping into ever higher realms of being,
Brightening into the radiant glow of feeling,
Till it turns into the white fire of thought.

God is in the faith
By which we overcome
The fear of loneliness, of helplessness,
Of failure and of death.

God is in the hope
Which, like a shaft of light
Cleaves the dark abysms
Of sin, of suffering, and of despair.

God is in the love
Which creates, protects, forgives.

His is the spirit
Which broods upon the chaos men have wrought
Disturbing its static wrongs,
And stirring into life the formless beginnings
Of the new and better world.

— MORDECAI MENAHEM KAPLAN, 1881-

Should one in boldness say, Lo, I am God!
Besides the One—Eternal—Infinite,
Then let him from the throne he has usurped
Put forth his power and form another globe,
Such as we dwell in, saying, This is mine.
Nor only so, but in this new domain
For ever let him dwell. If this he can,
Then verily he is a god proclaimed.

— PYTHAGORAS, sixth century B.C.

In one God I believe
Sole and eternal, moving all the heaven,
Himself unmoved, with love and with desire.
For such belief not only have I proofs
From physics and from metaphysics, but
'Tis also given me by the truth which flows
Through Moses and the Prophets and the Psalms,
Through the Evangel, and through you who wrote
As God's inspired guardians of the truth.

— DANTE ALIGHIERI, 1265-1321

That God exists can be proved in five Ways:—

1. The first and most evident Way is the argument from Motion. For it is certain and agrees with what our senses inform us that in this world some things are in motion. But anything which is moved, is moved by some other thing; for nothing is moved except in so far as there is in it the relation of potentiality with that towards which it is moved; but one thing moves another in so far as the former is in actuality, for to move is nothing else than to draw anything from potentiality into actuality. But nothing can be brought from potentiality into actuality except by means of something which is already

in actuality. Fire which is actual heat makes wood which is only potentially hot become actually hot, and by this means moves and alters it. Moreover, it is impossible for the same thing to be in potentiality and in actuality at the same time and in the same respect; it could be so only in different respects; for what is actually hot cannot be at the same time potentially hot, although it is at the same time potentially cold. It is impossible, therefore, that in the same respect and in the same manner anything should be both moving and moved, or be self-moved. Everything therefore which is moved must be moved by something else. If therefore that by which the first thing is moved should itself be moved this must be by motion from some third thing, and that third thing by some other in its turn. We cannot here proceed to infinity, for in that way there would be no first source of movement and consequently no other moving thing at all, because secondary moving things do not move except as they are moved by the first source of movement; a stick, for example, does not move except it is moved by a hand. We must then arrive at some first source of motion which is moved by nothing else: and such a source all men understand to be God.

2. The second Way is from consideration of efficient Causes. In things of sense we find an order of efficient causes; but it is not found, nor is it possible, that anything is the cause of itself, for this would mean that it is prior to itself, which is impossible. Finally, it is not possible in efficient causes to go back to infinity, for in all series of efficient causes first comes the cause of the intermediate, and the intermediate is the cause of the last whether the intermediate be many or only one. If then the Cause is removed so is the effect. Therefore, if there have not been a first among the efficient causes neither will there be a last, nor an intermediate. But if we proceed with efficient causes in infinity, there will be no first efficient cause, and so no last effect, nor any intermediate efficient causes; which is plainly false. We must therefore posit some first efficient Cause: and all men call this God.

3. The third Way is taken from consideration of the possible and the necessary, and proceeds as follows. Amongst things we find some which are capable of existing or not existing, for they are found to be generated and to be corrupted, and therefore can either exist or not exist. It is impossible, however, that all the things of this kind should always be in existence, because what is capable of not existing, at some time does not exist. If, therefore, all things are capable of not existing, there was a time when there was nothing in existence. But if this is true, even now there would be nothing in existence, for the

non-existent does not commence to exist except by virtue of some other thing which is already existing. If ever, therefore, there were nothing in existence, it is impossible that anything should commence to exist: and so there would be nothing in existence now: which is obviously false. Therefore it cannot be that all things are merely capable of existing; there must be among things some thing which is necessary.

Moreover, every necessary thing either has a cause of its necessity from some other quarter, or it has not. But it is not possible to proceed in infinity in things necessary which have a cause of their necessity, just as was proved for efficient causes. We must, therefore, posit something which has its necessity, not from some other quarter but *per se;* and which is itself a cause of necessity to other things. And this all men call God.

4. The fourth Way is the consideration of the grades or stages which are found in things. For we find in things something more or less good and true and noble, and so of other qualities of this kind. But "more" or "less" are spoken of different things, according to their different degrees of approach to what is greatest of all: as that thing is the hotter which more nearly approaches that which is hottest. There is, therefore, something which is most true and most good and most noble, and consequently is being in the highest degree: for what is true in the highest degree is also being in the highest degree, as is said in the *Metaphysics,* Bk. II. But whatever is called highest in any kind of being is the cause of all other things which are of that kind; as fire, which is the highest of the class of hot things is the cause of all hot things, as is said in the same book. There is, therefore, some being which to all beings is the cause that they exist, and that they are good, and so for every perfection. And this we call God.

5. The fifth Way is the consideration of the government of things. For we see that some things which have no power of knowing, such as natural bodies, work for ends, as is manifest from their constantly, or at least frequently, working in the same way for the attainment of that which is best; which shows that they arrive at their end not by chance but from intention. Now such things as have no power of knowing do not tend towards an end unless they are directed by some being which has knowledge and intelligence, as an arrow is directed by an archer. There is therefore some intelligent Being by which all natural things are directed towards ends. And this we call God.

— St. Thomas Aquinas, 1225?-1274

O Thou Perfect! Thou Eternal! Thou Only One!
Great Hawk that fliest with the flying Sun!
Between the Turquoise Sycamores that risest, young for ever,
Thine image flashing on the bright celestial river.

Thy rays are on all faces; Thou art inscrutable.
Age after age thy life renews its eager prime.
Time whirls its dust beneath thee; thou art immutable,
Maker of Time, thyself beyond all Time.

Thou passest through the portals that close behind the night,
Gladdening the souls of them that lay in sorrow.
The True of Word, the Quiet Heart, arise to drink thy light;
Thou art Today and Yesterday; Thou art Tomorrow!

—Ancient Egyptian Hymn

Most glorious of the immortals, thou of many names, omnipotent
    for aye,
O Zeus, founder of nature, who dost govern all things by law,
All hail! For mortals all enjoy the right to call upon thee,
Since we are thine offspring, the lot having fallen on us to be thine
    echo,
We alone, all mortal things that live and creep on earth.
Therefore will I hymn thee and sing thy might for ever.
All yonder world that wheels about the earth
Obeys thee, wheresoe'er thou leadest, and willingly is swayed by
    thee.
Such minister hast thou in thine unconquered hands,
The two-edged, fiery, ever-living thunderbolt,
For at its stroke all nature quakes.
By it thou dost direct the universal reason, which through all things
Runs, mingled with the lights both great and small.
So great art thou, a king supreme for ever.
Without thee, power divine, there is naught done on earth
Nor in heaven's holy vault, nor in the deep,
Save what bad men in their own folly perpetrate.
But thou dost know how best to make the uneven even,
To order the disorderly, and make the loveless loving.
So hast thou harmonized in one all good things with the bad
That they should form the Reason of the Eternal Universe,
Which evil men, fleeing, abandon,

Mortals ill-starred, who, coveting the gain of fancied good,
Do neither see nor hear God's universal law,
That law, to which obedience yielding they might lead a life of
   sense and virtue.
But they, strangers to goodness, seek their various ends:
Some on the feverish quest of glory all agog,
Others intent on lucre's sorry gain,
Others, voluptuous, all on ease and pleasure bent,
Wander this way and that, nor ever reach the goal.
But thou, O Zeus, all-bounteous, wrapt in dusky clouds, lord of the
   thunderbolt,
O save men from their baneful ignorance,
Disperse it, Father, from their soul afar; grant that we do attain
That wisdom, wherein trusting thou dost rule all things in justice,
To the end that we, honored by thee, may thee requite with honor,
Hymning thy works for evermore, as doth become
A mortal man; for sure nor men nor gods can win a guerdon greater
Than to hymn the universal law in righteousness for aye.

                              — CLEANTHES, third century B.C.

Magnified and praised be the living God;
He is, and there is no limit in time unto His being.
He is One, and there is no unity like unto His unity;
Inconceivable is He, and unending is His unity.

He hath neither bodily form nor substance;
We can compare naught unto Him in His holiness.

He was before anything that hath been created—even the first;
But His existence had no beginning. . . .

He watcheth and knoweth our secret thoughts;
He beholdeth the end of a thing before it existeth. . . .

Blessed forevermore be His glorious name.

                        — DANIEL BEN JUDAH, fourteenth century

CHAPTER EIGHT

The Light That Never Was on Land or Sea

Do you not seek a light, ye who are surrounded by darkness?

— THE DHAMMAPADA

· I ·

THE WORLD is charged with the grandeur of God.
  It will flame out, like shining from shook foil;
  It gathers to a greatness, like the ooze of oil
Crushed. Why do men then now not reck his rod?
Generations have trod, have trod, have trod;
  And all is seared with trade; bleared, smeared with toil;
  And wears man's smudge and shares man's smell: the soil
Is bare now, nor can foot feel, being shod.

And for all this, nature is never spent;
  There lives the dearest freshness deep down things;
And though the last lights off the black West went
  Oh, morning, at the brown brink eastward, springs—
Because the Holy Ghost over the bent
  World broods with warm breast and with ah! bright wings.

— GERARD MANLEY HOPKINS, 1844-1889

143

The physical facts of science are not cold, unless your soul and your heart are cold. There is white heat somewhere in every physical fact when we decipher correctly the message which it conveys to us. Fifty years ago, when as a member of a herdsman's squad of boys I watched the stars on the black background of a summer midnight sky, I felt that their light was a language proclaiming the glory of God. Has science changed that vision of the early childhood days? Fifty years ago, instructed by David's psalms, I found in the light of the stars a heavenly language which proclaims the glory of God, but I did not know how that language reached me, and I hoped that some day I might find out. That hope was in my soul when I landed at Castle Garden. Today science tells me that the stars themselves bring it to me. The light of the stars is a part of the life-giving breath of God. I never look now upon the starlit vault of the heaven without feeling this divine breath and its quickening action upon my soul.

We feel intuitively that science will never penetrate the mysteries beyond physical phenomena, but our faith encourages us in the belief that there behind the impenetrable veil of this eternal background is the throne of a Divine power, the soul of the physical world.

— MICHAEL PUPIN, 1858-1935

O Light Invisible, we praise Thee!
Too bright for mortal vision.
O Greater Light, we praise Thee for the less;
The eastern light our spires touch at morning,
The light that slants upon our western doors at evening,
The twilight over stagnant pools at batflight,
Moon light and star light, owl and moth light,
Glow-worm glowlight on a grassblade.
O Light Invisible, we worship Thee!

We thank Thee for the lights that we have kindled,
The light of altar and of sanctuary;
Small lights of those who meditate at midnight
And lights directed through the coloured panes of windows
And light reflected from the polished stone,
The gilded carven wood, the coloured fresco.
Our gaze is submarine, our eyes look upward
And see the light that fractures through unquiet water.
We see the light but see not whence it comes.
O Light Invisible, we glorify Thee!

In our rhythm of earthly life we tire of light. We are glad when the
day ends, when the play ends; and ecstasy is too much pain.
We are children quickly tired: children who are up in the night and
fall asleep as the rocket is fired; and the day is long for work or
play.
We tire of distraction or concentration, we sleep and are glad to
sleep,
Controlled by the rhythm of blood and the day and the night and the
seasons.
And we must extinguish the candle, put out the light and relight it;
Forever must quench, forever relight the flame.
Therefore we thank Thee for our little light, that is dappled with
shadow.
We thank Thee who hast moved us to building, to finding, to form-
ing at the ends of our fingers and beams of our eyes.
And when we have built an altar to the Invisible Light, we may set
thereon the little lights for which our bodily vision is made.
And we thank Thee that darkness reminds us of light.
O Light Invisible, we give Thee thanks for Thy great glory!

—T. S. Eliot, 1888-

O Lord, pardon my three sins:
I have in contemplation clothed in form Thee who art formless!
I have in praise described Thee who are ineffable!
And in visiting shrines I have ignored Thine omnipresence.

—Sankara

Formless, that self-luminous Being exists within and without, higher
than the highest. From Him issue life, and mind, and senses—ether,
air, water, fire, and the earth. . . . He is the innermost Self in all beings.
He who knows him hidden in the shrine of his heart cuts the knot of
ignorance even in his life. Self-luminous, ever present in the hearts
of all, is the great Being. He is the refuge of all. In Him exists all that
moves and breathes. Adorable is He. He is the supreme goal. He is
beyond the known, and beyond the knowable. He is self-luminous,
subtler than the subtlest; in Him exist all the worlds and those that
live therein. He is that imperishable *Brahman.* He is the life-prin-
ciple; He is the speech and the mind; He is the truth; He is immortal.
He is to be realized. Attain Him, O friend.

—Mundaka Upanishad

According to strict truth, God is incomprehensible, and incapable of being measured. For whatever be the knowledge which we are able to obtain of God, either by perception or reflection, we must of necessity believe that He is by many degrees far better than what we perceive Him to be. For, as if we were to see any one unable to bear a spark of light, or the flame of a very small lamp, and were desirous to acquaint such a one, whose vision could not admit a greater degree of light than what we have stated, with the brightness and splendour of the sun, would it not be necessary to tell him that the splendour of the sun was unspeakably and incalculably better and more glorious than all this light which he saw? So our understanding, when shut in by the fetters of flesh and blood, and rendered, on account of its participation in such material substances, duller and more obtuse, although, in comparison with our bodily nature, it is esteemed to be far superior, yet, in its efforts to examine and behold incorporeal things, scarcely holds the place of a spark or lamp. But among all intelligent, that is, incorporeal beings, what is so superior to all others—so unspeakably and incalculably superior—as God, whose nature cannot be grasped or seen by the power of any human understanding, even the purest and brightest?

But it will not appear absurd if we employ another similitude to make the matter clearer. Our eyes frequently cannot look upon the nature of the light itself—that is, upon the substance of the sun; but when we behold his splendour or his rays pouring in, perhaps, through windows or some small openings to admit the light, we can reflect how great is the supply and source of the light of the body. So, in like manner, the works of Divine Providence and the plan of this whole world are a sort of rays, as it were, of the nature of God, in comparison with His real substance and being. As, therefore, our understanding is unable of itself to behold God Himself as He is, it knows the Father of the world from the beauty of His works and the comeliness of His creatures.

—ORIGEN, 185?-?254

Let us reason again with an universal awe
The eternal Being of God, His absolute
    Entity and mystery, and His absolute law,
His absolute proclamation, though He be quite mute,
    His absolute foresight, though He be quite blind,

And His absolute deafness to violin or flute;
   And when we stagger, having such God in mind,
Let us not think that therefore He is not—
   Let us not, incomprehending, therefore unbind
Our manhood's cords, by hacking through the knot
   Which cannot in fact be unraveled, thus to claim
An ostensible liberty in which we rot;
   For however we may fidget, argue, or blame,
We live but in His illimitable thought
   And should be nameless but for His secret name;
And however we have scratched and screamed and fought
   To make ourselves dominant and unclean,
It still remains that we alone are as naught—
   It still remains that we are what we have been,
And shall be so to the ultimate generation;
   While ever about us, ever to be unseen,
Ever to be unheard, and beyond violation,
Blazes the Godhead; though, in our perturbation,
His image be lost to us by lack of contemplation.

     — ALASTAIR W. R. MILLER, contemporary

God's Spirit is no private empty shade,
But that great Ghost that fills both earth and sky,
And through the boundless universe doth lie,
Shining through purged hearts and simple minds,
When doubling clouds of thick hypocrisy
Be blown away with strongly brushing winds.
Who first this tempest feels, the Sun he after finds.

     — HENRY MORE, 1624-1687

To You the stars of morning upward sing,
From You the sources of their radiance spring.
And steadfast in their vigils, day and night,
The sons of God, flooded with fervor, ring
Your praise; they teach the holy ones to bring
Into Your house the breath of early light.

     — YEHUDAH HALEVI, 1085?-?1140

Veni, sancte Spiritus,
Et emitte caelitus
   Lucis tuae radium:
Veni, pater pauperum;
Veni, dator munerum;
Veni lumen cordium.

Holy Spirit, Lord of light,
From Thy clear celestial height
   Thy pure beaming radiance give;
Come, Thou Father of the poor,
Come, with treasures that endure,
   Come, thou light of all that live!

Thou, of all consolers best,
Thou, the soul's delightsome guest,
   Dost refreshing peace bestow;
Thou in toil art comfort sweet,
Pleasant coolness in the heat,
   Solace in the midst of woe.

Light immortal, light divine!
Visit Thou these hearts of thine
   And our inmost being fill:
If Thou take thy grace away,
Nothing pure in man will stay:
   All his good is turned to ill.

Heal our wounds, our strength renew,
On our dryness pour thy dew:
   Wash the stains of guilt away.
Bend the stubborn heart and will;
Melt the frozen, warm the chill;
   Guide the steps that go astray.

Thou, on those who evermore
Thee confess and Thee adore,
   In thy sevenfold gifts, descend;
Give them comfort when they die,
   Give them life with Thee on high,
   Give them joys that never end.

— Ascribed to STEPHEN LANGTON, died 1228

Undying Soul of this material ball,
Heaven- and Earth-Maker! Thou who first didst call
Time into being, and by Thy behest
Movest all things, Thyself alone at rest,
No outward power impelled Thee thus to mold
In shape the fluid atoms manifold,
Only the immortal image, born within,
Of perfect beauty! Wherefore Thou hast been
Thine own fair model, and the things of sense
The image bear of Thy magnificence!
Parts perfect in themselves, by Thy control,
Are newly wrought into a perfect whole;
The yoked elements obey Thy hand:
Frost works with fire, water with barren sand,
So the dense continents are fast maintained,
And heaven's ethereal fire to earth restrained.
Thou dost the life of threefold nature tame,
To serve the parts of one harmonious frame,—
That soul of things constrained eternally
To trace Thy image on the starry sky,
The greater and the lesser deeps to round,
And on Thyself return. Thou too hast found
For us, thy lesser creatures of a day,
Wherewith Thou sowest earth,—forms of a clay
So kindly-fragile naught can stay our flight
Backward, unto the source of all our light!
Grant, Father, yet the undethronéd mind!
A way unto the fount of truth to find,
And, sought, so long, the Vision of Thy face!
Lighten our flesh! Terrestrial vapours chase,
And shine in all Thy splendour! For Thou art
The final rest of every faithful heart,
The First, the Last! of the expatriate soul
Lord, Leader, Pathway, and Eternal Goal!

—Boethius, 480?-?524

· II ·

O Lord, who hast brought us through the darkness of night to the light
of the morning, and who by Thy Holy Spirit dost illumine the darkness of ignorance and sin; we beseech Thee, of Thy loving-kindness,

to pour Thy holy light into our souls, that we may ever be devoted to Thee by whose wisdom we were created, by whose mercy we were redeemed, and by whose Providence we are governed; to the honour and glory of Thy great name.

— BOOK OF HOURS

Void the mind,
Open the being to God;
Abide in stillness,
Life arises, and passes,
Birth, growth, and return,
A rhythmic arc from Source to Source.
In the rhythm is quietude,
A tranquil submission;
In the soul's submission is peace,
Absorption in Eternity.
And so, the Great Light!

— LAO-TSE, 604-531 B.C.

Deign, then, O Lord, to hear our prayers, pour Thyself upon our hearts, and with the splendour of Thy most holy fire illumine our darkness and, like a trusted guide, in this blind labyrinth show us the true path. Correct the falseness of our senses, and after our long pursuit of vanities give us true and solid good; make us to inhale those spiritual odours that quicken the powers of the intellect, and to hear the celestial harmony with such accord that there may no longer be room in us for any discord of passion; fill us at that inexhaustible fountain of content which ever delights and never satiates, and gives a taste of true beatitude to all who drink of its living and limpid waters; with the beams of Thy light purge our eyes of misty ignorance, to the end that they may no longer prize mortal beauty, and may know that the things which they seemed to see, are not, and that those which they saw not, really are.

— CONTE BALDASSARE CASTIGLIONE, 1478-1529

Religion alone brings the vivid revelation of Spirit other than the human—a Spirit so perfect and so richly real as Itself to be the ultimate, overflowingly self-conscious cause of man's very capacity for apprehending it. Nevertheless, such a Self-manifestation of Perfect Spirit, once found and accepted, gives a base, a setting and a crown to all those other self-manifestations of the lesser realities—a base, a setting and a crown which their graduated series, taken as a whole, so greatly requires and which indeed it dimly and semi-consciously prepares yet cannot itself effectuate. And this same Self-manifestation of Spirit and the human spirit's response to It, render superfluous all attempts, always more or less hopeless, to construct God *a priori,* or even to demonstrate Him, from the facts of nature and of human life, by any single, deductive argument of a strictly constraining force. Because Spirit, God, works in our midst and in our depths, we can and we do know Him; because God has been the first to condescend to us and to love us, can we arise and love Him in return.

—Baron Friedrich von Hügel, 1852-1925

Man, if you love some thing, you love no thing at all,
God is not this or that, so let the Something fall.

—Angelus Silesius, 1624-1677

Religion must define the relation of man to the source of all, the destiny of man which follows from this relation, and the rules of conduct from this destiny. And the universal religion, the fundamental principles of which are identical in all faiths, entirely satisfies these demands. It defines the relation of man to God as that of a part to the whole; it deduces from this relation the function of man as the increase in himself of the divine element; and from this function it deduces practical rules from the principle of acting toward others as one wishes others to act toward oneself.

The truths of the universal religion of today are so simple, comprehensible, and near to the heart of every one that it would seem sufficient for all parents, rulers, and teachers to instill into children and adults those clear simple truths of the religion common to all men—the metaphysical essence of which is that the spirit of God lives in man, and the practical rule of which is that man should act toward others as he wishes others to act toward himself—for the whole life of mankind to change of itself.

Religion is not a faith established once for all in supernatural events supposed to have taken place at some time or other, or in the necessity of certain prayers and rites; neither is it, as the scientists think, the remains of the superstitions of ancient unenlightenment which in our time have no significance or adaptation to life. Religion is the relation of man to eternal life, to God, in accordance with reason and contemporary knowledge, which alone moves man forward toward the end for which he is intended.

"The human soul is a lamp of God," says a wise Hebrew proverb. Man is a weak, miserable animal until in his soul there burns the fire of God. But when this fire kindles, and it kindles only in a soul illumined by religion, man becomes the most powerful being in the world. And this cannot be otherwise, because then it is no longer *his* power which works in him, but the power of God.

— Count Leo Tolstoy, 1828-1910

Thou art my life; if Thou but turn away,
My life's a thousand deaths: Thou art my way;
Without Thee, Lord, I travel not, but stray.

My light Thou art; without Thy glorious sight,
Mine eyes are darken'd with perpetual night.
My God, Thou art my way, my life, my light.

Thou art my way; I wander, if Thou fly:
Thou art my light; if hid, how blind am I!
Thou art my life; if Thou withdraw, I die.

Mine eyes are blind and dark, I cannot see;
To whom, or whither should my darkness flee,
But to the light? and who's that light but Thee?

My path is lost, my wand'ring steps do stray;
I cannot safely go, nor safely stay;
Whom should I seek but Thee, my path, my way? . . .

Thou art the pilgrim's path, the blind man's eye;
The dead man's life: on Thee my hopes rely;
If thou remove, I err, I grope, I die.

— Francis Quarles, 1592-1644

Learn, my good youth, that your mind, existing within your body, directs your body as it pleases; and it becomes you therefore to believe that the Intelligence pervading all things directs all things as may be agreeable to It, and not to think that while your eye can extend its sight over many furlongs, that of the Divinity is unable to see all things at once; or that while your mind can think of things here, or things in Egypt or Sicily, the mind of the Deity is incapable of regarding everything at the same time.

— SOCRATES, 470? - 399 B.C.

The intellectual love of the mind towards God is that very love of God whereby God loves himself, not in so far as He is infinite, but in so far as He can be explained through the essence of the human mind regarded under the form of eternity; in other words, the intellectual love of the mind towards God is part of the infinite love wherewith God loves Himself.

— BARUCH SPINOZA, 1632 - 1677

God bringeth not a new or strange spirit into us but He openeth with His spirit, namely the mystery of God's wisdom which lieth in every man.

— JAKOB BÖHME, 1575 - 1624

· III ·

As God dwells in a light from which every ray of light which illumines the world issues, yet by none of these ways can a man enter in order to see God; for the way of light changes to darkness if one faces the light: so love dwells in secret, or is hidden in the heart. . . . So it is love's wish and prayer that its secret source and its hidden life in the heart may remain a secret. . . .

Love's secret life is in the heart, unfathomable, and it also has an unfathomable connection with the whole of existence. As the peaceful lake is grounded deep in the hidden spring which no eye can see, so a man's love is grounded even deeper in the love of God. If there were at the bottom no wellspring, if God were not love, then there would be no quiet lake or human love. . . .

So the life of love is hidden; but its secret life is itself in motion and has eternity in it.

— SÖREN KIERKEGAARD, 1813-1855

But what is it that I love when I love You? Not the beauty of any
bodily thing, nor the order of seasons, not the brightness of light that
rejoices the eye, nor the sweet melodies of all songs, nor the sweet
fragrance of flowers and ointments and spices: not manna or honey,
not the limbs that carnal love embraces. None of these things do I
love in loving my God. Yet in a sense I do love light and melody
and fragrance and food and embrace when I love my God—the light
and the voice and the fragrance and the food and embrace in the
soul, when that shines upon my soul which no place can contain, that
voice sounds which no tongue can take from me, I breathe that
fragrance which no wind scatters, I eat the food which is not
lessened by eating, and I lie in the embrace which satiety never comes
to sunder. This it is that I love, when I love my God.

— St. Augustine, 354-430

O Lord, Thou hast searched me, and known me.

Thou knowest my downsitting and mine uprising, thou under-
standest my thought afar off.

Thou compassest my path and my lying down, and art acquainted
with all my ways.

For there is not a word in my tongue, but, lo, O Lord, Thou knowest it altogether.

Thou hast beset me behind and before, and laid Thine hand upon
me.

Such knowledge is too wonderful for me; it is high, I cannot attain
unto it.

Whither shall I go from Thy spirit? or whither shall I flee from
Thy presence?

If I ascend up into heaven, Thou art there: if I make my bed in
hell, behold, Thou art there.

If I take the wings of the morning, and dwell in the uttermost
parts of the sea;

Even there shall Thy hand lead me, and Thy right hand shall
hold me.

If I say, Surely the darkness shall cover me; even the night shall
be light about me.

Yea, the darkness hideth not from Thee; but the night shineth as
the day: the darkness and the light are both alike to Thee.

The Bible, Psalm 139:1-12

What is man in nature? A zero in comparison with infinity, an infinity in comparison with zero, a middle ground between nothing and all. At an infinite distance from understanding finalities, the ends of things as their beginnings are for him invincibly hidden in an impenetrable secret; equally incapable is he to see the zero from which he is drawn and the infinity in which he is engulfed.

Unable to bear the thought of the infinite, men boldly carry their challenge to nature, as though they had some part and lot in her. It is a thing out of the ordinary, is it not, that they have set their heart on understanding the nature of things, and next on arriving at perfect knowledge, by a presumption as boundless as their object. For it is without doubt that one may not sketch this design without a presumption or a capacity as infinite as nature itself.

Would then that man might contemplate nature as a whole in her high and full majesty, and that he might turn his gaze from the trifling objects that surround him; that he might look upon this splendor of light, set as an everlasting lamp to illumine the universe, that the earth might appear to him the center of a vast orbit described by this star, and that he might stand amazed before the thought that this vast circuit is no more than a trifling point in comparison with the revolutions of the stars of the firmament. . . . The visible world is no more than a hint of the ample bosom of nature. No idea can approach its grandeur. . . . It is a sphere whose center is everywhere and its circumference nowhere.

— Blaise Pascal, 1623-1662

Since it is the author of all that exists, and since the multiplicity in each thing is converted into a self-sufficing existence by this presence of the One, so that even the particular itself becomes self-sufficing, then clearly this principle, author at once of Being and of self-sufficingness, is not itself a Being, but is above Being and above even self-sufficing.

May we stop content with that? No: the soul is yet, and even more, in pain. Is she ripe, perhaps, to bring forth, now that in her pangs she has come so close to what she seeks? No: we must call upon yet another spell if anywhere the assuagement is to be found. All the need is met by a contact purely intellectual. At the moment of touch there is no power whatever to make any affirmation; there is no leisure; reasoning upon the vision is for afterwards. We may know we have had the vision when the soul has suddenly taken light.

This light is from the Supreme and is the Supreme; we may believe in the Presence when, like that other God on the call of a certain man, He comes bringing light: the light is the proof of the advent. Thus, the soul unlit remains without that vision; lit, it possesses what it sought. And this is the true end set before the soul, to take that light, to see the Supreme by the Supreme and not by the light of any other principle—to see the Supreme which is also the means to the vision, for that which illumines the soul is that which it is to see just as it is by the sun's own light that we see the sun.

But how is this to be accomplished?

Cut away everything. . . .

Our self-seeing there is a communion with the self restored to its purity. No doubt we should not speak of seeing, but instead of seen and seer speak boldly of a simple unity. For in this seeing we neither see nor distinguish, nor are there two. The man is changed, no longer himself nor self-belonging; he is merged with the Supreme, sunken into It, one with It; only in separation is there duality. This is why a vision baffles telling; for how could a man bring back tidings of the Supreme as detached when he has seen It as one with himself? It is not to be told, not to be revealed to any that has not himself had the happiness to see It. Since beholder was one with beheld, and it was not a vision compassed but a unity apprehended, the man formed by this mingling with the Supreme would, if he but remembered, carry Its image impressed upon him; he is become the Unity, having no diversity either in relation to himself or anything else; no movement now, no passion, no outlooking desire, once this ascent is achieved; reason is in abeyance and intellection and even the very self; caught away, God-possessed, in perfect stillness, the entire being calmed, he turns neither to this side nor to that, nor even inwards to himself; utterly resting, he has become rest itself. He has risen beyond Beauty, the choir of the virtues overpassed; like one who, having penetrated the inner sanctuary, leaves the temple images behind; for there his converse is not with image, nor with trace, but with the Deity Himself, in view of whom all the rest is but of secondary concern. This is the only seeing reserved for the sanctuary; look otherwise and there is nothing there.

Things here are but signs that show to the wise how the Supreme God is known; the enlightened priest reading the sign may enter the holy place and make the vision real. This Term, attained only by those that have overpassed all, is the All-Transcending. There is thus a converse in virtue of which the essential man outgrows Being, becomes identical with the Transcendent of Being. He that knows himself to be one with This has in himself the likeness of the Supreme; if from that heightened self he can pass higher still—image to archetype —he has won the term of all his journeying.

This is the life of gods and of godlike and blessed men—liberation from the alien that besets us here, a life taking no pleasure in the things of earth—a flight of the alone to the Alone.

—PLOTINUS, 205?-270

Spirit, which is ultimately addressed to pure Being, is not itself this pure Being. It is the gift of intuition, feeling, or apprehension: an overtone of animal life, a realization, on a hypostatic plane, of certain moving unities in matter. So, at least, I understand the word; but its original meaning was a breath or wind, and hence, often, an influence. In this last sense it is used in Christian theology; the Holy Ghost is not the Father nor the Son, but proceeds from them and animates the world, or at least the souls of the elect. It is the fountain of grace. We also read in the gospel that God is a spirit, to be worshipped in spirit and in truth. Here the word evidently bears more than one sense; the spirit in which God is worshipped is a disposition of the mind, whereas God himself, we may presume, is a spirit in the mighty sense in which Jehovah swept the void, a breath or a word, bringing order out of chaos; the same voice that spoke to Job out of the whirlwind, with the sheer authority of power. Spirit thus seems to be sometimes a creative energy, sometimes a sanctifying influence. . . .

This double function of spirit, if we investigate its origin, would bring back the double source of Christian doctrines, here Hebraic and there Platonic: a profound dualism which custom scarcely avails to disguise or theology to heal. Creative power and redeeming grace point in opposite directions; but a complete religion needs to look both ways, feeding piously at the breast of nature, yet weaning itself spiritually from that necessary comfort to the contemplation of superhuman and eternal things. The object of piety is necessity, power, the laws of life and prosperity, and to call these things spirit is pure mythology; they are indeed a great wind, sometimes balmy, sometimes terrible; and it is the part of wisdom to take shelter from it, or spread wings or sails in it, according as it lists to blow. But to what end? To live, to have spirit, to understand all these things.

There is also a conventional modern sense in which we speak of the spirit of an age, a place, or a book, meaning some vague tendency or inspiration either actually dominating that thing or suggested by it to the mind of a third person. This is a verbal survival of myth, poetry become cant: spirit here means those characters of a thing which a myth-making mind would have attributed to a spirit.

In contrast to all these uses I am employing the word spirit to mean something actual; indeed, the very fact of actuality. The gleam of intuition or feeling. But this gleam ordinarily serves only to light up material life and the perspectives in which it moves in time and in space: an incessant sketchy sense of the affairs of the body and of its world. The digestion, and preparation of action (as the behaviourists have shown) is a physical matter. In that business the spirit is entirely superfluous. The behaviourists even affect to deny its existence on the ground that it is invisible and would be a useless luxury in nature: excellent economy, as if a man, the better to provide for his future, should starve himself to death. The spirit in us is that which, morally, we actually are: if anything is to be expunged from the complex face of reality it might rather be our material and social setting and all the strange and incoherent stories told us in history and science. Certainly all these apparent or reported facts would be perfectly vain, if they did not create the spirit, and teach it to observe and enjoy them. So we are brought back to the immediate revelation of things, which is also their ultimate value: we are brought back to the spirit. Its life is composed of feelings and intuitions, in many stages and degrees; and when spirit is free and collected it has no life but this spiritual life, in which the ultimate is immediate. All the experiences of the spirit, until they are so exorcized and appropriated—so enshrined in pure Being—are sheer distraction.

— GEORGE SANTAYANA, 1863-1952

God is in all that liberates and lifts;
In all that humbles, sweetens, and consoles.
A mystery of purpose gleaming through the secular confusions of
    the world,
Whose will we darkly accomplish, doing ours.
Sometimes at waking, in the street sometimes, or on the hillside,
    always unforewarned,
Man sees a grace of being finer than himself, that beckons and is gone.
O Power, more near than life itself,
Or what seems life to us in sense immured,

Even as the roots, shut in the darksome earth, share in the tree-top's
   joyance, and conceive of sunshine and wide air and winged things,
   by sympathy of nature,
So do I have evidence of Thee so far above, yet in and of me.

              — JAMES RUSSELL LOWELL, 1819-1891

I have wander'd like a sheep that's lost,
To find Thee out in every coast.
Without I have long seeking been,
Whilst Thou the while abid'st *within*.
Through every broad street and strait lane
Of this world's city, but in vain,
I have enquir'd. The reason why?
I sought Thee ill; for how could I
Find Thee *abroad*, when Thou, mean space,
Had'st made *within* Thy dwelling-place?

I sent my messengers about
To try if they could find Thee out.
But all was to no purpose still,
Because, indeed they sought Thee ill;
For how could they discover Thee
That saw not when Thou enteredst me?

Mine eyes could tell me? If He were
Not colour'd, sure He came not there.
If not by sound, my ears could say
He doubtless did not pass my way.
My nose could nothing of Him tell,
Because my God He did not smell.
None such I relish'd said my taste,
And therefore me He never pass'd.
My feeling told me that none such
There enter'd, for He did none touch.
Resolv'd by them how should I be,
Since none of all these are in Thee?

In Thee! My God, Thou hast no hue
That man's frail optic sense can view;
No sound the ear hears; odour none
The smell attracts; all taste is gone

At Thy appearance; where doth fail
A body, how can touch prevail?
What even the brute beasts comprehend—
To think Thee such, I should offend
Yet when I seek my God, I enquire
For Light, than sun and moon much higher,
More clear and splendrous, 'bove all light,
Which eye receives not, 'tis so bright.

I seek a Voice beyond degree
Of all melodious harmony;
The ear conceives it not: a Smell
Which doth all other scents excel;
No flower so sweet, no myrrh, no nard
Or aloës, with it compar'd;
Of which the brain not sensible is.
I seek a sweetness—such a bliss
As hath all other sweets surpass'd
And never palate yet could taste.
I seek That to contain and hold
No touch can feel, no embrace enfold.

So far this Light the rays extends
As that no place it comprehends.
So deep this Sound that, though it speak,
It cannot by a sense so weak
Be entertain'd. A redolent grace
The air blows not from place to place.
A pleasant Taste, of that delight
It doth confound all appetite.
A strict embrace, not felt, yet leaves
That virtue, where it takes it cleaves.
This light, this sound, this savouring grace,
This tasteful sweet, this strict embrace,
No place contains, no eye can see,
My God is, and there's none but He.

— THOMAS HEYWOOD, 1574?-1641

CHAPTER NINE

The Ground on Which
Thou Standest

I am as rich as God: there's nothing any-
where
That I with Him (believe it!) do not share.

— ANGELUS SILESIUS, 1624-1677

·1·

WHILE Moses was tending the flock of his father-in-law, Jethro, the priest of Midian, he led the flock to the western side of the desert, and came to the mountain of God, Horeb. Then the angel of the Lord appeared to him in a flame of fire, rising out of a bush. He looked, and there was the bush burning with fire without being consumed! So Moses said,

"I will turn aside and see this great sight, why the bush is not burned up."

When the Lord saw that he had turned aside to look at it, God called to him out of the bush.

"Moses, Moses!" He said.

"Here I am!" said he.

"Do not come near here," He said; "take your sandals off your feet; for the place on which you are standing is holy ground." "I am the God of your father," He said, "the God of Abraham, Isaac, and Jacob."

Then Moses hid his face; for he was afraid to look at God.

"I have indeed seen the plight of my people who are in Egypt," the Lord said, "and I have heard their cry under their oppressors; for I know their sorrows, and I have come down to rescue them from the Egyptians and bring them up out of that land to a land, fine and large, to a land flowing with milk and honey, to the country of the Canaanites, Hittites, Amorites, Perizzites, Hivvites, and Jebusites. Now the cry of the Israelites has reached me, and I have also seen how the Egyptians are oppressing them; so come now, let me send you to Pharaoh, that you may bring my people, the Israelites, out of Egypt."

But Moses said to God,

"Who am I, to go to Pharaoh and bring the Israelites out of Egypt?"

"I will be with you," He said; "and this shall be the sign for you that I have sent you. When you bring the people out of Egypt, you shall serve God at this mountain."

"But," said Moses to God, "in case I go to the Israelites and say to them, 'The God of your fathers has sent me to you,' and they say to me, 'What is his name?' what am I to say to them?"

"I am who I am," God said to Moses. Then He said, "Thus you shall say to the Israelites: '"I am" has sent me to you.'"

God said further to Moses,

"Thus you shall say to the Israelites:

"'Yahweh [the Lord], the God of your fathers, the God of Abraham, Isaac, and Jacob, has sent me to you.' This has always been my name, and this shall remain my title throughout the ages. Go and assemble the elders of Israel, and say to them, 'The Lord, the God of your fathers, the God of Abraham, Isaac, and Jacob, has appeared to me, saying, "I have given careful heed to you and your treatment in Egypt, and I have resolved to bring you up out of your tribulation in Egypt to the land of the Canaanites, Hittites, Amorites, Perizzites, Hivvites, and Jebusites, to a land flowing with milk and honey."' They will heed your appeal, and then you and the elders of Israel shall come to the king of Egypt and say to him, 'The Lord, the God of the Hebrews, has paid us a visit; so now, let us make a three days' journey into the desert to offer sacrifices to the Lord our God.' I know, however, that the king of Egypt will not let you go without the use of force; so I will stretch out my hand and smite Egypt with all the marvels that I shall perform in it; after that he will let you go."

— THE BIBLE, Exodus, 3:1-20

Great Majesty, since Thou art everywhere,
Oh, why should I misdoubt Thy Presence here?
I long have sought Thee, but my ranging heart
Ne'er quests, and cannot see Thee where Thou art:
There's no defect in Thee, Thy light hath shin'd,
Nor can be hid, Great God, but I am blind.
Oh, clear mine eyes, and with Thy holy fire
Inflame my breast, and edge my dull desire:
Wash me with hysop, cleanse my stained thoughts,
Renew my spirit, blur forth my secret faults;
Thou tak'st no pleasure in a sinner's death,
For Thou art Life; Thy mercy's not beneath
Thy sacred justice: Give Thy servant power
To seek aright, and, having sought, discover
Thy glorious Presence; let my blemish'd eye
See my salvation yet before I die.

— FRANCIS QUARLES, 1592-1644

God exists in all things, not as a part of their essence or as one of
their accidents, but He exists in them as an agent is present in that
which it works upon. For an agent must be in immediate relation
with that upon which it works, it must touch it by its efficacious
power; from which Aristotle demonstrates in his *Physics* that the
thing moved and the mover must exist at one and the same time.
Now since God is existence itself by His own essence, it follows that
created existence must be His proper effect, in the same way as to
ignite is the proper effect of fire. This effect God produces in things
not only when they are first given being, but as long as they con-
serve it; in the same way as light is produced by the sun as long as the
earth remains illuminated. Thus, so long as a thing exists, so long is
God present to its being. But the being of a thing is that which is
most intimate to it, it is that which most deeply resides in it, since
being is the form of all that which it encloses. Hence God is in all
things, and is intimately in them.

— ST. THOMAS AQUINAS, 1225?-1274

If thou would'st see
God's laws with purest mind,
Thy sight on heaven must fixéd be,

Whose settled course the stars in peace doth bind.
            The sun's bright fire
        Stops not his sister's team,
        Nor doth the northern bear desire
Within the ocean's wave to hide her beam.
            Though she behold
        The other stars there couching,
        Yet she uncessantly is rolled
About high heaven, the ocean never touching.
            The evening light
        With certain course doth show
        The coming of the shady night,
And Lucifer before the day doth go.
            This mutual love
        Courses eternal makes,
        And from the starry spheres above
All cause of war and dangerous discord takes.
            This sweet consent
        In equal bands doth tie
        The nature of each element,
So that the moist things yield unto the dry.
            The piercing cold
        With flames doth friendship keep,
        The trembling fire the highest place doth hold,
And the gross earth sinks down into the deep.
            The flowery year
        Breathes odours in the spring
        The scorching summer corn doth bear,
The autumn fruit from laden trees doth bring.
            The falling rain
        Doth winter's moisture give.
        These rules thus nourish and maintain
All creatures which we see on earth to live.
            And when they die,
        These bring them to their end,
        While their Creator sits on high,
Whose hand the reins of the whole world doth bend.
            He as their King
        Rules them with lordly might.
        From Him they rise, flourish, and spring,
He as their law and judge decides their right.

Those things whose course
Most swiftly glides away
His might doth often backward force,
And suddenly their wandering motion stay.
Unless His strength
Their violence should bound,
And them which else would run at length,
Should bring within the compass of a round,
That firm decree
Which now doth all adorn
Would soon destroyed and broken be,
Things being far from their beginning borne.
This powerful love
Is common unto all,
Which for desire of good do move
Back to the springs from whence they first did fall.
No worldly thing
Can a continuance have
Unless love back again it bring
Unto the cause which first the essence gave.

—BOETHIUS, 480?-?524

Il mondo è il libro dove il Senno eterno
scrisse i propri concetti, e vivo tempio
dove, pingendo i gesti e'l proprio esempio,
di statue vive ornò l'imo e'l superno;
perch'ogni spirto qui l'arte e'l governo
leggere e contemplar, per non farsi empio,
debba, e dir possa: Io l'universo adempio,
Dio contemplando a tutte cose interno.
Ma noi, strette alme a'libri e tempii morti,
copiati dal vivo con più errori,
gli anteponghiamo a magistero tale.
O pene, del fallir fatene accorti,
liti, ignoranze, fatiche e dolori:
deh torniamo, per Dio, all'originale!

The world is the book where the eternal Wisdom wrote its own concepts, and the living temple where, depicting its deeds and own example, it adorned the depth and the height with statues;

that every spirit here, lest it become impious, may learn and contemplate art and law, and can say: I fulfil the universe, by contemplating God within all things.

But we, souls fettered to books and dead temples, copied from the truth with many errors, place them above such teaching.

O suffering, discord, ignorance, labour, grief, make us aware of our mistake. Ah, by God, let us return to the original.

— TOMMASO CAMPANELLA, 1568-1639

Any one thing of those which exist would be enough to make a man perceive the providence of God. And speak not now to me of great things, but only of this, that milk is produced from grass, and cheese from milk, and wool from skins. Who made these things or devised them? Are these the only works of Providence toward us? And what words can adequately express their praise?

For if we had understanding, ought we to do anything else both jointly and severally than to sing hymns to God and to laud Him and tell of His benefits? Ought we not when we are digging and ploughing and eating to sing this hymn to God: Great is God?

For what else can I, a lame old man, do but sing hymns to God? Were I a nightingale, I would act the part of a nightingale; a swan, the part of a swan; but since I am a reasonable creature, it is my duty to praise God. Nor will I ever desert this post as long as it is vouchsafed me; and I exhort you to join me in the same song.

— EPICTETUS, first century

Who may see to the bottom of the marvellous works of God, how He made all things of nothing, how the very framework of the world is arranged with a marvellous mightiness of power, and the heaven hung above the atmosphere and the earth balanced above the abyss, how this whole universe consists of things visible and invisible, how He created man, so to say, gathering together in a small compass another world, yet a world of reason; how constituting this world of soul and flesh, He mixed the breath and the clay by an unsearchable disposal of His might? A part, then, of these things we know, and a part we even are. Yet we omit to admire them, because those things which are full of marvels for an investigation deeper than we can reach, have become cheap from custom in the eyes of men.

— ST. GREGORY THE GREAT, 540?-604

All the things of the earth do shew that Thou art to be praised. What things? The dragons, and all the abysses; fire, hail, snow, ice, stormy winds, they fulfill Thy word; mountains and all hills and fruitful trees and cedars; the beasts and all the cattle; all creeping things and all flying fowl whatsoever; all the kings of the earth and all the peoples; all the princes and all the judges of the land; all young men and maidens, old men and children; let them praise Thy name. Seeing also these in Heaven praise Thee, praise Thee, O our God, in the heights, Thine angels and all thy hosts, sun, moon, stars and light, the very heaven of heavens and all the waters that are above the heavens, seeing that they praise Thy name, I do not desire better than to praise Thee.

—St. Augustine, 354-430

Thales was asked, What God was: That, he said, which hath neither beginning nor end. Of all things, the oldest is God. All things are full of God. The mind of the universe is God.

— Thales, 640?-546 b.c.

· II ·

In all things there is mystery and the greatest mystery we can approach is the soul of man. For the mystery of God is beyond our conceiving and it is for this reason that, strive as we may, it is as impossible to define God as it is to see Him. To define is to limit, for definition is merely the indication of limitations. Limits relate only to the finite. We refer to that spirit which we name God (men have given it countless names) as infinite and by the use of this word we imply that God is outside definition. The Infinite manifests Itself in the finite and would we find the Creator, we must seek Him in the made; since only through realization shall we approach Him, and we can only realize that which lies within the scope of our experience. And thus it is that St. Augustine's definition of the nature of God is probably the best, for it defines the impossibility of definition—the nature of God is as a circle whose centre is everywhere, and its circumference nowhere.

— Claude Houghton, 1889-

God is the most obvious thing in the world. He is absolutely self-evident—the simplest, clearest and closest reality of life and consciousness. We are only unaware of Him because we are too complicated, for our vision is darkened by the complexity of pride We seek Him beyond the horizon with our noses lifted high in the air, and fail to see that He lies at our very feet. We flatter ourselves in premeditating the long, long journey we are going to take in order to find Him, the giddy heights of spiritual progress we are going to scale, and all the time are unaware of the truth that "God is nearer to us than we are to ourselves." We are like birds flying in quest of the air, or men with lighted candles searching through the darkness for fire.

The self-evidence of God is the result of His love, and is one with the gift of union with Himself which He bestows upon us. For God is not niggardly in His self-revelation; He creates us to know Him, and short of actual compulsion does everything possible to present Himself to our consciousness. In saying that God gives us union with Himself here and now, we are saying also that here and now He exposes Himself right before our eyes. In this very moment we are looking straight at God, and He is so clear that for us complex human beings He is peculiarly hard to see. To know Him we have to simplify ourselves, and the mind is so dominated by the complexity of pride that it will resort to every conceivable subtlety to resist and avoid a truth so wholly simple.

God and union with God is Reality; nothing is more real, more concrete, more actual, and more present. At the same time, Reality is infinitely alive. It, He, cannot be grasped in any finite form, whether physical, mental or emotional. Therefore, as long as we *try* to grasp God, we shall never realize Him. Life itself, as we experience it moment by moment, proceeding as it does directly from God, is the perfect analogy of this truth, for to grasp life is to kill it, or rather, to miss it, and more than ever is this true of God—the Life of life. Pluck a flower, and it dies. Take up water from the stream, and it flows no longer. Pull down the blind, but the sunbeam is not trapped in the room. Snatch the wind in a bag, and you have only stagnant air. This is the root of every trouble: man loves life, but the moment he tries to hold on to it he misses it. . . .

Religion, as it is generally practised, is simply an attempt to hang on to life and the still more lively mystery which informs it—God. Hence religion as generally practised is idolatry. God cannot be held in theologies; theism, deism, pantheism—none of them can grasp His truth. Nor can states of mind and feeling contain Him; ecstasy, rapture, quiet, *samadhi*—these are only the secondary and unessential effects of His presence. Our various intellectual and emotional idols, our doctrines, holy books, sacraments, religious feelings, creeds and churches, are of use so long as they are understood as approximating and pointing to God. But when we try to possess Him within them, they must sooner or later become millstones about our necks.

God, and the living creation which proceeds from His hands, cannot be possessed. To enjoy and to know Reality we must let go of it and realize that it possesses us. Beauty grasped turns into pain, for God is the source both of the beauty and of the pain of life. In its beauty he calls us to Him; in the pain which comes from grasping He warns us that we cannot come to Him in a possessive spirit, because in so doing we shall miss the very thing that we desire. To clutch the splendour of flame is to be burned. To enjoy anything living, whether it be fire, water, air, earth, flesh and blood, our own lives, or God Himself, we must let go of it and let it be free to be itself. . . .

The Reality which we term union with God simply *is*, whether we realize it or not, whether we are doing something about it or nothing about it. Any attempt to grasp it, by action or by inaction, suggests that it is not absolutely present. The moment we look for union with God, we imply that we do not already have it, and this is true even when we look for it by not looking. . . .

The focal point of Reality is now—this present moment, this elusive image of eternity, so small that it has no temporal length and yet so long that we can never escape from it. Here in this present moment life is most lively; here alone do we really exist. The past is dead; the future as yet is not. The moment assumes a hundred different forms—moments of pleasure, moments of pain, moments of elation, moments of depression, moments of quiet, moments of agitation; but it will not stay, it cannot be grasped, in any of its forms. This moment is our life, but the more we try to hold it, the faster it slips away. We look for it and cannot find it because it is too small to see, too slippery to hold, and yet this is where we are given union with God. If we do not discover it in this moment, we shall never discover it. . . .

But while we cannot grasp the moment, arresting that flow of life which we call time, there remains the fact that we cannot get away from it. . . . However hard we may fight to retain the past or to hurry on into the future, we cannot get out of the present moment. The more we try to hold it, the more we fail to perceive that it holds us. The moment always carries us in its embrace, and wherever we go or whatever we do, it cannot be escaped. To understand this is simplicity itself.

And here is the perfect analogy of our union with God—a reality which possesses and holds us as surely and as presently as the moment, a reality which in some sense *is* this moment. For the moment is not its forms; it is not space; it is not time; it is infinitesimal and thus Infinite; it is Reality, Being, the eternal presence of God. In this moment we live and move and have our being, and nowhere else. What we have to realize, therefore, is not the getting of union with God, but the not being able to get away from it. It is in, it *is* this Eternal Now, wherein God so lovingly holds us.

—ALAN WATTS, 1915-

Thy breath, O God! flitted by me and I was scorched,
Thy fingertip, one little moment, made my heartstrings tremulous,
And there I crawled mute, and held in check the surging of my spirit;
My heart swooned within me, and my inner music could not billow
    forth;
Wherewith dare I enter the sanctuary, and how can my prayer be
    pure,
While my language, O God! has become defiled, is all uncleanliness,
Not a word therein but is besmirched down to its root,
Not a phrase but filthy lips have befouled,
Not a thought but has been dragged to the house of shame? . . .
Where can I remove myself from this smell?
O, where can I hide from this empty tumult?
Where is the Seraph to cleanse my mouth with his fiery coal?
I will go forth to the birds of the field that chirp at dawn,
Or arise and go now to the children playing by the gate;
I will go and mingle with them in their multitude, will learn their
    speech and their chatter—
Will be purified by their breath, and wash my lips with their cleanli-
    ness.

—CHAIM NAHMAN BIALIK, 1873-1934

The Kobriner turned to his Hasidim and said: "Do you know where God is?" He took a piece of bread, showed it to them all, and continued: "God is in this piece of bread. Without the Lord's manifestation of His power in all nature, this piece of bread would have no existence."

— HASIDIC SAYING

The quest for God is the quest for an ideal Source of Help and Object of Devotion: a being so much greater, more enduring, and more worthful than ourselves that we may confidently lean on it for support and unreservedly give ourselves to its service.

All ideas of God, even the most fragmentary, are at least partial or supposed solutions of the great problem involved in this quest. Amid all the welter of naïve personification and untamed primitive imagination that makes the god-world of polytheism look so unreal to us today, certain underlying realities can be discerned, which the most sophisticated modern would admit to be truly worthy of man's devotion and reliance.

(1). *There is something deservedly sacred and holy in the social ties that bind us together in families, tribes, and nations.* There may be much that is fanciful in the Roman worship of Lares and Penates, or in the Chinese worship of the family oven and household gate, or in the Shinto rites that have done so much to bind the Japanese people into one great family with the Emperor as its beloved head; but there is solid truth beneath all this poetry and mythology; so much so, that many Western-educated Orientals, completely devoid of literalistic belief in ancestral ghosts, sun-goddesses, and the like, hold firmly to their ancient worship as if their life depended on it— as indeed it does, in a very real sense. The truth is that we all do owe religious reverence to our family, our community, our nation—from which the very stuff of our life is so largely drawn; and they do repay our loyalty to them by increasing our strength and security and the meaningfulness of our existence. *Meaning* is largely a matter of *interrelationship and connection;* in proportion as we devote ourselves to our social group, it extends the meaning of our personality by enmeshing it in a network of social conections that goes out as far as the group has influence, and backwards and forwards in history to include the dead and the unborn. We grow greater, longer-lived, more meaningful in proportion as we identify ourselves with the larger social life that surrounds us. This is what the humanistic gods have always been supposed to do for their worshipers, and what the reality beneath their fanciful forms always *has* done.

(2). *There is something deservedly sacred and holy in the powers of nature by which man's life is surrounded and supported.* In some parts of the world, where man's struggle with his environment is hard and tense, the idea of "Mother Nature" is not so persuasive as in those climates where man's relation with his environment is more passively dependent; yet in all environments men have reckoned upon the support of *some* powers as allies in their struggle with the more unfriendly forces. Sun, rain, soil, and the mysterious power of fertility that rises from the dead in the springtime have been recognized as gods and goddesses in every quarter of the globe, with local variations easily traceable to climatic differences.

In modern urban civilization, the sense of almost personal relationship with the supporting natural forces has been lost, and the sentiment of grateful dependence has largely atrophied because of the multiplication of intermediate mechanical devices; but man is still the child of nature, and if he persistently refuses to give reverent obedience to her laws, he succumbs to degenerative or nervous disease. When a man thus succumbs and wishes to be cured, it is customary to take him from his artificial environment and send him "back to nature," to bask in the rays of the sun and swim in the brine from which his animal ancestors emerged. If he does not then begin to feel a religious sentiment toward nature, and half believe in Apollo and Poseidon, he is less than a man and devoid of sensibility. Doubtless, he does not feel the same sort of devotion toward nature that he feels toward his family or his country, since he has given up the habit of personifying her forces; yet he feels a kind of trustful dependence, a delicious inflow of refreshing power, as from an inexhaustible fountain of youth, when he puts himself back in harmony with her laws and begins to recuperate.

(3). *There is something deservedly sacred and holy in man's inward sense of unrealized possibilities, which makes him turn rebel against himself and his environment and dream of better things yet to be.* If it is perilous to idealize the world of existent things, and people it with fanciful sprites, it is even more perilous to view things unimaginatively and baldly, with no sense of their ideal possibilities. The voice of the gods has always been heard in the utterances of certain men who, when filled with the "divine afflatus," have cried out against the existing order of things, prophesied doom in the midst of general prosperity, and painted glowing pictures of a new and better age in times of disaster and despair. Such men have been called "seers" not because their sense-perceptions differed from those of other men, but because they were gifted with "second sight," or the ability to discern the hidden possibilities of the existing situation and the shadows that coming events are said to cast before them. . . .

All highly organized religions are at one in the verdict that *man's trust and allegiance can rightly be offered to a being or beings made manifest partly through human institutions, partly through nature, and partly through prophetic discernment of ideal values and possibilities.*

— WALTER MARSHALL HORTON, 1895-

In God there is a creative dynamic process which is accomplished in eternity. This must not be understood as meaning that God depends upon the world and the process that goes on in the world, but that the process which goes on in the world is inwardly linked with the process which goes on in God, in eternity not in time; that is to say it is linked with the divine drama, and it is on this account only that what happens in the world and in man acquires an eternal meaning. A world and man which were on no grounds at all necessary to God would be a mere matter of chance and by that very fact would be destitute of all meaning. We must be bold enough to recognize God's need of man, and such a need by no means limits God. What actually would not only limit God but also degrade Him is a stony, insensitive immobility and self-sufficiency. There is in God a yearning for the loved one and this confers the highest significance upon the loved one. Belief in God is belief in the highest Truth and Right, exalted above the wrongness of the world. But this Truth demands the creative participation of man and of the world. It is divine-human; in it the ideal humanity operates.

— NICOLAS ALEKSANDROVICH BERDYAEV, 1874-1948

In the deep cave of the heart, far down, running under the outward shows of the world and of people,
Running under continents, under the fields and the roots of the grasses and trees,
Under the little thoughts and dreams of men, and the history of races,
I see, feel and hear wondrous and divine things.
I seem to see the strands of affection and love, so tender, so true and life-long, holding together the present and past generations.

The currents of love and thought streaming in the watches of the night from far and near, from one to another,

Streaming all the more powerfully for the very hindrances and disasters which arrive or threaten.

I dream that these are the fibres and nerves of a body that lies within the outer body of society;

A network, an innumerable vast interlocked ramification, slowly being built up;

All dear lovers and friends, all families, groups, all peoples, nations, all times, all worlds perhaps,

Members of a body, archetypal, eternal, glorious, the centre and perfection of life.

The organic growth of God himself in time.

— EDWARD CARPENTER, 1844-1929

The emeralds are singing on the grasses
And in the trees the bells of the long cold are ringing,—
My blood seems changed to emeralds like the spears
Of grass beneath the earth piercing and singing.

The flame of the first blade
Is an angel piercing through the earth to sing
"God is everything!
The grass within the grass, the angel in the angel, flame
Within the flame, and He is the green shade that came
To be the heart of shade."

The grey-beard angel of the stone,
Who has grown wise with age, cried "Not alone
Am I within my silence,—God is the stone in the still stone, the silence laid
In the heart of silence" . . . then, above the glade
The yellow straws of light
Whereof the sun has built his nest, cry "Bright
Is the world, the yellow straw
My brother,—God is the straw within the straw:—All things are Light."

He is the sea of ripeness and the sweet apple's emerald lore.
So you, my flame of grass, my root of the world from which all Spring shall grow,
O you, my hawthorn bough of the stars, now leaning low

Through the day, for your flowers to kiss my lips, shall know
He is the core of the heart of love, and He, beyond labouring seas,
  our ultimate shore.

—EDITH SITWELL, 1887-

> Religion's all or nothing; it's no mere smile
> O' contentment, sigh of aspiration, sir—
> No quality o' the finelier-tempered clay
> Like its whiteness or its lightness; rather, stuff
> O' the very stuff, life of life, and self of self.

—ROBERT BROWNING, 1812-1889

· III ·

At my entrance into religion, I took a resolution to give myself up
to God, as the best return I could make for His love, and, for the
love of Him, to renounce all besides.

For the first year I commonly employed myself during the time
set apart for devotion with the thought of death, judgment, heaven,
hell, and my sins. Thus I continued some years, applying my mind
carefully the rest of the day, and even in the midst of my business,
to the presence of God, whom I considered always as *with* me, often
as *in* me.

At length I came insensibly to do the same thing during my set
time of prayer, which caused in me great delight and consolation.
This practice produced in me so high an esteem for God that *faith*
alone was capable to satisfy me in that point.

Such was my beginning, and yet I must tell you that for the first
ten years I suffered much. As for what passes in me at present, I cannot express it. I have no pain or difficulty about my state, because I
have no will but that of God, which I endeavor to accomplish in all
things, and to which I am so resigned that I would not take up a
straw from the ground against His order, or from any other motive
but purely that of love of Him.

—BROTHER LAWRENCE, 1611-1691

The childlikeness of an adequate religion lies not on this but on the
other side of sophistication. It is not the childlikeness of primitive

ignorance but the childlikeness of a wisdom which has learned the limits of human knowledge. It therefore approaches life with awe, hope and fear. With awe, because it knows that the mystery of life is something more than an unknown region not yet explored by an advancing science; with hope because "it doth not yet appear what we shall be" and no record of past history gives us an adequate clue of what creative omnipotence may bring forth out of the infinite possibilities of existence; with fear, because it knows the possibilities of evil, which appear at each new turn in history, are never adequately anticipated by any analysis of the past. The wisdom of such childlikeness will prefer its hopes to its fears, knowing that good is more primary than evil, that the world could not exist at all if it were not good, creation being a triumph over chaos. It will therefore approach life fearful and yet unafraid. Its serenity will be more lasting than that of a culture which based its confidence upon the illusion that human intelligence had overcome the chaos of the nature about us and the nature in us.

— Reinhold Niebuhr, 1892-

God is our refuge and strength, a very present help in trouble.

Therefore will not we fear, though the earth be removed, and though the mountains be carried into the midst of the sea;

Though the waters thereof roar and be troubled, though the mountains shake with the swelling thereof.

There is a river, the streams whereof shall make glad the city of God, the holy place of the tabernacles of the most High.

God is in the midst of her; she shall not be moved: God shall help her, and that right early.

The heathen raged, the kingdoms were moved: He uttered His voice, the earth melted.

The Lord of hosts is with us; the God of Jacob is our refuge.

Come, behold the works of the Lord, what desolations He hath made in the earth.

He maketh wars to cease unto the end of the earth; He breaketh the bow, and cutteth the spear in sunder; He burneth the chariot in the fire.

Be still, and know that I am God: I will be exalted among the heathen, I will be exalted in the earth.

The Lord of hosts is with us; the God of Jacob is our refuge.

— The Bible, Psalm 46

One aspect of religious experience is the wondering, the marveling, the becoming aware of life and of one's own existence, and of the puzzling problem of one's relatedness to the world. Existence, one's own existence and that of one's fellow men, is not taken for granted but is felt as a problem, is not an answer but a question. Socrates' statement that wonder is the beginning of all wisdom is true not only for wisdom but for the religious experience. One who has never been bewildered, who has never looked upon life and his own existence as phenomena which require answers and yet, paradoxically, for which the only answers are new questions, can hardly understand what religious experience is.

Another quality of religious experience is what Paul Tillich has called the "ultimate concern" . . . an ultimate concern with the meaning of life, with the self-realization of man, with the fulfillment of the task which life sets us. This ultimate concern gives all desires and aims, inasmuch as they do not contribute to the welfare of the soul and the realization of the self, a secondary importance; in fact they are made unimportant by comparison with the object of this ultimate concern. It necessarily excludes division between the holy and the secular because the secular is subordinated to and molded by it.

Beyond the attitude of wonder and of concern there is a third element in religious experience, the one which is most clearly exhibited and described by the mystics. It is an attitude of oneness not only in oneself, not only with one's fellow men, but with all life and, beyond that, with the universe. Some may think that this attitude is one in which the uniqueness and individuality of the self are denied and the experience of self weakened. That this is not so constitutes the paradoxical nature of this attitude. It comprises both the sharp and even painful awareness of one's self as a separate and unique entity and the longing to break through the confines of this individual organization and to be one with the All. The religious attitude in this sense is simultaneously the fullest experience of individuality and of its opposite; it is not so much a blending of the two as a polarity from whose tension religious experience springs. It is an attitude of pride and integrity and at the same time of a humility which stems from experiencing oneself as but a thread in the texture of the universe.

—ERICH FROMM, 1900-

· IV ·

The way to attain . . . [a] sense of awe is to realize the following
two veritable facts: first, that the Divine Presence exists everywhere
in the universe; and second, that God exercises His providence over
everything, both great and small. Nothing is hidden from His sight.
Nothing is too great or too small for Him to see. He beholds and discerns equally all things, whether trivial or important. . . .

When a man is convinced that, wherever he is, he always stands in
the presence of God, blessed be He, he is spontaneously imbued with
fear lest he do anything wrong, and so detract from the exalted glory
of God. "Know what is above thee," said our Sages, "a seeing eye
and a hearing ear, and all thy deeds written in a book."

— MOSES HAYYIM LUZATTO, 1707-1747

Why hast thou said, "I have sinned so much,
And God in His mercy has not punished my sins"?
How many times do I smite thee, and thou knowest not!
Thou art bound in my chains from head to foot.
On thy heart is rust on rust collected
So that thou art blind to divine mysteries.
When a man is stubborn and follows evil practices,
He casts dust in the eyes of his discernment.
Old shame for sin and calling on God quit him;
Dust five layers deep settles on his mirror,
Rust spots begin to gnaw his iron,
The colour of his jewel grows less and less.

— JALAL-UD-DIN RUMI, 1207-1273

Our Father holds it for better that in all things one should endeavour
to find God, rather than that long continuous periods of time should
be applied to prayer, . . . in conversation, in walking, seeing, tasting,
hearing, thinking, and in fact in all kinds of activity, for of a truth
the majesty of God is in all things. This kind of meditation, in which
one finds God in everything, is easier than the other, and prepares
the soul to receive great graces from God, without it being necessary
to spend a long time in prayer.

— ST. IGNATIUS OF LOYOLA, 1491-1556

Religion is the complete life in that it surveys the entire objective world, all its ideas and all its doings. It brings together all aspects of life in one complete experience. It sees beyond the provincial to the worldwide: it seeks to be lifted above the particular to the general, above the local to the universal: it attempts to transcend partiality and achieve completeness of life. It ignores nothing. It is the supreme effort of the imagination to attempt a sweeping survey of all the facts and factors of life whatsoever, known or conceived, past, present or future.

Religion is the complete life in that it not only surveys all the facts and factors of the outer world but employs all the faculties of the inner self, mind and heart and will. It is not only a scientific and philosophic interest in the forces of reality, both proximate and ultimate, but a life interest in them, an esthetic appropriation of them, an ethical discrimination and devotion respecting them. It engages all the powers of thinking and feeling and willing in an effort of the whole man towards the fulfilment of his highest capacities. After religion surveys all knowledge, all systems of faith and morals, it calls men to the adoption of a faith and to a decision of the will to further those projects which appear to be the highest and best. It affords men, moreover, an occasion of celebration, fellowship and joy. It is not only thinking about life and duty but the immediate enjoyment of life to the full, never forgetting that present joy cannot be fulfilled without the continued devotions of the future.

Religion as the complete survey of factors and the complete enjoyment of faculties is thus different in kind from every other experience or action. The religious moment transcends all lesser categories, it is the comprehending category. It is not merely truth but also beauty, not merely goodness but also truth. . . .

Religion is a marvelous amalgam. It seeks truth and duty and joy not separately but together. The duties are derived from the truths, and the joys from both, and both from the joys. These elements do not become religion until they take on an inner union, in which the actions of thinking and feeling and willing are commingled into one. They are not isolated parts but interrelated and mutually engaged components of one whole fabric. Religion is truly the bread of life because the wheaten flour of its truth, the milk of its kindness and the sugar of its apprehensions are not just set out upon the table, they are stirred together and baked by the welding fires of religious devotion. The ingredients of religion do not become religion until merged by the alchemy of an inner union. The life of cultivation does not become culture until blended by the amalgam of the religious cult.

Religion is a marvelous universality. Its knowledge is cosmic, its morals determined in the light of all things, its art symbolic of the wholeness of life. Its elements do not become religion until they take on an outer extension by which they are carried to the farthest possible bounds. Religion seeks truths not only in their proximate connections but in their total relations. It can never cease the quest for universal knowledge. It requires duties selected not by local factors but by the light of all factors. It can never fall short of the effort to perform the full duty of life. It apprehends goods both severally and connectedly. It cannot be satisfied short of communion with the Life of All Things. . . .

Wherever men gather all the facts of their knowledge and all the essays of their faith to make of them the best system of thought they can conceive, and derive from the best purposes they can approve, and the highest satisfaction they can enjoy, they are acting religiously. Religion is the perpetual effort to achieve the truest thought, the noblest purposes and the highest happiness.

Religion is thus the supreme experience of life. It is the presumptuous effort of comprehension: to remember and embrace all things; all sorts and conditions of men; all facts of nature; all factors of the political and social life of nations; all affairs and toils of humanity; all inner powers and potencies of persons; all states of mind and heart of any and every man; all fortunes and misfortunes, disasters and achievements of individuals and of the race; all sciences and philosophies; all faiths and virtues; all hopes and dreams of mankind.

It is at the same time the high art of apprehension. It moves beyond the intellectual labors of survey to those vivid realizations that are appropriative and apprehending. It gathers all the bright glory of the earth, of seas and skies and flowers, of gay youth and venerable age, of human minds in the fulness of their powers; it sweeps forward beyond the solemn resolutions of evil in the tragic arts of the great poets until it can see some lineaments of the beauty of holiness, the sublime life and glory of All Things.

It is, finally, the response of commitment, of sharing and partnership, the acceptance of the common lot, the assumption of responsibility by those who can freely offer the sacrifices of praise because they have offered the works of their hands and the labors of their lives.

— VON OGDEN VOGT, 1879-

You do say grace at meals and thank and praise God for your daily bread, so far so good, but thank and praise Him now for everything.

When a man is in God's grace and free from mortal sin, then everything that he does, so long as there is no sin in it, gives God glory and what does not give Him glory has some, however little, sin in it. It is not only prayer that gives God glory, but work. Smiting on an anvil, sawing a beam, whitewashing a wall, driving horses, sweeping, scouring, everything gives God some glory. . . . To go to communion worthily gives God great glory, but to take food in thankfulness and temperance gives Him glory too. To lift up the hands in prayer gives God glory, but a man with a dungfork in his hand, a woman with a sloppail, give Him glory too. He is so great that all things give Him glory if you mean they should. So then, my brethren, live.

—GERARD MANLEY HOPKINS, 1844-1889

CHAPTER TEN

The One Remains, the Many Change and Pass

Up from the world of the many
To the Over world of the One
Back to the world of the many
To fulfill the life of the One.

— VON OGDEN VOGT, 1879-

· I ·

La gloria di colui che tutto muove
per l'universo penetra, a risplende
in una parte più, e meno altrove.

DANTE

The One remains, the many change and pass;
Heaven's light forever shines, Earth's shadows fly;
Life, like a dome of many-colored glass,
Stains the white radiance of Eternity,
Until Death tramples it to fragments. Die,
If thou wouldst be with that which thou dost seek!
Follow where all is fled! Rome's azure sky,
Flowers, ruins, statues, music, words, are weak
The glory they transfuse with fitting truth to speak.

That Light whose smile kindles the Universe,
That Beauty in which all things work and move,
That Benediction which the eclipsing Curse
Of birth can quench not, that sustaining Love
Which through the web of being blindly wove
By man and beast and earth and air and sea,
Burns bright or dim, as each are mirrors of
The fire for which all thirst, now beams on me,
Consuming the last clouds of cold mortality.

The breath whose might I have invoked in song
Descends on me; my spirit's bark is driven
Far from the shore, far from the trembling throng
Whose sails were never to the tempest given;
The massy earth and sphered skies are riven!
I am borne darkly, fearfully, afar;
Whilst burning through the inmost veil of Heaven,
The soul of Adonaïs, like a star,
Beacons from the abode where the Eternal are.

— PERCY BYSSHE SHELLEY, 1792-1822

Thou alone, O Lord, art what Thou art and who Thou art. For that
which is one thing in its whole and another in its parts, and in which
there is anything mutable, is not what it is, in an absolute sense. And
that which begins from non-existence and can be conceived of as not
existing, and which unless it subsist through something else, must
return to non-existence; also whatever has a past which is now no
longer, and a future, which is yet to come, this does not exist in
proper and absolute sense. But Thou art what Thou art; because
whatsoever Thou art at any time or in any manner, Thou art this at
all times and absolutely. And Thou art who Thou art properly and
simply; because Thou hast neither a past nor a future, but only a
present, neither canst Thou be conceived of as not existing at any
moment. But Thou art life and light and wisdom and blessedness and
eternity, and many things good of this nature, and yet Thou art none
other than the one supreme Good, absolutely self-sufficient, need-
ing nothing, but whom all things else need in order to their existence
and well-being.

— ST. ANSELM, 1033-1109

One Being, yet unique in unity; a mystery of Oneness measureless.

— THE SIDDUR

The soul of him, who is self-conquered and full of peace, is fixed on the Supreme, in cold and heat, in pleasure and pain, in honor and dishonor. . . .

With soul at peace, with fear gone, standing firm in the vow of service of the Eternal, controlling the mind, with heart set on Me, let him dwell in union, intent on Me. . . .

The seeker for union, thus ever joining himself in union, his darkness gone, happily attains the infinite joy of union with the Eternal.

He sees his soul as one with all beings, and all beings as one with his soul; his soul joined in union, beholding Oneness everywhere.

Who sees Me everywhere, and sees all in Me, him I lose not, nor will he lose Me. . . .

They who strive for freedom from age and death, taking refuge in Me, know the Eternal, the All, the highest self, the perfect Work.

They who know Me as the highest Being, the highest Divinity, the highest Sacrifice, even in death perceive Me, their hearts united to Me. . . .

I am the offering, I am the sacrifice, I am the oblation, I am the libation; I am the chant, I am the holy oil, I am the fire, I am what is offered.

I am the father of this world, the mother, the guardian, the father's father; I am the end of knowledge, the purifier, the sacred syllable, the hymn, the chant, the sacred sentence.

I am the way, the supporter, the lord, the witness, the home, the refuge, the beloved; the forthcoming and withdrawing, the place, the treasure, the everlasting seed. . . .

I am equal toward all beings; nor is any hated or favored of Me; but they who love Me with dear love, they are in Me and I in them.

— BHAGAVAD-GITA

O God, who art, and wast, and art to come, before whose face the generations rise and pass away, age after age the living seek Thee and find that of Thy faithfulness there is no end. Our fathers in their pilgrimage walked by Thy guidance, and rested on Thy compassion. Still to their children be Thou the cloud by day, and the fire by night. Where but in Thee have we a covert from the storm, or shadow from the heat of life? In our manifold temptations, Thou alone knowest and art ever nigh; in sorrow, Thy pity revives the fainting soul; in our prosperity and ease, it is Thy spirit only that can keep us from pride and keep us humble.

— JAMES MARTINEAU, 1805-1900

In the midst of this City Celestial,
Where the eternal Temple should have rose,
Lighten'd the Idea Beatifical:
End and Beginning of each thing that grows,
Whose self no end, nor yet beginning knows,
    That hath no eyes to see nor ears to hear,
    Yet sees and hears and is all-eye, all-ear,
That nowhere is contained and yet is everywhere.

Changer of all things, yet immutable,
Before and after all, the first and last,
That, moving all, is yet immovable,
Great without quantity, in whose forecast
Things past are present, things to come are past,
    Swift without motion, to whose open eye
    The hearts of wicked men unbreasted lie,
At once absent and present to them, far and nigh.

— GILES FLETCHER, 1588?-1623

The quietude of a soft wind
Will not rescind
My debts to God, but gentle-skinned
His finger probes. I lull myself
In quiet in diet in riot in dreams,
In dopes in drams in drums in dreams
Till God retire and the door shut
But
Now I am left in the fire-blaze
The peacefulness of the fire-blaze
Will not erase
My debts to God for His mind strays

Over and under and all ways
All days and always.

— LOUIS MacNEICE, 1907 -

Infinity!
O who can scan, who measure Thee, for Whom
Whole worlds are days and men a moment's flash.
Mayhap e'en now a thousandth sun may wheel
And thousands yet remain. Rolling apace
A sun like some vast timepiece animate
With balanced weight, hastens inspired by might
Of God. Its springs run down, another strikes.
But Thou, Infinity, Thou remainest
And dost not count their sun.

— ALBRECHT VON HALLER, 1708 - 1777

I admire thee, master of the tides,
Of the Yore-flood, of the year's fall;
The recurb and the recovery of the gulf's sides,
The girth of it and the wharf of it and the wall;
Stanching, quenching ocean of a motionable mind;
Ground of being, and granite of it: past all
Grasp God, throned behind
Death with a sovereignty that heeds but hides, bodes but abides.

— GERARD MANLEY HOPKINS, 1844 - 1889

· II ·

All creatures seek after unity; all multiplicity struggles toward it—
the universal aim of all life is always this unity. All that flows outward is to flow backward into its source—God.

— JOHANNES TAULER, 1300? - 1361

I say in the heart of the seas to the quaking heart,
Fearing exceedingly because they lift up their waves:
If thou believest in God who made
The sea, and whose Name doth stand unto all eternity,

The sea shall not affright thee when the waves thereof arise,
For with thee is One who hath set a bound to the sea.

— YEHUDAH HALEVI, 1085?-1140

In man's every contact with reality, whether with nature through
sense-experience, or with beauty through appreciation, or with a
divine Comforter through personal communion, he is in immediate
contact with the Supernatural, with the eternal and active God. To
put the point otherwise, it is assumed that man's very awareness of
reality and his desire to comprehend it can be rightly interpreted
only as his response to the prior movement of the living divine Spirit
upon him. "Thou wouldst not seek me hadst thou not already possessed me." . . .

The very first datum for our thought—as it is certainly the first
fact of all experience—is the indubitable existence of that most certainly real, most incomprehensibly mysterious, most persistently
alluring Reality which is the *fons et origo* of all knowledge as of all
existence. And the achievement of knowledge by man now becomes
a painstaking, ever baffled but ever persistent, ever incomplete but
ever more nearly complete, effort to discern and define more precisely the features of that Reality. No longer is it the aim of philosophy and of religious apologetic to construct a neat and tight system
or to unify the findings of the various sciences without remainder.
Indeed their purpose is not to "construct" anything, but rather to
reveal the inner logic of mankind's varied types of experience and
their interpretation in the different sciences, to show their harmonies
and the points at which harmonization is not at present possible. The
proper function of the mind in knowledge is not creation but
reception. . . .

The energies of reflection should be directed to the better *understanding* of the "given" data of experience. As to God, the *fact* of
God is assumed as beyond dispute from the outset. Theology's task
is the ever more accurate and adequate comprehension of the precise
character of that fact. Finally, the same logic which points to a truer
view of God demands a sounder estimate of the significance of religion. For it is obvious to common-sense that, if religion has any
validity at all, it is not "one among" the interests of life correlative
with art and mathematics and politics—an "elective in the university
of life"—but the central and regnant concern in which all others find
their completion and their meaning. In this truer perspective, religion
as the experience of the soul's communion with the Ultimate Real-

ity, far from being a dubious matter recognized if at all by the leave of the special sciences, becomes life's first and final preoccupation as it has to do with life's initial and ultimate relationship.

— HENRY P. VAN DUSEN, 1897-

The Spirit of God, in countless variety of forms, neither above, nor in any way without, but intimately within all things, is really present, with equal integrity and fullness, in the sunbeam ninety millions of miles long, and the wandering drop of water as it evaporates therein.

The divine consciousness has the same relation to the production of things as the human intelligence to the production of true thoughts concerning them. Nay! Those thoughts are themselves actually God in man, a loan to man also of His assisting Spirit, who, in Truth, is the Creator of things, in and by his contemplation of them. For Him, as for man in proportion as man thinks truly, thought and being are identical, and things existent only as they are known. And God the Spirit, the soul of the world, being therefore really identical with the soul of Bruno, he too becomes a sharer in the divine joy. In a certain mystic sense, he, too, is the creator; himself actually a participator in the divine function.

— WALTER PATER, 1839-1894

The supreme critic on the errors of the past and the present, and the only prophet of that which must be, is that great nature in which we rest as the earth lies in the soft arms of the atmosphere, that unity, that Over-Soul, within which every man's particular being is contained and made one with all other. Within man is the soul of the whole, the wise silence, the universal beauty, to which every part and particle is equally related, the eternal One.

— RALPH WALDO EMERSON, 1803-1882

In these moments of communion with the infinite, how different does our life here seem. How all that occupies us, engrosses us, impassions us becomes suddenly before our eyes puerile, frivolous and vain. We seem mere marionettes who play at being serious in a fantastic parade and who mistake baubles for treasures. How different everything seems to us then. Reality appears to us less real than the fable. The purpose of all this is the development of the soul. The soul is the only reality, the rest is the sublime fantasmagoria created to brighten it and to give it shape.

Fairy stories and legends seem more directly true than natural history and even more so—for at least they are more transparent emblems. Immortal, lasting, alone completely real, is the soul. The world is only a majestic fireworks. The soul is an entire universe and her sun is love.

—Henri Frédéric Amiel, 1821-1881

His the fact of the fact, the life of the life, the soul of the soul, the incomprehensible, the sum of all contradictions, the unity of all diversity. . . . He is not a being, yet apart from Him there is no being —there is no apart from Him.

—John Burroughs, 1837-1921

All things which are, are in God, and must be conceived through God, therefore God is the cause of those things which are in Him. Further, besides God there can be no substance, that is nothing in itself external to God. God, therefore, is the indwelling cause of all things.

—Baron Gottfried Wilhelm von Leibniz, 1646-1716

What, then, is that which really exists? It is the Eternal, the Un-created, the Undying, to whom time brings no change. For time is always flowing and never stays: it is a vessel charged with birth and death: it has a before and after, a "will be" and a "has been": it belongs to the "is not" rather than to the "is." But God is: and that not in time but in eternity, motionless, timeless, changeless eternity, that has no before or after: and being One, He fills eternity with one Now, and so really "is," not "has been," or "will be," without beginning and without ceasing.

—Plutarch, 46?-?120

For He is one, no second shares His nature or His loneliness.

—The Siddur

· III ·

Seers of the Infinite have ever been quiet souls. They abide alone with themselves and the Infinite, or if they do look around them, grudge to no one who understands the mighty word his own peculiar way. By means of this wide vision, this feeling of the Infinite, they are able to look beyond their own sphere. There is in religion such a capacity for unlimited many-sidedness in judgment and in contemplation, as is nowhere else to be found. . . . Religion is the natural and sworn foe of all narrow-mindedness and of all one-sidedness. . . .

The man who only thinks methodically, and acts from principle and design, and will accomplish this or that in the world, unavoidably circumscribes himself, and makes everything that does not forward him an object of antipathy. Only when the free impulse of seeing and of living is directed towards the Infinite and goes into the Infinite, is the mind set in unbounded liberty. Religion alone rescues it from the heavy fetters of opinion and desire.

— FRIEDRICH SCHLEIERMACHER, 1768-1834

For there is one universe made up of all things, and one God who pervades all things, and one substance, and one law. . . . Observe constantly that all things take place by change, and accustom thyself to consider that the nature of the Universe loves nothing so much as to change the things which are and to make new things like them. . . . For we are made for co-operation, like feet, like hands, like eyelids, like the rows of the upper and lower teeth. . . . We are all working together to one end, some with knowledge and design, and others without knowing what they do. . . . But men co-operate after different fashions; and even those co-operate abundantly, who find fault with what happens and those who try to oppose it and to hinder it; for the universe had need even of such men as these.

— MARCUS AURELIUS, 121-180

The essence of man is constituted by certain modifications of the attributes of God. For the being of substance does not belong to the essence of man. That essence therefore is something which is in God, and without God can neither be nor be conceived, whether it be a modification or a mode which expresses God's nature in a certain conditioned manner.

— BARUCH SPINOZA, 1632-1677

>   . . . 'Tis the sublime of man,
> Our noontide majesty, to know ourselves
> Parts and proportions of one wondrous whole!
> This fraternises man, this constitutes
> Our charities and bearings. But 'tis God
> Diffused through all, that doth make all one whole.

— SAMUEL TAYLOR COLERIDGE, 1772-1834

We know that even our nearest friends enter into us but partially, and hold intercourse with us only at times; whereas the consciousness of a perfect and enduring Presence, and it alone, keeps the heart open. Withdraw the Object on which it rests, and it will relapse again into its state of confinement and constraint; and in proportion as it is limited, either to certain seasons or to certain affections, the heart is straitened and distressed. If it be not overbold to say it, He who is infinite can alone be its measure; He alone can answer to the mysterious assemblage of feelings and thoughts which it has within it. . . .

Life passes, riches fly away, popularity is fickle, the senses decay, the world changes, friends die. One alone is constant; One alone is true to us; One alone can be true; One alone can be all things to us; One alone can supply our needs; One alone can train us up to our full perfection; One alone can give a meaning to our complex and intricate nature; One alone can give us tune and harmony; One alone can form and possess us.

— CARDINAL JOHN HENRY NEWMAN, 1801-1890

>   Authentic tidings of invisible things,
> Of ebb and flow and ever 'during power, and central peace
> Subsisting at the heart of endless agitation.

— WILLIAM WORDSWORTH, 1770-1850

If one is not clear about God, one will always tend to shy away toward something more accessible, like one's own conscious states. To talk about commitment brings one face to face with the question of God, so that one cannot dodge it. . . . God is that within and beyond the universe which expresses the greatest good which now is and ever can be: the direction of life against death, the direction of unity against discord, the direction of creation and increasing growth against destruction and decay. God is the power of good in all its various forms: in the order and structure of inorganic matter, in the process of growth and sensitivity in the realm of life, in the conditions of intelligence, co-operation, appreciation and creative love on the human level.

This cosmic reach in our description of God must not distract our attention from the specific human focus within which our experiences of the good are most intense and most decisive. It is here most of all that we know God as a daily fact. We have tried the ways of ambition, of self-aggrandizement, of aggressive opportunism, and we have seen the kind of flimsy success to which they lead, we have tasted the bitter poisons they generate, we have known the conflict, the disgust, the inner division, the outer isolation that follow in their wake. We have also tried in some small measure the other way, and known that every man and woman must have love; that there is no life or peace without love; only strife, waste, madness, destruction, death. There is that in life which makes it necessary that men should find the way of truth, of understanding, of justice, or else destroy themselves and each other. You have not seen it? You cannot move a step but you stumble into it; it is in the structure of your world; you cannot live a day or an hour without saying either yes or no to it, without finding life through it or death without it.

Even a faint glimpse of this reality brings you back to yourself. Whither do you move? With it or without it? The alternatives are simple—terrifyingly simple and clear. To compromise in this matter is to decide; to waver is to decide; to postpone and evade decision is to decide; to hide the matter is to decide. There is no escape. You must say yes, or no. There are a thousand ways of saying no; one way of saying yes; and no way of saying anything else.

—GREGORY VLASTOS, 1907-

A genuine faith must recognize the fact that it is through a dark glass that we see; though by faith we do penetrate sufficiently to the heart of the mystery not to be overwhelmed by it. A genuine faith resolves the mystery of life by the mystery of God. It recognizes that no aspect of life or existence explains itself, even after all known causes and consequences have been traced. All known existence points beyond itself. To realize that it points beyond itself to God is to assert that the mystery of life does not dissolve life into meaninglessness. Faith in God is faith in some ultimate unity of life, in some final comprehensive purpose which holds all the various, and frequently contradictory, realms of coherence and meaning together.

— REINHOLD NIEBUHR, 1892 -

The relation of God to the universe . . . may be best understood by thinking of Him as both transcendent and immanent. God transcends the universe because He is its ground, because His nature is wholly characterized by Truth, Beauty, and Goodness, and because His purpose is far richer in content than the sum-total of actualized value in the universe. God is immanent in the universe because He is actively present in the order, organization, and achieved values of the world as a conserver of value, and because He is purposefully at work throughout the historic process of the world as a creator of value.

— EUGENE WILLIAM LYMAN, 1872 - 1948

· IV ·

God minus the world equals God;
The world minus God equals nothing.

— WILLIAM TEMPLE, 1881 - 1944

He who flees from God, flees into himself. For there are two kinds of mind, the mind of the universe, and that is God, and the mind of individual man. And the one flees from his own mind to the mind of the universe—for whoever leaves his own mind, avows therewith that the works of the mortal mind are as nothing, and ascribes everything to God. But the other flees from God, and declares that not God is the cause of anything at all, but that he himself is the cause of all that comes to pass. Thus there are many who believe that all the things in the world go their own course by themselves, without a guide, and that it is the spirit of man that has invented the arts, crafts, laws, customs, state institutions, and the rights of the individual and the community, both in regard to men and to beasts, that are without reason. But you, O my soul, see the difference between these two points of view. For the one leaves the perishable mortal mind, which has been created, and chooses for its true aid the primordial and immortal mind of the universe. But the other, which sets aside God, foolishly courts as its ally the human mind, which is not even able to help itself.

— PHILO JUDAEUS, late first century B.C. and early first century A.D.

We know that in religion we withdraw ourselves from what is temporal, and that religion is for our consciousness that region in which all the enigmas of the world are solved, all the contradictions of deeper-reaching thought have their meaning unveiled, and where the voice of the heart's pain is silenced—the region of eternal truth, of eternal rest, of eternal peace. Speaking generally, it is through thought, concrete thought, or, to put it more definitely, it is by reason of his being Spirit, that man is man; and from man as Spirit proceed all the many developments of the sciences and arts, the interests of political life, and all those conditions which have reference to man's freedom and will. But all these manifold forms of human relations, activities, and pleasures, and all the ways in which these are intertwined; all that has worth and dignity for man, all wherein he seeks his happiness, his glory, and his pride, finds its ultimate centre in religion, in the thought, the consciousness, and the feeling of God. Thus God is the beginning of all things, and the end of all things. As all things proceed from this point, so all return back to it again. He is the centre which gives life and quickening to all things, and which animates and preserves in existence all the various forms of being. In religion man places himself in a relation to this centre, in which all other relations concentrate themselves, and in so doing he rises up to the highest level of consciousness and to the region which is free from relation to what is other than itself, to something which is absolutely self-sufficient, the unconditioned, what is free, and is its own object and end.

— GEORG WILHELM FRIEDRICH HEGEL, 1770-1831

No coward soul is mine,
No trembler in the world's storm-troubled sphere;
   I see Heaven's glories shine,
And faith shines equal, arming me from fear.

O God within my breast,
Almighty, ever-present Deity!
   Life—that in me has rest,
As I—undying life—have power in thee!

Vain are the thousand creeds
That move men's hearts: unutterably vain;
   Worthless as withered weeds,
Or idlest froth amid the boundless main.

To waken doubt in one
Holding so fast by thine infinity;
   So surely anchored on
The steadfast rock of immortality.

With wide-embracing love
Thy Spirit animates eternal years,
   Pervades and broods above,
Changes, sustains, dissolves, creates and rears.

Though earth and man were gone,
And suns and universes ceased to be,
   And Thou were left alone,
Every existence would exist in Thee.

There is not room for Death
Nor atom that his might could render void:
   Thou—Thou art Being and Breath,
And what Thou art may never be destroyed.

                    —EMILY BRONTË, 1818-1848

Belief in God necessarily delivers a man from fear and from self-centeredness, because it *is* his consciousness that he is not responsible for himself nor for the world in which he lives. It involves the recognition that his own life is a small, yet an essential part of the history of mankind, and that the life of mankind is a small but essential part of the universe to which it belongs. It involves the recognition that the control and the determination of all that happens in the world lies in the hands of a power that is irresistible and yet friendly. It is more than the recognition of this; it is the capacity to live as if this were so. It is the habit of living in the light of this faith. This is not all that is contained in the belief in God, but it is a fundamental and necessary element in it. Anyone who does behave in this way believes in God at least so far, whatever he himself may say about it. The opposite attitude, which is the core of real atheism, expresses itself in that individualism which makes a man feel alone and isolated in a world against which he must defend himself. Such a man may often be overwhelmed with a sense of his individual responsibility. He feels that what happens to him depends upon himself. If he is responsible in a smaller or a greater degree for other people he feels that what happens to them depends upon himself. Consequently all that happens beyond his own control in the world appears as a series of fortunate or unfortunate accidents to which he must perpetually adjust himself. This *is* to disbelieve in God. For belief in God, whatever else it may involve, at least includes the capacity to live as part of the whole of things in a world which is unified. If we believe in God we live as if the fortunes of the world did not depend on us; we live as if the world could be trusted to work out its own destiny and to use us, even through our mistakes and our failures, for its own good purposes.

— JOHN MACMURRAY, 1891-

A hasty kind of reasoning may hold that praying is an unprofitable act, because a man's prayer does not really change the Unchangeable; but even if this in the process of time were desired, might not changeable man come easily to regret that he had changed God? The true kind of reasoning is therefore the only desirable kind as well; prayer does not change God, but changes him who prays.

— SÖREN KIERKEGAARD, 1813-1855

Hast thou not known? hast thou not heard, that the everlasting God, the Lord, the Creator of the ends of the earth, fainteth not, neither is weary? there is no searching of his understanding.

He giveth power to the faint: and to them that have no might he increaseth strength.

Even the youths shall faint and be weary, and the young men
shall utterly fall:

But they that wait upon the Lord shall renew their strength; they
shall mount up with wings as eagles; they shall run, and not be
weary; and they shall walk, and not faint.

— THE BIBLE, Isaiah 40:28-31

· v ·

Our Father, whose creative Will
   Asked Being for us all,
Confirm it that Thy Primal Love
May weave in us the freedom of
The actually deficient on
   The justly actual.

Though written by Thy children with
   A smudged and crooked line,
The Word is ever legible,
Thy Meaning unequivocal,
And for Thy Goodness even sin
   Is valid as a sign.

Inflict Thy promises with each
   Occasion of distress,
That from our incoherence we
May learn to put our trust in Thee,
And brutal fact persuade us to
   Adventure, Art, and Peace.

— W. H. AUDEN, 1907-

Man entereth the world,
And knoweth not why;
He rejoiceth
And knoweth not wherefore;
He liveth,
And knoweth not for how long.
In his childhood he walketh in his own stubbornness,
And when the spirit of lust beginneth in its season
To stir him up to gather power and wealth,

Then he journeyeth from his place
To ride in ships
And to tread in the deserts,
And to carry his life to dens of lions,
Adventuring in among wild beasts;
And when he imagineth that great is his glory
And that mighty is the spoil of his hand,
Quietly stealeth the spoiler upon him,
And his eyes are opened and there is naught.

At every moment he is destined to troubles
That pass and return,
At every hour evils,
At every moment chances,
On every day terrors.
If for an instant he stand in security,
Suddenly disaster will come upon him,
Either war shall come and the sword will smite him,
Or the bow of brass transpierce him;
Or the sorrows will overpower him,
Or the presumptuous billows flow over him,
Or sickness and steadfast evils shall find him,
Till he become a burden on his own soul,
And shall find the gall of serpents in his honey.

When his pain increaseth
His glory decreaseth,
And youth make mock of him,
And infants rule him,
And he becometh a burden to the issue of his loins,
And all who know him become estranged from him.
When his hour hath come, he passeth from the courts of his house
        to the court of Death,
And from the shadow of his chambers to the shadow of Death.
He shall strip off his broidery and his scarlet
And shall put on corruption and the worm,
And lie down in the dust
And return to the foundation from which he came.

O man, whom these things befall,
When shall he find a time for repentance
To scour away the rust of his perversion?

For the day is short and the work manifold,
And the task-masters irate,
Hurrying and scurrying,
And Time laughs at him,
And the Master of the House presses.

Therefore I beseech Thee, O my God,
Remember the distresses that come upon man,
And if I have done evil
Do Thou me good at my latter end,
Nor requite measure for measure,
To man whose sins are measureless,
And whose death is a joyless departure.

— SOLOMON IBN-GABIROL, 1021? -? 1058

Your character is developed according to your faith. This is the primary religious truth from which no one can escape. Religion is force of belief cleansing the inward parts. For this reason the primary religious virtue is sincerity, a penetrating sincerity.

A religion, on its doctrinal side, can thus be defined as a system of general truths which have the effect of transforming character when they are sincerely held and vividly apprehended.

In the long run your character and your conduct of life depend upon your intimate convictions. Life is an internal fact for its own sake, before it is an external fact relating itself to others. The conduct of external life is conditioned by environment, but it receives its final quality, on which its worth depends, from the internal life which is the self-realization of existence. Religion is the art and the theory of the internal life of man, so far as it depends on the man himself and on what is permanent in the nature of things.

This doctrine is the direct negation of the theory that religion is primarily a social fact. Social facts are of great importance to religion, because there is no such thing as absolutely independent existence. You cannot abstract society from man; most psychology is herd-psychology. But all collective emotions leave untouched the awful ultimate fact, which is the human being, consciously alone with itself, for its own sake.

Religion is what the individual does with his own solitariness. It runs through three stages, if it evolves to its final satisfaction. It is the transition from God the void to God the enemy, and from God the enemy to God the companion.

Thus religion is solitariness; and if you are never solitary, you are never religious. Collective enthusiasms, revivals, institutions, churches, rituals, bibles, codes of behaviour, are the trappings of religion, its passing forms. They may be useful, or harmful; they may be authoritatively ordained, or merely temporary expedients. But the end of religion is beyond all this.

Accordingly, what should emerge from religion is individual worth of character. But worth is positive or negative, good or bad. Religion is by no means necessarily good. It may be very evil. The fact of evil, interwoven with the texture of the world, shows that in the nature of things there remains effectiveness for degradation. In your religious experience the God with whom you have made terms may be the God of destruction, the God who leaves in His wake the loss of the greater reality.

In considering religion, we should not be obsessed by the idea of its necessary goodness. This is a dangerous delusion. The point to notice is its transcendent importance; and the fact of this importance is abundantly made evident by the appeal to history.

— Alfred North Whitehead, 1861-1947

Lord, thou hast been our dwelling place in all generations.

Before the mountains were brought forth, or ever Thou hadst formed the earth and the world, even from everlasting to everlasting, Thou art God.

Thou turnest man to destruction; and sayest, Return, ye children of men.

For a thousand years in Thy sight are but as yesterday when it is past, and as a watch in the night.

Thou carriest them away as with a flood; they are as a sleep: in the morning they are like grass which groweth up.

In the morning it flourisheth, and groweth up; in the evening it is cut down, and withereth.

For we are consumed by Thine anger, and by Thy wrath are we troubled.

Thou hast set our iniquities before Thee, our secret sins in the light of Thy countenance.

For all our days are passed away in Thy wrath: we spend our years as a tale that is told.

The days of our years are threescore years and ten; and if by reason of strength they be fourscore years, yet is their strength labour and sorrow; for it is soon cut off, and we fly away.

Who knoweth the power of Thine anger? even according to Thy fear, so is Thy wrath.

So teach us to number our days, that we may apply our hearts unto wisdom.

Return, O LORD, how long? and let it repent Thee concerning Thy servants.

O satisfy us early with Thy mercy; that we may rejoice and be glad all our days.

Make us glad according to the days wherein Thou hast afflicted us, and the years wherein we have seen evil.

Let Thy work appear unto Thy servants, and Thy glory unto their children.

And let the beauty of the LORD our God be upon us: and establish Thou the work of our hands upon us; yea, the work of our hands establish Thou it.

— THE BIBLE, Psalm 90

CHAPTER ELEVEN

Imago Dei

When we know God, some likeness of God
comes to be in us.

— St. Thomas Aquinas, 1225?-1274

·I·

THREE things conspire together in mine eyes
To bring the remembrance of Thee ever before me,
And I possess them as faithful witnesses:
Thy heavens, for whose sake I recall Thy name,
The earth I live on, that rouseth my thought
With its expanse which recalleth the expander of my pedestal,
And the musing of my heart when I look within the depths of myself.
Bless the Lord, O my soul, for ever and aye!

— Solomon ibn-Gabirol, 1021?-?1058

Everything harmonizes with me which is harmonious to thee, O Universe! Nothing for me is too early or too late which is in due time for thee. Everything is fruit to me which thy seasons bear, O Nature! From thee are all things, in thee are all things, to thee all things return. Could the poet say of Athens, Thou lovely city of Cecrops; and shalt not thou say of the world, Thou lovely city of God?

— Marcus Aurelius, 121-180

202

I have not seen Thee, yet I tell Thy praise,
Nor known Thee, yet I image forth Thy ways . . .
They [the prophets] told of Thee, but not as Thou must be,
Since from Thy work they tried to image Thee.

— ANONYMOUS

I have gone the whole round of creation: I saw and I spoke;
I, a work of God's hand for that purpose, received in my brain
And pronounced on the rest of his handwork—returned him again
His creation's approval or censure: I spoke as I saw:
I report, as a man may of God's work—all's love, yet all's law.
Now I lay down the judgeship he lent me. Each faculty tasked
To perceive him, has gained an abyss, where a dewdrop was asked.
Have I knowledge? confounded it shrivels at Wisdom laid bare.
Have I forethought? how purblind, how blank, to the Infinite Care!
Do I task any faculty highest, to image success?
I but open my eyes,—and perfection, no more and no less,
In the kind I imagined, full-fronts me, and God is seen God
In the star, in the stone, in the flesh, in the soul and the clod.
And thus looking within and around me, I ever renew
(With that stoop of the soul which in bending upraises it too)
The submission of man's nothing-perfect to God's all-complete,
As by each new obeisance in spirit, I climb to his feet.

— ROBERT BROWNING, 1812-1889

I

Shall all of the responses be now apportioned to the birds?
    To leap be the lamb's peculiarity? to flit, the flying-fish's?
Cows, quiet as bronzes, let radiance seep to the bone,
    While man, looking at creation through the miasma of his wishes,
Finds it fit either for nothing or for a few bitter words?
Shall the oppressed jay and starling in clownish tone
    Chatter, and make shimmer their target-forming feathers,
While man, who thinks himself the paragon of the earth,
    Uses his prerogative in all sorts of weathers
To make reasons for groaning, and then to proceed to groan?
And to make of his unique means of expressing mirth
    A vehicle for sourness, turned-in on itself, and brittle,

While the unlaughing otters cavort down muddy banks?
    Shall the squirrel still scamper, though acorns be few and little,
While man fires his wheatfields and complains of a dearth?
I say, if we think ourselves better than the incalculable ranks
    Of our dread, or gentle, or comical contemporaries,
Let us then show it in our presenting of praise;
    For between the three bears and the three beautiful Marys
What gulf is fixed, save in the gift of giving thanks?
And if I feel my heart, in these almost doomed days,
    In this valley of grinding teeth, to grow heavy and to harden,
Let me remember still that the due love is still due;
    For the earth is a granary, the earth is a garden,
And my despair is the necessary product of my own ways;
My strength and virtue lessen, and compass my own rue;
    But the unspeakable and unimaginable glory
Of the divine working of circling beauty and power
    Blazes, no less transcendent than in the earliest story,
And quite impractical flowers grow where they always grew.
Let me then constantly adore, in however harassed an hour,
    The inconceivable Maker of the inconceivable but daily
Procession of mysteries which rounds the daily round;
    And though the long shadow fall, let my heart rise gaily,
For the shadow is my own: beyond me is founded the tower.
The shadow is my own, lain in mourning along the ground,
    But the tower for ever stands, from bedrock to highest distance,
Made firm by the indivisible, infinitely divided One:
    Whose deaf ears are drummed on by each sequestered existence,
Whose sightless eyes beacon from the empyrean to the profound,
Whose mouth is my neighbor's, Whose hard heart is a sun,
                                    And Whose will shall be done.

II

Many are the wonders of the world, and man is the most
    Wonderful; and of man the beauties also are many,
But more purely beautiful are ocean, and sky, and hill.
    Among the beauties and wonders is nutriment too much for any
However avid intelligence between womb-fruit and ghost.
Thus, considering the firmament and my own so fallible will,
    Let me constantly adore the inconceivable Maker,
And, adoring the Maker, let me marvel at my kind again;
    For the pigment of the painter and the leaven of the baker

Equally attest to the glory of God and to human skill.
Innumerable are His residences, and one is in every brain.
　The accomplishments of men are the works of God, but ever
Are the works of God distinguishable from the accomplishments of
　　men;
　Godward from man the absolute chasms eternally sever,
But manward from God the universe is an inseparable chain.
Then first let me stir my idle, my shamefully unpractised pen
　In homage to the whole of the impersonal creation,
The revolving stage where each acts a partly written part.
　Let my heart rise gaily, buoyed upon constant adoration,
Seeing the huge majesty of the surges, or the anxiety of the wren;
Or hearing among the leaves the spasmodic tattle-tale start
　Sibilantly and suddenly, at the end of the dry season,
When heavy marbles of rain are the hissing gossip's theme;
　And then at the smell of the wet dust moved beyond reason,
Moved with an ancient worship, let me worship in my heart;
And so, also, as the sky splits along its eastern seam
　In the flushed summer at five o'clock in the morning
When the sun upon talon-tips springs onto the forested bowl,
　Complicating the already complicated spiders' webs, adorning
Them with the complications of his tiger-colored beam;
Or when a night grows goblin'd by an instantaneous owl;
　Or when, at noon, an apparently artificial backdrop of ranges
Of mountains, clear, hard, inorganic, and remote,
　Dances to life at the slithering of a cloud-shade, changes
From a land beyond loving to an Eden, given a soul
By one feather of immaculate moisture perilously afloat,
　A temporary nimbus over a converted region
Where the streams now are loquacious, the trees subject to whim,
　Where little songs and sorties among the bushes are legion,
And the rock is a tambourine for the feet of the goat;
Or when, in the evening, on the hushed seashore, the dim
　Evening dimly welds the pale sands to the pale ocean,
And the faint knocking of the breaking wavelets is soon unheard,
　While in the air a hovering of silence is all the motion
And among the farther waters only teeming silences swim. . . .
But these are simply casual impressions, called, by a word,
　Or a shape, or a smell, or some uncertain thread of association,
Back into the mystery of one all but insignificant mind;
　Which cannot grasp the notion of the residue of creation,

From the animus which inhabits to the outermost skies which gird—
The creation wherein man preys upon his own kind,
    And upon the beasts; and the beasts also prey upon each other,
And upon man; in every time and in every place:
    Where what devours enriches, what rots enlivens; ever another
Day after night, another birth after death; ever behind
Summer shall autumn drop, behind winter shall spring chase,
    As Africa chases Asia for ever around the equator,
And the whole world forever chases the moon around the sun.
    I can only constantly adore the unthinkable Creator,
Who abides in the heart of the flea, Who wheels in space,
Who endlessly continues what has been endlessly begun,
                Until His will shall have been done.

III

To consider God as one stares giddily at the starred sky
    Is instinctive, and both in time and in place universal;
The celestial circuits stagger one's mind into a shame,
    Only capable of a more or less mechanical rehearsal
Of one's sense of insignificance and of being about to die.
But I say that to be burdened with this awe is to proclaim
    The very splendor of man, by which his look may be lifted
From the prostrate shadow to the tower's circumference;
    For man is miserable precisely because he is gifted,
And the measure of his infamy serves also to measure his fame.
Thus when, during the intervals of his inept violence,
    His meditations concern themselves with the unlimited pavilion
Which is imperial upon him whether he regards it or not,
    An each sees himself as one among many a million
Two-leggéd worries bickering wistfully hence—
Then let the agitations, which bedevil him and besot,
    Perish in a pride at possessing even such a vision;
For of all the made mysteries only man has inward eyes,
    And only man harbors simultaneously both unity and division
And can symbolize complexity in the grace of the gavotte.
Therefore let me constantly adore the manifestations, in any guise,
    Of the mystery working through the minds and hands of people:
Whether in the simple purposefulness of a fisherman's net,
    Or in the elegant aspiration of a tapered steeple,
Or in the international language of lullabies,
Or in the varying rituals in which we are born and we beget,
    The making of works of art out of natural urges,

The touching of lips, the removal of hats, the shaking of hands—
   Any at all of the telling symbols in which emerges
A hankering for order from the jumbled everyday alphabet;
Any of the skills by which the seemingly fortuitous strands
   Of experience are loomed into satisfying traditions,
Wherein man is ever childish, and ever childishly sage,
   Hanging silver balls on fir trees, brazen bells on missions,
And perpetuating bountiful ecstasies in reticent sarabands.
Let us constantly adore, in however disheartening an age,
   The inconceivable Maker of the inconceivable but daily
Augmented procession of inconceivable man.
   The shadows are our own: let our hearts rise gaily;
For the turmoil which unmakes us, the abandon, the ethic rage,
The hunger for assertion which frenzies the partizan,
   The nausea making us pious, the fear making us aggressive—
These are the reverse of the obverse: but the coin is still of gold;
   And the identical passions are equally expressive
Of the celestial quickening by which our kind began.
Let us now remember what a noble river of music rolled
   From the vast intellectual brow of an otherwise peasant-
Faced, snubnosed, deaf, and uncouth mortal, a stream
   Now coarsely boisterous, now pellucidly pleasant,
Now sad with all the sorrows ever told or left untold;
And let us remember every figment of the too, too solid dream
   Which is populated with such palpitating creatures
That history is outdone, and which was thin air, before
   A provincial from by the Avon, with slightly foolish features,
Set out to make a living and to bolster his self-esteem.
These let us remember; let us remember a thousand more;
   Let us ever be aware of millions whom we cannot remember
Because we have never heard of them: their vision is our eyes.
   Let the winds of emulation fan the ashy ember
Till flowers of flame decorate the holy and hidden core;
For, that the core is within us, all perception testifies,
   And the core is always holy however unclean its raiment.
The light has been given us: let each give back his light.
   Whatever the nature or the extent of the repayment
The cowardly and reprehensible shall gleam with the just and the
     wise,
If only each, keeping a corner of his own darkness bright,
   Liberal in responses, deliberately living,
Improvident in acceptance, ashamed only to shun,

Constantly adore the unthinkable Creator, constantly giving
Adoration throughout the daytime, and trust during the night
That His pulse is in each of us, though His will be in none;
And that His will shall be done.

—ALASTAIR W. R. MILLER, contemporary

Most high, omnipotent, good Lord,
Thine are praise, glory, honour and all benediction,
To Thee alone, Most High, do they belong:
And no man is there, worthy Thee to name.
Praise be to Thee, my Lord, with all Thy creatures,
Chiefest of all, Sir Brother Sun,
Who is our day, through whom Thou givest light:
Beautiful is he, radiant with great splendour:
Of Thee, Most High, he is a true revealer.

Praise be to Thee, my Lord, for Sister Moon and for the stars;
In heaven hast Thou formed them, bright, precious and fair.
Praise be to Thee, my Lord, for Brother Wind, and for the air and
for the clouds, for clear sky and all weathers,
By which Thou givest nourishment to all Thy creatures.
Praise be to Thee, my Lord, for Sister Water,
She most useful is, and humble, precious pure.

Praise be to Thee, my Lord, for Brother Fire, by whom Thou light-
est up the night:
And fair he is, and merry, mighty and strong.
Praise be to Thee, my Lord, for our Sister, Mother Earth,
The which sustains and keeps us:
She brings forth divers fruits, the many-hued flowers and grass.

O Creatures all! praise and bless my Lord, and grateful be,
And serve Him with deep humility.

Praise be to Thee, my Lord, for those who pardon grant for love of
Thee,
And weakness bear and buffetings:
Blessed are they who in peace abide,
For by Thee, Most High, they shall be crowned.

Praise be to Thee, my Lord, for our Sister, bodily Death,
From whom no man living can flee;

Woe is it to them who die in mortal sin,
But blessed they who shall find themselves in Thy most holy will.
To them the second death shall do no ill.

— ST. FRANCIS OF ASSISI, 1182-1226

The worship of God is: Honouring His gifts in other men, each according to his genius, and loving the greatest men best; those who envy or calumniate great men hate God, for there is no other God.

The Angel, hearing this, almost became blue; but mastering himself he grew yellow and at last white, pink and smiling.

— WILLIAM BLAKE, 1757-1827

And whence are we? Of thy divine love-store,
Loving, hast Thou our slender love-life made,
That unafraid
We may thy dazzling love see and adore.

— ANONYMOUS

· II ·

No organism corresponds completely to the Idea that lies at its root; behind every one the higher Idea is hidden. That is my God, that is the God we all seek after and hope to find, but we can only feel Him, we cannot see Him.

— JOHANN WOLFGANG VON GOETHE, 1749-1832

It was only from the spring of 1906 onwards, when I had finished with the *Quest of the Historical Jesus* and had given up the headship of the college, that I could give to my new course of study the time it required. But then I set to work with eagerness at the natural sciences. Now at last I was able to devote myself to what had held most attraction for me when I was at the Gymnasium: I was at last in a position to acquire the knowledge I needed in order to feel the firm ground of reality under my feet in philosophy!

But study of the natural sciences brought me even more than the increase of knowledge I had longed for. It was to me a spiritual experience. I had all along felt it to be psychically a danger that in the so-called humanities with which I had been concerned hitherto, there is no truth which affirms itself as self-evident, but that a mere opinion can, by the way in which it deals with the subject matter, obtain recognition as true. The search for truth in the domains of history and philosophy is carried on in constantly repeated endless duels between the sense of reality of the one and the inventive imaginative power of the other. The argument from facts is never able to obtain a definite victory over the skillfully produced opinion. How often does what is reckoned as progress consist in a skillfully argued opinion putting real insight out of action for a long time!

To have to watch this drama going on and on, and deal in such different ways with men who had lost all feeling for reality I had found not a little depressing. Now I was suddenly in another country. I was concerned with truths which embodied realities, and found myself among men who took it as a matter of course that they had to justify with facts every statement they made. It was an experience which I felt to be needed for my own intellectual development.

Intoxicated as I was with the delight of dealing with realities which could be determined with exactitude, I was far from any inclination to undervalue the humanities as others in a similar position often did. On the contrary. Through my study of chemistry, physics, zoology, botany, and physiology I became more than ever conscious to what an extent truth in thought is justified and necessary, side by side with the truth which is merely established by facts. No doubt something subjective clings to the knowledge which results from a creative act of the mind. But at the same time such knowledge is on a higher plane than the knowledge based only on facts.

The knowledge that results from the recording of single manifestations of Being remains ever incomplete and unsatisfying so far as it is unable to give the final answer to the great question of what we are in the universe, and to what purpose we exist in it. We can find our right place in the Being that envelops us only if we experience in our individual lives the universal life which wills and rules within it. The nature of the living Being without me I can understand only through the living Being which is within me. It is to this reflective knowledge of the universal Being and of the relation to it of the individual human being that the humanities seek to attain. The results they reach contain truth so far as the spirit which is creatively active in this direction possesses a sense of reality, and has passed through the stage of gaining a knowledge of facts about Being to reflection about the nature of Being.

— ALBERT SCHWEITZER, 1875-

God cannot be distilled to a well-defined idea. All concepts fade when applied to His essence. To the pious man knowledge of God is not a thought within his grasp, but a form of thinking in which he tries to comprehend all reality. It is the untold secret of the soil in which all knowledge becomes a seed of sense, a secret by which we live and which we never truly understand; a soil from which the roots of all values derive perpetual vitality. Over and against the split between man and nature, self and thought, time and timelessness, the pious man is able to sense the interweaving of all, the holding together of what is apart, the love that hovers over acts of kindness, mountains, flowers, which shine in their splendor as if looked at by God.

How do we identify the divine?

Divine is a message that discloses unity where we see diversity, that discloses peace when we are involved in discord. God is He who holds our fitful lives together, who reveals to us that what is empirically diverse in color, in interest, in creeds—races, classes, nations—is one in His eyes and one in essence.

God means: No one is ever alone; the essence of the temporal is the eternal; the moment is an image of eternity in an infinite mosaic. God means: *Togetherness of all beings in holy otherness.*

God means: What is behind our soul is beyond our spirit; what is at the source of our selves is at the goal of our ways. He is the heart of all, eager to receive and eager to give.

When God becomes our form of thinking we begin to sense all men in one man, the whole world in a grain of sand, eternity in a moment. To worldly ethics one human being is less than two human beings, to the religious mind if a man has caused a single soul to perish, it is as though he had caused a whole world to perish, and if he has saved a single soul, it is as though he had saved a whole world.

If in the afterglow of a religious insight I can see a way to gather up my scattered life, to unite what lies in strife; a way that is good for all men as it is for me—I will know it is His way.

— ABRAHAM JOSHUA HESCHEL, 1907-

"Picture men in an underground cave-dwelling, with a long entrance reaching up towards the light along the whole width of the cave; in this they lie from their childhood, their legs and necks in chains, so that they stay where they are and look only in front of them, as the chain prevents them turning their heads round. Some way off, and higher up, a fire is burning behind them, and between the fire and the prisoners is a road on higher ground. Imagine a wall built along this road, like the screens which showmen have in front of the audience, over which they show the puppets. . . . Then picture also men carrying along this wall all kinds of articles which overtop it, statues of men and other creatures in stone and wood and other materials; naturally some of the carriers are speaking, others are silent."

"A strange image and strange prisoners," he said.

"They are like ourselves," I answered. "For in the first place, do you think that such men would have seen anything of themselves or of each other except the shadows thrown by the fire on the wall of the cave opposite to them?"

"How could they," he said, "if all their life they had been forced to keep their heads motionless?"

"What would they have seen of the things carried along the wall? Would it not be the same?"

"Surely."

"Then if they were able to talk with one another, do you not think that they would suppose what they saw to be the real things?"

"Necessarily."

"Let us suppose one of them was released, and forced suddenly to stand up and turn his head, and walk and look towards the light. What do you think he would say if he were told by some one that before he had been seeing mere foolish phantoms. And, further, if each of the several figures passing by were pointed out to him, and he were asked to say what each was, do you not think that he would be perplexed, and would imagine that the things he had seen before were truer than those now pointed out to him?"

"Yes, much truer," he said.

"Then if he were forced to look at the light itself, would not his eyes ache, and would he not try to escape and turn back to things which he could look at, and think that they were really more distinct than the things shown him?"

"Yes," he said.

"But," I said, "if some one were to drag him out up the steep and rugged ascent, and did not let go till he had been dragged up to the light of the sun, would not his forced journey be one of pain and annoyance; and when he came to the light would not his eyes be so full of the glare that he would not be able to see a single one of the objects we now call true?"

"Certainly, not all at once," he said.

"Yes, I fancy that he would need time before he could see things in the world above. At first he would most easily see shadows, then the reflections in water of men and everything else, and, finally, the things themselves. Last of all, I fancy he would be able to look at the sun and observe its nature, not its appearance in water or on alien material, but the very sun itself in its own place?"

"Inevitably," he said.

"And that done, he would then come to infer concerning it that it is the sun which produces the seasons and years, and controls everything in the sphere of the visible, and is in a manner the author of all those things which he and his fellow-prisoners used to see?"

"It is clear that this will be his next conclusion," he said.

"Well, then, if he is reminded of his original abode and its wisdom, and those who were then his fellow-prisoners, do you not think that he will pity them and count himself happy in the change?"

"Certainly."

"Would he not rather suffer anything rather than be so the victim of seeming and live in their way?"

"Yes," he said, "I certainly think that he would endure anything rather than that."

"Then consider this point," I said. "If this man were to descend again and take his seat in his old place, would not his eyes be full of darkness because he had just come out of the sunlight?"

"Most certainly," he said.

"And suppose that he had again to take part with the prisoners there in the old contest of distinguishing between the shadows, while his sight was confused and before his eyes had got steady (and it might take them quite a considerable time to get used to the darkness), would not men laugh at him, and say that having gone up above he had come back with his sight ruined, so that it was not worth while even to try to go up? And do you not think that they would kill him who tried to release them and bear them up, if they could lay hands on him, and slay him?"

"Certainly," he said.

"Now this simile, my dear Gloucon, must be applied in all its parts to what we said before. In the world of knowledge the Form of the good is perceived last and with difficulty, but when it is seen it must be inferred that it is the cause of all that is right and beautiful in all things, producing in the visible world light and the lord of light, and being itself lord in the intelligible world and the giver of trust and reason and this Form of the good must be seen by whosoever would act wisely in public or in private."

— PLATO, 427?-347 B.C.

Where power and mercy are combined, there is God manifest; where we see righteousness or love, we see the character of God; where we see these triumphing we see God in action; where we see them achieve their purpose despite all calculable probabilities, there we acknowledge God signally self-revealed. We do not know that it costs Him more (to speak humanly), to work the most startling so-called miracle, than to maintain the habitual motion of the planets; but where that happens which former experience leads us to expect, we are less impelled to ponder on the divine nature as therein disclosed, than when our expectation is negatived by an exhibition of that character in ways unpredictable by us. All is of God, but not all things equally display His character, and not all things equally call our attention to His character as displayed.

— WILLIAM TEMPLE, 1881-1944

· III ·

The purposiveness of the world, of life, of historical happenings, of our knowledge, and of moral endeavor lead me to acknowledge a creator, and director of all, a personal being, spiritual, and infinitely perfect. God himself is reason, is νοῦς λόγος. The Greeks understood this when they freed themselves from mythological polytheism and fetishism. "Reason," said Anaxagoras, "is an organizer of the cosmos," and Aristotle praised him for that because "he came like one sober among the drunk." . . .

A man who would completely deny the order in the world, with its consequences, and the purpose of everything, even of his own life—I ask you, how could he exist with such an idea? Reason, after all, itself ascertains, and to a certain extent it also constructs, an intelligent order in everything it conceives. Reason from its nature seeks for order and purpose; it itself formulates aims. To speak of chance, and aimlessness in the world is contrary to reason; reason itself is the agent of order and of teleology. A purposeful order in the world is provided by reason; our knowledge itself is teleological. . . .

I think that philosophy need not refute pessimism and justify God. God has no need of an advocate. And to refute pessimism? Illness, misery, crime, and so on cannot be refuted with words. Don't think that I should close my eyes to physical and spiritual incongruities and misery. When recently I visited Zidichovice in Moravia I heard the nightingales singing there, well, beautifully! They told me that this year the nightingales were singing because they had plenty of mosquitoes. And a thought passed through my mind: do those nightingales sing their praises to the Good Lord for those mosquitoes? And those mosquitoes—that buzzing of theirs, is that also a song of praise because the nightingales are swallowing them as they fly? Teleology—a hard nut, but even if you can't crack it, it is more likely to get into the palm of your hand than a theory of aimlessness, chance, and chaos.

Perhaps after death we shall be given fuller and more complete knowledge, also knowledge of God; it may be that life after death is an asymptote approaching to God: always and always nearer, eternally nearer—well yes, this also is a continuation of life upon earth, because God is the chief and foremost object of our thinking, knowing, and striving. God and the soul. One is connected with the other. The soul and God, that is the dual problem of our thinking and striving—I should say, the true task of life.

I do believe, I must believe in Providence which governs the development of the world, and of humanity, and of any one of us. Once I acknowledge God the creator, and director, I must see in everything some order, plan, and reasonable aim.

— TOMAS MASARYK, 1850-1937

The heavens declare the glory of God; and the firmament sheweth his handywork.

Day unto day uttereth speech, and night unto night sheweth knowledge.

There is no speech nor language, where their voice is not heard.

Their line is gone out through all the earth, and their words to the end of the world. In them hath He set a tabernacle for the sun,

Which is as a bridegroom coming out of his chamber, and rejoiceth as a strong man to run a race.

His going forth is from the end of the heaven, and his circuit unto the ends of it: and there is nothing hid from the heat thereof.

The law of the LORD is perfect, converting the soul: the testimony of the LORD is sure, making wise the simple.

The statutes of the LORD are right, rejoicing the heart: the commandment of the LORD is pure, enlightening the eyes.

The fear of the LORD is clean, enduring for ever: the judgments of the LORD are true and righteous altogether.

More to be desired are they than gold, yea, than much fine gold: sweeter also than honey and the honeycomb.

Moreover by them is Thy servant warned: and in keeping of them there is great reward.

Who can understand His errors? cleanse thou me from secret faults.

Keep back Thy servant also from presumptuous sins; let them not have dominion over me: then shall I be upright, and I shall be innocent from the great transgression.

Let the words of my mouth, and the meditation of my heart, be acceptable in Thy sight, O LORD, my strength, and my redeemer.

— THE BIBLE, Psalm 19

God is known as that of which I am primarily certain; and being certain, am certain of self and of my world of men and men's objects.

I shall always be more certain *that* God is, than *what* He is: it is the age-long problem of religion to bring to light the deeper characteristics of this fundamental experience. But the starting point of this development ... is no mere That Which, without predicates. Substance is known as Subject: reality from the beginning is known as God. The idea of God is not an attribute which in the course of experience I come to attach to my original whole-idea: the unity of my world which makes it from the beginning a whole, knowable in simplicity, is the unity of other Selfhood.

God then is immediately known, and permanently known, as the Other Mind which in creating Nature is also creating me. Of this knowledge nothing can despoil us; this knowledge has never been wanting to the self-knowing mind of man.

— WILLIAM ERNEST HOCKING, 1873-

As to the Personal God, it has now become a prevalent fashion angrily to proclaim, or complacently to assume, the utter absurdity of anything Personal about the Infinite; since Personality, of every degree and kind, essentially implies, indeed largely consists of, limitations of various kinds, and is a gross anthropomorphism the moment we apply it to anything but man himself. Yet it is interesting to note the readiness with which these same thinkers will hypostatise parts, or special functions, of our human personality, and will indeed do so largely with concepts which we know to be specially characteristic of spatially extended bodies. Thus Thought or Love or Law, or even Substance, nothing of all this is, for such thinkers, anthropomorphic or sub-human; but anything personal is rank anthropomorphism. Yet it is only self-conscious spirit that we know well, since it alone do we know from within. Self-conscious spirit is immensely rich in content; and self-conscious spirit is by far the widest and yet deepest reality known to us at all. True, Natural Science and even Philosophy do not, of themselves, fully find the Personal God, since Natural Science is not, as such, busy with the like ultimate questions, and since Philosophy . . . appears, of itself, to bring us indeed to certain more than human orders or laws, but hardly fully to the Orderer. But there is nothing intrinsically unreasonable in thinking of the ultimate Cause, Ground and End of the world as certainly not less than, as somehow not all unlike, what we know our own self-conscious mind, feeling and will to be, provided we keep the sense that God is certainly not just one Object amongst other objects, or even simply one Subject amongst other subjects; and that, though variously present and operative in all subjects and objects, He is not only more perfect than, but distinct and different from, them all. In so thinking we find in, or we attribute to, the supreme Reality what we ourselves possess that is richest in content, that is best known to us, and that is most perfect within our own little yet real experience —we have done what we could; and life and history abound with warnings how easy it is here to go apparently further and to fare in fact very much worse.

— Baron Friedrich von Hügel, 1852-1925

The old Eleatic argument carried out consistently is, that if there is but one Infinite or one God, the soul also can in its true essence be nothing but God. Religions which are founded on a belief in a transcendent yet personal God, naturally shrink from this conclusion as irreverent and as almost impious. Yet this is their own fault. They have first created an unapproachable Deity, and they are afterwards afraid to approach it; they have made an abyss between the human and the divine, and they dare not cross it. . . .

When the original oneness of earth and heaven, of the human and the divine natures has once been discovered, the question of the return of the soul to God assumes a new character. It is no longer a question of an ascension to heaven; an approach to the throne of God, an ecstatic vision of God and a life in a heavenly Paradise. The vision of God is rather the knowledge of the divine element in the soul, and of the consubstantiality of the divine and human natures.

— FRIEDRICH MAX MÜLLER, 1823-1900

Our universe . . . is a creative process, and the Power behind it is best thought of as Creator. But—it is a creative process in which the task of creation is increasingly shared by the Creator with the creatures created. All the highest values within our experience—art, poetry, invention, philosophy, homes, character, love, sacrifice, noble devotion —cannot be brought into being by God alone; they are possible only as men will to become fellow-creators. Further, the relative importance of God's part and man's part in the task of creation is not to be thought of as fixed. It alters as the process advances—alters by the diminishing influence of the divine control, the progressive increase of human freedom and responsibility. In the creation of the highest values, man's contribution is more central, indispensable. The process is marked then, by an increasing voluntary self-limitation of the Creator. Therefore I think we are not mistaken in the statement that God has willed to create an age-long evolutionary process the final culmination of which shall be dependent upon the wisdom, the courage, the devotion of mortal men. That part of the cosmic purpose which is to be discovered on this planet waits for its further advance upon the voluntary co-operation of mankind. Does this not suggest the figure of a father, begetting and rearing children, initiating great enterprises and high purposes, and then entrusting the fate of his concerns to their care? Could there be a more impressive indication of the significance of human freedom? Or a more lofty and compelling interpretation of human destiny?

— HENRY P. VAN DUSEN, 1897-

I have shown that He necessarily exists; that He is one God; that from the necessity alone of His own nature He is and acts; that He

is, and in what way He is, the free cause of all things; that all things
are in Him and so depend upon Him that without Him they can
neither be nor be conceived; and finally, that all things have been
pre-determined by Him, not indeed from freedom of the will, or
from absolute good pleasure, but from His absolute nature or infinite
power.

— BARUCH SPINOZA, 1632 - 1677

My God, I heard this day
That none doth build a stately habitation
    But he that means to dwell therein.
    What house more stately hath there been,
Or can be, than is Man? to whose creation
    All things are in decay.

    For Man is ev'ry thing,
And more: he is a tree, yet bears no fruit;
    A beast, yet is, or should be, more:
    Reason and speech we only bring;
Parrats may thank us, if they are not mute,
    They go upon the score.

    Man is all symmetrie,
Full of proportions, one limbe to another,
    And all to all the world besides;
    Each part may call the farthest brother,
For head with foot hath private amitie,
    And both with moons and tides.

    Nothing hath got so farre
But Man hath caught and kept it as his prey;
    His eyes dismount the highest starre;
    He is in little all the sphere;
Herbs gladly cure our flesh, because that they
    Find their acquaintance there.

    For us the windes do blow,
The earth doth rest, heav'n move, and fountains flow;
    Nothing we see but means our good,
    As our delight or as our treasure;
The whole is either our cupboard of food
    Or cabinet of pleasure.

The starres have us to bed,
Night draws the curtain, which the sunne withdraws;
  Musick and light attend our head,
  All things unto our flesh are kinde
In their descent and being; to our minde
    In their ascent and cause.

  Each thing is full of dutie:
Waters united are our navigation;
  Distinguished, our habitation;
  Below, our drink; above, our meat;
Both are our cleanlinesse. Hath one such beautie?
    Then how are all things neat!

  More servants wait on Man
Than he'l take notice of: in ev'ry path
  He treads down that which doth befriend him
  When sickness makes him pale and wan.
Oh mightie love! Man is one world, and hath
    Another to attend him.

  Since then, my God, Thou hast
So brave a palace built, O dwell in it,
  That it may dwell with Thee at last!
  Till then afford us so much wit,
That, as the world serves us, we may serve Thee,
    And both Thy servants be.

                           — GEORGE HERBERT, 1593-1633

What time this world's great Workmaster did cast
To make all things such as we now behold,
It seems that He before His eyes had plac'd
A goodly Pattern, to whose perfect mould
He fashion'd them as comely as He could,
That now so fair and seemly they appear,
As nought may be amended anywhere.

That wondrous Pattern, wheresoe'er it be,
Whether in earth laid up in secret store,
Or else in heaven, that no man may it see
With sinful eyes, for fear it to deflore,

Is perfect Beauty, which all men adore;
Whose face and feature doth so much excel
All mortal sense, that none the same may tell.

Thereof as every earthly thing partakes
Or more or less, by influence divine,
So it more fair accordingly it makes,
And the gross matter of this earthly mine,
Which closeth it thereafter, doth refine,
Doing away the dross which dims the light
Of that fair beam which therein is empight.

But that fair lamp, from whose celestial ray
That light proceeds, which kindleth lover's fire,
Shall never be extinguish'd nor decay;
But when the vital spirits do expire,
Unto her native planet shall retire,
For it is heavenly born and cannot die,
Being a parcel of the purest sky.

So every spirit, as it is most pure,
And hath in it the more of heavenly light,
So it the fairer body doth procure
To habit in, and it more fairly dight
With cheerful grace and amiable sight:
For of the soul the body form doth take;
And soul is form, and doth the body make.

— EDMUND SPENSER, 1552?-1599

The supreme power, wisdom, and benevolence of the Creator is reflected in all created things, as is reported in threefold fashion by the sense of the flesh to the interior sense. For the sense of the flesh lends itself to the intellect when it investigates with reason, believes with faith, or contemplates with intellect. In contemplating, it considers the actual existence of things; in believing, their habitual course; in reasoning, their potential pre-excellence.

The first point of view, which is that of contemplation, considering things in themselves, sees in them weight, number, and measure; weight, which marks the point to which they tend; number, whereby they are distinguished; measure, whereby they are limited;

and whereby it sees in them mode, species, order, as well as substance, virtue, and action, from which it may rise, as from footsteps, to understand the power, wisdom, and boundless goodness of the Creator.

The second point of view, which is that of faith, considering this world, attends to its origin, course, and termination. For by faith we believe that the ages were arranged by the word of life; by faith we believe that the epochs of the three laws—the law of nature, the law of Scripture, and the law of grace—succeed each other and have elapsed in the most perfect order; by faith we believe that the world will be terminated by a final judgment. In the first we observe the power; in the second, the providence; in the third, the justice of the supreme principle.

The third point of view—that of reason—investigating, sees that some things are only, and some are and live only, whereas some are, live, and discern; and that the first are inferior; the second, middle; the third, superior. It sees, likewise, that some are only corporeal, and some partly corporeal, partly spiritual; whence it concludes that there are some purely spiritual, as better and worthier than either. It sees, moreover, that some are mutable and corruptible, as terrestrial things; others mutable and incorruptible, as supercelestial things. From these visible things therefore it rises to consider God's power, wisdom and goodness, as being, living, and intelligent, as purely spiritual, incorruptible, and intransmutable. This consideration, again, is extended according to the sevenfold condition of created things, which is the sevenfold witness of the divine power, wisdom, and goodness, if we consider the origin, magnitude, multitude, beauty, plenitude, action and order of all things. For the origin of things, in respect to creation, distinction, and adornment, as far as the works of the six days are concerned, proclaims the divine power, producing all things from nothing; the divine wisdom, as clearly distinguishing all things; the divine goodness, as generously adorning all things.

The magnitude of things—in respect to the bulk of length, breadth, and depth; in respect to the excellence of the power extending itself in length, breadth, and depth, as is manifest in the diffusion of light; in respect to the efficacy of action, intimate, continuous, and diffused as is manifested in the action of fire—clearly indicates the immensity of the power, wisdom, and goodness of the threefold God, who exists uncircumscribed in all created things, through power, presence, and essence.

The multitude of things—in respect to their diversity, general,

special, and individual, in substance, in form of figure, and in efficacy, beyond all human estimation—manifestly involves and displays
the immensity of the three above-named conditions in God.

The beauty of things—in respect to the variety of lights, figures,
and colors, in bodies simple, mixed, and organized, as in the heavenly
bodies and minerals, as in stones and metals, plants and animals—
plainly proclaims the above three things.

The plenitude of things—in that matter is full of forms, in respect
to seminal reasons, form is full of virtue as to active power, and
virtue is full of effects as to efficiency—manifestly declares this same
thing. . . .

He, therefore, who is not enlightened by all these splendors of
created things is blind; he who is not waked by such callings is deaf;
he who from all these effects does not praise God is dumb; he who
after such intimation does not observe the first principle is foolish.

— St. Bonaventure, 1221-1274

The creation of wholes, and ever more highly organized wholes, and
of wholeness generally as a characteristic of existence, is an inherent
characteristic of the universe. There is not a vague indefinite creative
energy or tendency at work in the world. This energy has specific
characters, the most fundamental of which is whole-making. . . .

We thus arrive at the conception of a universe which is not a col-
lection of accidents externally put together like an artificial patch-
work, but which is synthetic, structural, active, vital, and creative
in increasing measure all through, the progressive development of
which is shaped by one unique holistic activity operative from the
humblest inorganic beginnings to the most exalted creations of the
human and of the universal Spirit.

— Jan Christiaan Smuts, 1870-1950

· IV ·

Whoever wants to know the deepest that is in man, the hidden forces
that drive him onward, should become a student of mysticism. And
if knowing man is not knowing God, it is nevertheless only when in
possession of an adequate knowledge of man that metaphysics may
expect to fashion an acceptable conception of the Ultimate.

— James Henry Leuba, 1868-1948

It is in *man* that God reveals Himself most fully and that the most veridical clue to His mind and will are to be found; in man, moreover, when he is at his manliest and best. "He made man in his own image"—there, if they had only realised it, lay the secret which the diviners and the augurs and the soothsayers made the object of their ancient quest.

Yet we must try to give our meaning something of a sharper definition than this. For it might well be asked: "Is not this the maddest and most groundless of all megalomanias, that a particular animal species inhabiting a comparatively insignificant planet should find in its own specific nature the key to the nature of the Eternal Being?" And our answer to that question can only be that it is not in our own specific animal nature (not in our nature as vertebrates or as mammals or as bipeds, nor yet in the particular bundle of instincts which mark us from our nearest brutish relatives, nor in what the old moralists called "the particular constitution of human nature") that we find the footprints of Divinity, but only in our nature as moral personalities. So once again we find ourselves led to our old conclusion, that it is in our human values that we find God revealed. Not in the procession of the stars, not in the flight of birds, not in the guttural frenzy of the Delphic maid, but in "the milk of human kindness" is the character of God made plain and His will made known. Not in the sound of thunder but in the voice of conscience do we hear Him speak most plainly. Not in hepatoscopic markings, nor yet on tables of stone, but on the tables of the human heart, are His words most plainly to be deciphered.

— JOHN BAILLIE, 1886-

The monumental evidence of God is, I believe, the fact of spiritual personality through which divine traits of character are revealed. Stars and mountains and ordered processes of nature reveal law and mathematics and beauty, but they reveal and can reveal no traits of character, no qualities of personality, no warmth and intimacy of heart and mind. If we are ever to be convinced that self-giving love is a reality of God's nature, we shall be convinced by seeing this love break through some human organ of His Spirit. . . . As the sap flows through the branches of the vine and vitalizes the whole organism so that it bursts into the beauty and glory of foliage and blossom and finally into fruit, so through the lives of men and women, inwardly responsive and joyously receptive, the life of God as Spirit flows, carrying vitality, awakening love, creating passion for goodness, kindling the fervor of consecration and producing that living body, that organism of the Spirit, that "blessed community," which continues through the centuries the revelation of God as love and tenderness and eternal goodness.

— RUFUS M. JONES, 1863-1948

The seed of God is in us. Given an intelligent and hard-working farmer, it will thrive and grow up to God, whose seed it is; and accordingly its fruits will be God-nature. Pear seeds grow into pear trees, nut seeds into nut trees, and God seed into God.

— MEISTER ECKHART, 1260? -? 1327

There is no conflict between God and man, no hostility between spirit and body, no wedge between the holy and the secular. Man does not exist apart from God. The human is the borderline of the divine.

— ABRAHAM JOSHUA HESCHEL, 1907-

In the most noble part of the soul, the domain of our spiritual powers, we are constituted in the form of a living and eternal mirror of God; we bear in it the imprint of his eternal image and no other image can enter there. This image is found essentially and personally in all men; each man possesses it whole and entire and all men together possess no more of it than does each one. In this way we are all one, united in our eternal image which is the image of God, and the source in us all of our life and our coming into existence. Our created essence and our life are joined to it immediately as to their eternal cause. Yet our created being does not become God any more than the image of God becomes a creature.

— JAN VAN RUYSBROECK, 1293-1381

Those are red-letter days in our lives when we meet people who thrill us like a fine poem, people whose handshake is brimful of unspoken sympathy, and whose sweet, rich natures impart to our eager, impatient spirits a wonderful restfulness which in its essence is divine. The perplexities, irritations, and worries that have absorbed

us pass like unpleasant dreams, and we wake to see with new eyes
and hear with new ears the beauty and harmony of God's real world.
The solemn nothings that fill our everyday life blossom suddenly
into bright possibilities. In a word, while such friends are near us we
feel that all is well. Perhaps we never saw them before, and they may
never cross our life's path again; but the influence of their calm,
mellow natures is a libation poured upon our discontent, and we feel
its healing touch.

The hands of those I meet are dumbly eloquent to me. There are
those whose hands have sunbeams in them, so that their grasp warms
my heart.

I count it one of the sweetest privileges of my life to have known
and conversed with many men of genius. Only those who knew
Bishop Brooks can appreciate the joy his friendship was to those
who possessed it. As a child I loved to sit on his knee and clasp his
great hand with one of mine, while Miss Sullivan spelled into the
other his beautiful words about God and the spiritual world. I heard
him with a child's wonder and delight. My spirit could not reach up
to his, but he gave me a real sense of joy in life, and I never left him
without carrying away a fine thought that grew in beauty and depth
of meaning as I grew. Once, when I was puzzled to know why there
were so many religions, he said: "There is one universal religion,
Helen—the religion of love. Love your Heavenly Father with your
whole heart and soul, love every child of God as much as ever you
can, and remember that the possibilities of good are greater than the
possibilities of evil." His life was a happy illustration of this great
truth. In his noble soul love and widest knowledge were blended
with faith that had become insight. He saw

> God in all that liberates and lifts,
> In all that humbles, sweetens, and consoles.

— HELEN KELLER, 1880-

His [Origen's] words were so kind and affectionate that love sprang
up in my soul as if kindled by a spark; love not only for him, but for
all that is good, and for the divine Logos of whom he is the friend
and advocate. He incited us to virtue much more by what he did
than by what he said. The sum of all his teaching and example was
this: Be pure in mind, and so become like God that you may draw
near Him and abide in Him.

— GREGORY THAUMATURGUS, 213?-?270

It is said that mercy is the attribute that God shows forth in all His works; therefore a merciful person is a truly God-like man. For mercy is brought forth by love and kindness. Therefore the true friends of God are much more merciful and more ready to believe in the sinful and suffering than those who are not loving. Mercy is born of that love which we ought to exercise towards each other. . . . St. Dominic asked one of his companions who was weeping bitterly why he wept. When he replied, "Dear father, because of my sins," the Saint said: "No, dear son, they have been sufficiently mourned for; but I beseech thee, dear son, to weep for those who will not weep for themselves."

— Johannes Tauler, 1300?-1361

There are two kinds of love: one man loves whatever his clever son does and says, and boasts about his doing clever things and speaking clever words; the other loves his son for himself, no matter what he may say or do.

It is the same with the love of God for man. When a tried and proven man keeps the commandments and does good works wisely and well, God loves what he does and is present in all that he does, and thus the outer being of the universe is bound to God. But when the tried and proven man clings to God with his own being, then God loves him even when he does not work wisely and well, but goes his way with a simple mind and clings to God. God loves him just for that reason. And so the inner being of the universe is lifted to God.

— Hasidic Saying

All the length of our conscious life, God for whom we were made, in whom alone we can find what we want and understand what we mean, presents Himself to the apprehension of our soul, tempts our desire, pursues our will. To this pressure we must react, either with it or against it.

— R. H. J. Steuart, 1874-1948

All things whatsoever observe a
mutual order; and this the form that maketh
the universe like unto God.

Herein the exalted creatures trace the impress of
the Eternal Worth, which is the goal whereto
was made the norm now spoken of.

In the order of which I speak all things incline,
by diverse lots, more near and less unto their
principle.

— DANTE ALIGHIERI, 1265-1321

See how beautiful it is. All the beauty of the world proclaims the
majesty of God. Look at the animals. They, too, are beautiful. The
beauty of these forms proclaims the art of God, and we ourselves,
our faces and our eyes so appropriately placed and all the other
senses—surely they speak of divinity! Is not the world a house where
everything is kept in the utmost neatness and order, and surely this
house has a master, and the master himself is more beautiful than the
stars or any part of the known world.

— MARCUS MINUCIUS FELIX, third century

Man sleeps, but the forces of nature rest not either night or day: no
one considers how they go on—while all take delight in the beauty
of the fields and the fruit of the pastures. So is love manifest in the
same way; it presupposes that love is present like the germ in the
corn, and if it succeeds in bringing that to growth, then has the love
concealed itself, as if it were hidden, whereas it was working early
and late. Nevertheless, this is the edifying wonder in nature: you see
all this glory and then it impresses you edifyingly if you happen to
consider how strange it was that you did not see at all the one who
produced it.

— SÖREN KIERKEGAARD, 1813-1855

· v ·

Sooner or later philosophy must return to its Father's house, which is
Wisdom and Truth, and realize that as all fires mount to the sun, and
all waters flow into the sea, so too all men must return to God, for
whom they were made and in whom they find their rest, their peace,
their perfection: their *rest*, for "Our hearts are disquieted until they

rest in Thee, O Lord"; their *peace*, for peace is the tranquillity of order, and order is never tranquil unless man loves God; their *perfection:* for in Him is found the plenitude of the human heart's quest for Being, Truth and Love. A godless universe cannot exist for it cannot bear the sorrow of not knowing its Cause and its Author; nor can a Godless humanity exist for it cannot bear the burden of its own heart.

—FULTON J. SHEEN, 1895-

When therefore among the creatures the man cleaveth to that which is the best that he can perceive, and keepeth steadfastly to that, in singleness of heart, he cometh afterward to what is better and better, until, at last, he findeth and tasteth that the Eternal Good is a Perfect Good, without measure and number above all created good. Now if what is best is to be dearest to us, and we are to follow after it, the One Eternal Good must be loved above all and alone, and we must cleave to Him alone, and unite ourselves with Him as closely as we may. And now if we are to ascribe all goodness to the One Eternal Good, as of right and truth we ought, so must we also of right and truth ascribe unto Him the beginning, middle, and end of our course, so that nothing remain to man or the creature. So it should be of a truth, let men say what they will.

— THEOLOGIA GERMANICA

He manifests all things, but is not manifested; He is not Himself brought into being in images presented through the senses, but He presents all things to us in such images. It is only things which are brought into being that are presented through sense; coming into being is nothing else than presentation through sense. It is evident then that He who alone has not come into being cannot be presented through sense; and that being so, He is hidden from our sight.

But He presents all things to us through our senses, and thereby manifests Himself through all things, and in all things. . . . For thought alone can see that which is hidden, inasmuch as thought itself is hidden from sight; and if even the thought which is within you is hidden from your sight, how can He, being in Himself, be manifested to you through your bodily eyes? But if you have power to see with the eyes of the mind, then, my son, He will manifest

Himself to you. For the Lord manifests Himself ungrudgingly through all the universe; and you can behold God's image with your eyes, and lay hold on it with your hands.

— CORPUS HERMETICUM

Never did eye see the Sun unless first it had become Sun-like. Never can the soul see Primal Beauty unless itself be beautiful. Therefore let each man become Godlike and beautiful who aspires to see Beauty and God.

— PLOTINUS, 205?-270

Oh! Supreme and Eternal Good, who has moved Thee, Infinite God, to illuminate me, Thy finite creature with the light of Thy Truth? Thou, the same Fire of Love art the cause, because it is always love which constrained and constrains Thee to create us in Thine image and similitude, and to do us mercy, giving immeasurable and infinite graces to Thy rational creatures.

— ST. CATHERINE OF SIENA, 1347-1380

CHAPTER TWELVE

The Kingdom of God

Is Within You

To get at the core of God at his greatest, one must first get into the core of himself at his least, for no one can know God who has not first known himself. Go to the depths of the soul, the secret place of the Most High, to the roots, to the heights; for all that God can do is focused there.

— MEISTER ECKHART, 1260? -? 1327

·I·

SEARCH yourself and you will find God.

— KURDISH PROVERB

I wonder at those who seek the House of God in this world; why do they not seek to contemplate Him in their hearts? For sometimes they find the House, and sometimes they fail to find it, and contemplation they might always find. If it is incumbent on them to visit a stone, where they may behold Him, once a year, surely there is a greater obligation to visit the heart, where He may be contemplated hundreds of times each day. For the true sanctuary is the place where contemplation is; and only that one to whom the whole world is the trysting-place where he draws near to God and a place of retreat where he finds fellowship with Him, knows what it is to be the friend of God. When the veil has been removed, the whole world is his sanctuary, but while he is still veiled, the world will remain dark to him, for the darkest of things is the dwelling-place of the Beloved, without the Beloved.

— MUHAMMAD B. AL-FADL, 1339-1401

Know ye not that ye are the temple of God, and that the Spirit of God dwelleth in you?

If any man defile the temple of God, him shall God destroy; for the temple of God is holy, which temple ye are.

Let no man deceive himself. If any man among you seemeth to be wise in this world, let him become a fool, that he may be wise.

For the wisdom of this world is foolishness with God. For it is written, He taketh the wise in their own craftiness.

And again, The Lord knoweth the thoughts of the wise, that they are vain.

— THE BIBLE, I Corinthians 3:16-20

In thee
In me
In all men
There dwelleth the One God

In all
He suffers
And he suffers
For all;

In all everywhere,
See thyself.
Abandon this thy ignorant conceit,
Which holds that thou art separate from other men.

— ANONYMOUS

Every one hath the key to God in himself, let him but seek it in the right place.

— JAKOB BÖHME, 1575-1624

We do not need to uplift our hands towards heaven, or to beg the keeper of the temple to admit us to his idol's ear. God is near you, He is with you, He is within you. A holy spirit dwells within us who marks our good and evil deeds and is our guardian.

If ever you have come upon a grove that is full of ancient trees grown to an unusual height, shutting out a view of the sky by a veil of pleached and intertwining branches, then the loftiness of the forest, the seclusion of the spot will prove to you the presence of the Deity.

Or if a cave holds up a mountain on its arch, a place not built with hands, but hollowed out into such spaciousness by natural causes, your soul will be deeply moved by a certain intimation of the existence of God.

If you see a man unterrified in the midst of dangers, untouched by desires, happy in adversity, peaceful amid the storm, will you not say: A divine power has descended upon that man?

Just as the rays of the sun do indeed touch the earth, but still abide at the source from which they are sent; even so the great and hallowed soul does indeed associate with us, but still cleaves to its origin; on that source it depends, thither it turns its gaze and strives to go.

— LUCIUS ANNAEUS SENECA, 4 B.C.-65 A.D.

> The buried statue through the marble gleams,
> Praying for freedom, an unwilling guest,
> Yet flooding with the light of her strange dreams
> The hard stone folded round her uncarved breast.
>
> Founded in granite, wrapped in serpentine,
> Light of all life and heart of every storm,
> Doth the uncarven image, the Divine,
> Deep in the heart of each man, wait for form.

— EVA GORE-BOOTH, 1870-1926

Great is the blindness and exceeding the folly of many souls that are
ever seeking God, continuously sighing after God, and frequently
desiring God: whilst, all the time, they are themselves the tabernacles
of the living God . . . since their soul is the seat of God, in which He
continuously reposes. Now who but a fool deliberately seeks a tool
which he possesses under lock and key? or who can use and profit by
an instrument which he is seeking? or who can draw comfort from
food for which he hungers, but which he does not relish at leisure?
Like unto all this is the life of many a just soul, which ever seeks God
and never tarries to enjoy Him; and all the works of such an one are,
on this account, less perfect.

— St. Thomas Aquinas, 1225? - 1274

I laugh when I hear that the fish in the water is thirsty:
You do not see that the Real is in your own home,
And you wander from forest to forest listlessly!
Here is the truth! Go where you will, to Benaras or to Mathura;
If you do not find God in your own soul, the world is meaningless
    to you.

— Kabir, 1450? - 1518

You are a distinct portion of the essence of God, and contain a certain part of Him in yourself. Why then are you so ignorant of your
noble birth? Why do you not consider whence you came? Why do
you not remember when you are eating, who you are who eat and
whom you feed? When you are conversing, when you are exercis-
ing, when you are disputing, do you not know that it is God you
feed, God you exercise? You carry God about with you, wretch,
and know nothing of it.

Do you suppose I mean some god without you, of gold or silver?
It is within yourself you carry Him and profane Him without being
sensible of it, by impure thought and unclean actions.

If even the image of God were present, you would not dare to act
as you do; and when God is within you, and hears and sees all, are
you not ashamed to think and act thus, insensible of your own nature
and hateful to God? Have you not God? Do you seek any other
while you have Him?

If you were a statue of Phidias, either Zeus or Athena, you would remember both yourself and the artist, and if you had any sense, you would endeavor to do nothing unworthy of Him who formed you, or of yourself, nor to appear in an unbecoming manner to spectators.

And are you now careless how you appear, because you are the workmanship of Zeus? And yet, what comparison is there, either between the artists or the things they have formed? What work of any artist contains in itself those faculties which are shown in forming it? Is it anything but marble, or brass, or gold or ivory?

The Athena of Phidias, when its hand is once extended and a Victory placed in it, remains in that attitude forever. But the works of God are endued with motion, breath, and the use of appearances, judgment.

Being, then, the work of such an artist, will you dishonour Him, especially when He has not only formed you, but has entrusted you and given the guardianship of you to yourself? Will you not only be forgetful of this, but also dishonour the trust?

If God had committed some orphan to your charge, would you have been thus careless of him? He has delivered you to your own care, and says: I had no one fitter to be trusted than you. Keep this person for me just what he is by nature, modest, faithful, noble, unterrified, dispassionate, tranquil.

And will you not keep him such?

— EPICTETUS, first century

Thy God was making hast into thy roofe,
    Thy humble faith, and feare, keepes him aloofe:
Hee'l be thy guest, because he may not be,
    Hee'l come—into thy house? no, into thee.

— RICHARD CRASHAW, 1613?-1649

His kingdom dwelleth in thee; lo! the riches of heaven are within thy soul, if thou be willing! Enter in, leaving the wandering of pleasures and the corruption of lusts, the errors of the love of money, and

the business that harmeth thee. Enter thou in and dwell in thine
own self in the cleared ground of thine own mind and seek there
the Kingdom. Enter thou in and dwell within thine own heart, for
lo! there is God; for it is not He that goeth forth from thee, but
thou that goest forth from Him.

— EPHRAEM SYRUS, 306?-373

My dear, dear God! I do not know
What lodg'd Thee then, nor where, nor how;
But I am sure Thou dost now come
Oft to a narrow, homely room,
Where Thou too hast but the least part;
My God, I mean my sinful heart.

— HENRY VAUGHAN, 1622-1695

God in me, God without! Beyond compare!
A Being wholly here and wholly there!

— ANGELUS SILESIUS, 1624-1677

· II ·

I missed Him when the sun began to bend;
I found Him not when I had lost his rim;
With many tears I went in search of Him,
Climbing high mountains which did still ascend,
And gave me echoes when I called my friend;
Through cities vast and charnel-houses grim,
And high cathedrals where the light was dim,
Through books and arts and works without an end,
But found Him not—the friend whom I had lost.
And yet I found Him—as I found the lark,
A sound in fields I heard but could not mark;
I found Him nearest when I missed Him most;
I found Him in my heart, a life in frost,
A light I knew not till my soul was dark.

— GEORGE MACDONALD, 1824-1905

The breeze of Divine grace is blowing upon us all. But one needs to set the sail to feel this breeze of grace.

— RAMAKRISHNA, 1834-1886

Though God is everywhere present, yet He is only present to thee in the deepest and most central part of thy soul. The natural senses cannot possess God or unite thee to him; nay, thy inward faculties of understanding, will and memory can only reach after God, but cannot be the place of his habitation in thee. But there is a root or depth of thee from whence all these faculties come forth, as lines from a centre, or as branches from the body of the tree. This depth is called the centre, the fund or bottom of the soul. This depth is the unity, the eternity—I had almost said the infinity—of thy soul; for it is so infinite that nothing can satisfy it or give it rest but the infinity of God.

— WILLIAM LAW, 1686-1761

He who proclaims the existence of the Infinite—and none can avoid it—accumulates in that affirmation more of the supernatural than is to be found in all the miracles of all the religions; for the notion of the Infinite presents that double character, that it forces itself upon us and yet is incomprehensible. When this notion seizes upon our understanding we can but kneel . . . I see everywhere the inevitable expression of the Infinite in the world; through it the supernatural is at the bottom of every heart. The idea of God is a form of the idea of the Infinite. As long as the mystery of the Infinite weighs on human thought, temples will be erected for the worship of the Infinite . . . Men will be seen kneeling, prostrated in the thought of the Infinite . . . Blessed is he who carries within himself God, an ideal, and who obeys it: ideal of art, ideal of science, ideal of the gospel virtues, therein lie the springs of great thoughts and great actions; they all reflect light from the Infinite.

— LOUIS PASTEUR, 1822-1895

Happy is the man who by continually effacing all images and who by introversion and the lifting up of his mind to God, at last forgets and leaves behind all images. By this means he works inwardly with a naked, simple, pure intellect and affection about that most pure and simple object, God. See then that your whole exercise about God within you depend wholly and only on your naked intellect, affection and will. For indeed this exercise cannot be discharged by any corporeal organs or the external senses but by that which constitutes (essentially) a man—understanding and love. . . .

Work to simplify the heart that being immovable and at peace from any invading vain fantasms you may always stand fast in the Lord within, to that degree as if your soul had already entered into that always present Now of eternity, that is, of the Deity. To mount to God is to enter into oneself. For he who so mounting and entering goes above and beyond himself, truly mounts up to God. The mind must then raise itself above itself and say, He whom above all I need is above all I know. And so, carried into the darkness of the mind, gathering itself into that all sufficient good the mind learns to stay so at home and with whole affection cleave and become habitually fixed in the supreme good within. So do until you become immutable and arrive at that true life which is God himself: perpetually, without any vicissitude of space or time reposing in that inward quiet and secret mansion of the Deity.

—St. Albertus Magnus, 1193?-1280

The Lord is my shepherd; I shall not want.

He maketh me to lie down in green pastures: He leadeth me beside the still waters.

He restoreth my soul: He leadeth me in the paths of righteousness for His name's sake.

Yea, though I walk through the valley of the shadow of death, I will fear no evil: for Thou art with me; Thy rod and Thy staff they comfort me.

Thou preparest a table before me in the presence of mine enemies: Thou anointest my head with oil; my cup runneth over.

Surely goodness and mercy shall follow me all the days of my life: and I will dwell in the house of the Lord for ever.

—The Bible, Psalm 23

That measureless Love which is God Himself, dwells in the pure deeps of our spirit, like a burning brazier of coal. And it throws forth brilliant and fiery sparks which stir and enkindle heart and senses, will and desire, and all the powers of the soul, with a fire of love. . . . As air is penetrated by the brightness and heat of the sun, and iron is penetrated by fire; so that it works through fire the works of fire, since it burns and shines like the fire . . . yet each of these keeps its own nature—the fire does not become iron, and the iron does not become fire, for the iron is within the fire and the fire within the iron, so likewise God is in the being of the soul. The creature never becomes God as God never becomes creature. . . . The union takes place in God through grace and our home-turning love. . . . The pure soul feels a constant fire of love, which desires above all things to be one with God, and the more the soul obeys the attraction of God the more it feels it, and the more it feels it the more it desires to be with God. . . . The inward stirring and touching of God makes us hungry and yearning; for the Spirit of God hunts our spirit: and the more it touches it, the greater our hunger and our craving.

—Jan van Ruysbroeck, 1293-1381

Put out my eyes, and I can see you still; slam my ears to, and I can hear you yet; and without any feet can go to you; and tongueless, I can conjure you at will. Break off my arms, I shall take hold of you and grasp you with my heart as with a hand; arrest my heart, my brain will beat as true; and if you set this brain of mine afire, then on my bloodstream I will carry you.

—Rainer Maria Rilke, 1875-1926

· III ·

Religion . . . is the sphere of the sacred: the ultimate wonder and mystery of all existence as mirrored in the living consciousness of man. From this standpoint, a single cycle of life in the tiniest of organisms discloses something about the nature of the entire cosmic process that a whole eon of stellar evolution, without that stir of life, would not reveal; while what is relatively even a moment of significant consciousness in the life of man, transforms him from a mere speck lost in an almost boundless universe, into a progressively boundless mind, capable of devouring that universe. Where sentience, feelings, and thought exist the dumb universe has found a spokesman and its blind forces a commander.

—Lewis Mumford, 1895-

Every one of us may call himself a son of God. Just as our bodies are linked to the material universe, subject while we live to the same forces, resolved when we die into the same elements, so by virtue of reason our souls are linked to and continuous with Him, being in reality parts and offshoots of Him. There is no movement of which He is not conscious, because we and He are part of one birth and growth; to Him "all hearts are open, all desires known"; as we walk or talk or eat, He himself is within us, so that we are His shrines, living temples and incarnations of Him.

— EPICTETUS, first century

So true is it, what I then said, that *the Fraction of Life can be increased in value not so much by increasing your Numerator as by lessening your Denominator*. Nay, unless my Algebra deceive me, *Unity* itself divided by *Zero* will give *Infinity*. Make thy claim of wages a zero, then; thou hast the world under thy feet. Well did the Wisest of our time write: "It is only with Renunciation (*Entsagen*) that Life, properly speaking, can be said to begin."

I asked myself: What is this that, ever since earliest years, thou hast been fretting and fuming, and lamenting and self-tormenting, on account of? Say it in a word: is it not because thou art not HAPPY? Because the THOU (sweet gentleman) is not sufficiently honored, nourished, soft-bedded, and lovingly cared-for? Foolish soul! What Act of Legislature was there that *thou* shouldst be Happy? A little while ago thou hadst no right to *be* at all. What if thou wert born and predestined not to be Happy, but to be Unhappy! Art thou nothing other than a Vulture, then, that fliest through the Universe seeking after somewhat to *eat;* and shrieking dolefully because carrion enough is not given thee? Close thy *Byron;* open thy *Goethe.*

Es leuchtet mir ein, I see a glimpse of it! there is in man a HIGHER than Love of Happiness: he can do without Happiness, and instead thereof find Blessedness! Was it not to preach-forth this same HIGHER that sages and martyrs, the Poet and the Priest, in all times, have spoken and suffered; bearing testimony, through life and through death, of the Godlike that is in Man, and how in the Godlike only has he Strength and Freedom? Which God-inspired Doctrine art thou also honored to be taught; O Heavens! and broken with manifold merciful Afflictions, even till thou become contrite, and learn it! O, thank thy Destiny for these; thankfully bear what yet remain: thou hadst need of them; the Self in thee needed to be annihilated. By benignant fever-paroxysms is Life rooting out the deep-seated chronic Disease, and triumphs over Death. On the roaring billows of Time, thou art not engulfed, but borne aloft into the azure of Eternity. Love not Pleasure; love God. This is the EVERLASTING YEA, wherein all contradiction is solved: wherein whoso walks and works, it is well with him. . . .

Meanwhile what are antiquated Mythuses to me? Or is the God present, felt in my own heart, a thing which Herr von Voltaire will dispute out of me; or dispute into me? To the *Worship of Sorrow* ascribe what origin and genesis thou pleasest, *has* not that Worship originated, and been generated; is it not *here?* Feel it in thy heart, and then say whether it is of God! This is Belief; all else is Opinion, —for which latter whoso will, let him worry and be worried.

— THOMAS CARLYLE, 1795-1881

Oh, who will give me a voice that I may cry aloud to the whole world that God, the all highest, is in the deepest abyss within us and is waiting for us to return to Him. Oh, my God, how does it happen in this poor old world, that Thou art so great and yet nobody finds Thee, that Thou callest so loudly and nobody hears Thee, that Thou art so near and nobody feels Thee, that Thou givest Thyself to everybody and nobody knows Thy name! Men flee from Thee and say they cannot find Thee; they turn their backs and say they cannot see Thee; they stop their ears and say they cannot hear Thee!

— JOHANNES DENK, 1495?-1527

It is written: "The tree of life also in the midst of the garden." Whenever man studies or prays, he should think that he is in the garden of paradise, where there is no envy and no lust and no pride, and he will surely be safe from distraction. But how can he think in this way, since he knows that he is in this world and among people he is acquainted with? This is how: when man studies or prays with reverence and devoutness begotten of love, and fastens and binds his spirit to God and remembers that nothing is void of him and without him, but that everything is filled with life granted by the Creator, then, in all he sees, he sees the living power of the Creator and hears His living voice. That is the meaning of the words: "The tree of life in the midst of the garden." He who clings to the life of God is in the midst of the garden.

— HASIDIC SAYING

What is the nature of God's work? God's work is twofold: that which remains within Him and that which flows out of Him. The work that remains within Him is God's being and nature, that which flows out of Him is His creation. And just as His creatures have flowed from God, in the same way they shall flow back into Him. And that is why God works in the soul, so that He may bring it back to the source from which it first flowed out, for all its own works are not enough to bring the soul back to its source. And, therefore, it is needful that man learns to receive the works of God so that these works may bring him to God again. That is why our Lord said: "But one thing is needful." And without this one thing no one can return to God.

As God comprises all things, so a man who is pure and poor comprises all virtue in a love that is simple and single, and in this love he performs all virtuous acts, and all the virtues are within him and exist side by side with poverty. For only he is poor in the right way to whom virtues have become as his own nature.

— THE BOOK OF THE POOR IN SPIRIT

Meister Eckhart wrote, "As thou art in church or cell, that same frame of mind carry out into the world, into its turmoil and its fitfulness." Deep within us all there is an amazing inner sanctuary of the soul, a holy place, a Divine Center, a speaking Voice, to which we may continuously return. Eternity is at our hearts, pressing upon our time-torn lives, warming us with intimations of an astounding destiny, calling us home unto Itself. Yielding to these persuasions, gladly committing ourselves in body and soul, utterly and completely, to the Light Within, is the beginning of true life. It is a dynamic center, a creative Life that presses to birth within us. It is a Light Within which illumines the face of God and casts new shadows and new glories upon the face of men. It is a seed stirring to life if we do not choke it. It is the Shekinah of the soul, the Presence in the midst. Here is the Slumbering Christ, stirring to be awakened, to become the soul we clothe in earthly form and action. And He is within us all.

— THOMAS R. KELLY, 1893-1941

· IV ·

Foodless am I, and shelterless,
No home have I,
For me no children's prattle riseth at the eventide:

Yet am I rich beyond compute,
All love I have, all joy:

For I have God,
His grace I know, His love:

Come pain,
Come all adversity,
With Thee, my God, enthroned within,
No ill can overtake me:

Let transcience pass,
A dream it came,
A dream it goes again:

For me abideth Permanence,
Immortal Joy,
In inward touch of soul with Thee, my God.

— TUKARAM, 1608-1649

It is foolish to seek for God outside of oneself. This will result either in idolatry or in scepticism. To seek God within oneself is better, but there is danger lest this will result in ego-mania, in becoming an opponent of order or a nihilist.

Therefore, he who truly seeks God should discover the unchangeable laws which operate outside of himself and recognize within himself a profound and mysterious purpose. Through being cognizant of a power which pervades both within and without, cognizant also of a world of growth which is common to both, recognizing, moreover, the immutability of the moral order and recognizing the fact that God as life fills both the inner and the outer, that He is the creator of absolute values, the preserver and unfolder of all things, thus and thus only will one be able to cease going astray.

—Toyohiko Kagawa, 1888-

Let us invoke God Himself, not in mere form of words, but by elevating our souls to Him in prayer. And the only way truly to pray is to approach alone the One who is Alone. To contemplate that One, we must withdraw into the inner soul, as into a temple, and be still.

—Plotinus, 205?-270

Begin to search and dig in thine own field for this pearl of eternity that lies hidden in it; it cannot cost thee too much, nor canst thou buy it too dear, for it is *all;* and when thou hast found it thou wilt know that all which thou hast sold or given away for it is as mere a nothing as a bubble upon the water.

—William Law, 1686-1761

Little one, wait.
Let me assure you this is not the way
To gain the terminal of outer day.

Its single gate
Lies in your soul, and you must rise and go
By inward passage from what earth you know.

The steps lead down
Through valley after valley, far and far
Past the five centuries where the pleasures are,

And past all known
Maps of the mind and every colored chart
And past the final outcry of the heart.

No soul can view
Its own geography; love does not live
In places open and informative,

Yet, being true,
It grants to each its Raphael across
The mist and night through unknown lands of loss.

Walk till you hear
Light told in music that was never heard
And softness that was not a word.

The soul grows clear
When its five senses have been fused in one:
Savor and scent and sound to splendor run.

The smothered roar
Of the eternities, their vast unrest
And infinite peace are deep in your own breast.

That light-swept shore
Will shame the data of grief upon your scroll.
Child, have none told you? *God* is in your soul.

— JESSICA POWERS, contemporary

Betimes awake thee,
And unto sad and serious contemplation,
Dull soul, betake thee;
    Thyself retire,
And after the great God of thy salvation
    With care enquire.
Withdraw thyself within thy heart's close centre,
Whither, save Him alone, let nothing enter.

Then let thine heart
Thus say: My God, let me behold Thy face;
Show in what part,
    Or in what ground
Of the vast world, what corner or what place,
    Thou mayest be found.
How shall I find Thee, if Thou be'st not here?
Or why not present, being everywhere?

— THOMAS HEYWOOD, 1574? - 1641

"Hear, my son, the instruction of thy father, and forsake not the teaching of thy mother." Accustom yourself to speak calmly to all men, at all times, and you will save yourself from anger, which is an ill thing that brings man into sin.

And thus spake our teachers, blessed be their memory: Every kind of damnation has power over him who is angry, as it is written: "Remove vexation from thy heart, and put away evil from thy flesh"; but evil means nothing else than the pale of damnation.

And when you have saved yourself from anger, the way of humility will open in your heart, and that is better than all good ways, as it is written: "The reward of humility is the fear of the Lord."

And by virtue of humility, the fear of God will rise within your heart, for always will you take to heart "whence you have come, and whither you are bound," and that you are as worms and vermin, even in your life, and how much more in your death, and "in whose presence you will in time give account of yourself and reckoning"—before the King of glory, as it is written: "Behold, heaven and the heaven of heavens cannot contain Thee"; how then the hearts of men! And if you consider all this, you will fear your Creator, and save yourself from sin; and thanks to these ways, you will rejoice in your portion.

And if you constantly accustom yourself to the way of modesty, that you feel humility before every man, and fear God and fear sin, then the Divine Presence will rest upon you with the light of its splendor, and you will live the life in the coming world.

And now, my son, know and see: He who cherishes pride in his heart, and sets himself above all creatures, is a rebel against the kingdom of heaven, for he flaunts the raiment of the Omnipresent, as it is written: "The Lord reigneth; He is clothed in majesty." But of what should the heart of man be proud? Of riches? "The Lord maketh poor, and maketh rich." Of honors? Do they not belong to God? As it is written, "Both riches and honor come of Thee," and how could he boast of the honor of his Maker? Would he boast of wisdom? "He removeth away the speech of men of trust, and taketh away the sense of the elders."

And so we find that before God all are equal, for in His wrath He humbles the proud, and if it is His will, He raises the humbled. Therefore, do you humble yourself, and the Omnipresent will raise you up.

—Moses Nahmanides, 1194-1270

When you have shut your doors, and darkened your room, remember never to say that you are alone; for God is within, and your genius is within, and what need have they of light to see what you are doing?

— EPICTETUS, first century

CHAPTER THIRTEEN

Seers of the Infinite

Off and on, in some rare moments of our spiritual life, the soul becomes aware of the presence of the Divine. A strange awe and delight invade the life of the soul and it becomes convinced of the absoluteness of the Divine, which inspires and moulds every detail of our life.

— SIR SARVEPALLI RADHAKRISHNAN, 1888-

· I ·

As THE flowing rivers in the ocean
Disappear, quitting name and form,
So the knower, being liberated from name and form,
Goes unto the heavenly Person, higher than the high.

— MUNDAKA UPANISHAD

Let any true man go into silence: strip himself of all pretense, and selfishness, and sensuality, and sluggishness of soul; lift off thought after thought, passion after passion, till he reaches the inmost depth of all; remember how short a time and he was not at all; how short a time again, and he will not be here; open his window and look upon the night, how still its breaths, how solemn its march, how deep its perspective, how ancient its forms of light; and think how little he knows except the perpetuity of God, and the mysteriousness of life:—and it will be strange if he does not feel the Eternal

Presence as close upon his soul as the breeze upon his brow; if he does not say, "O Lord, art thou ever near as this, and have I not known thee?"—if the true proportions and the genuine spirit of life do not open on his heart with infinite clearness and show him the littleness of his temptations and the grandeur of his trust. He is ashamed to have found weariness in toil so light, and tears where there was no trial to the brave. He discovers with astonishment how small the dust that has blinded him, and from the height of a quiet and holy love looks down with incredulous sorrow on the jealousies and fears and irritations that have vexed his life. A mighty wind of resolution sets in strong upon him and freshens the whole atmosphere of his soul, sweeping down before it the light flakes of difficulty, till they vanish like snow upon the sea. He is imprisoned no more in a small compartment of time, but belongs to an eternity which is now and here. The isolation of his separate spirit passes away; and with the countless multitude of souls akin to God, he is but as a wave of his unbounded deep. He is at one with Heaven, and hath found the secret place of the Almighty.

— James Martineau, 1805-1900

As men who once have seen
White sun on snow, white fire on ice,
And in a wide noon, shadowless,
Gone blind with light,
So these men walk who once have seen
God without veils,—the mind's
Momentary and blinding birth of sight.

To them henceforth we are but shape and shadow,
Fog-forms, hands moving in a mist,
Our houses dark, our halls are winding tunnels,
Our little triumphs less than little straws
Balanced above a sparrow's nest.

And from that hour we call them dangerous men and strange,
Bigoted, fierce, loud croakers of a dream;
—Anarchists, atheists, we say
Who walk, eyes stretched, as blind men walk,
But ask no man the way.

— Josephine Winslow Johnson, 1910-

You, neighbour God, if sometimes in the night
I rouse you with loud knocking, I do so
only because I seldom hear you breathe;
I know: you are alone.
And should you need a drink, no one is there
to reach it to you, groping in the dark.
Always I hearken. Give but a small sign.
I am quite near.

Between us there is but a narrow wall,
and by sheer chance; for it would take
merely a call from your lips or from mine
to break it down,
and that all noiselessly.

The wall is builded of your images.

They stand before you hiding you like names,
And when the light within me blazes high
that in my inmost soul I know you by,
the radiance is squandered on their frames.

And then my senses, which too soon grow lame,
exiled from you, must go their homeless ways.

— RAINER MARIA RILKE, 1875-1926

Who are you, any one, who can remain unmoved when the Light
    breaks upon you?
Who can say it does not concern him?
Who can say it is just as well not to see as to see?
Who can ever be the same child or woman or man again after the
    Day has broken?
Who can admit there is anything else in the world, after this has
    come to the world?
I brushed all obstructions from my doorsill and stepped into the
    road;
And though so many cried to me, I did not turn back;
And though I was very sorrowful having to leave so many friends
    behind, I did not turn back;
And though the ground was rough and I was overtaken by fierce
    storms, I did not turn back;

For when the soul is once started on the soul's journey, it can never
   turn back. . . .
Can you now go on with your old life as if nothing had happened?
The whole universe has happened;
All your forgotten kinship to the people has happened;
All the terrible thirst for justice has happened;
And all sad things have happened in gladness at last;
And all things out of place have happened at last;
And all old enmity has happened in friendship at last;
The golden age is in my heart today.

— ANONYMOUS

If you ask me concerning God, my God:
"Where is He that we may worship him with resonant song?"
Here on earth, too, He is: the heavens are not for him—
But the earth He has given to man.

The beautiful tree, the beautiful plough-land—therein also the like-
   ness of his image;
Upon every mountainside He plays hide and seek;
Wherever there is an awareness of life in the flesh and blood,
There He invests himself in the plant, in the clod.

His next of kin—all that is: the doe, the turtle,
The scrawny bush and the dark cloud pregnant with thunder;
For He is not the God of would-be spirits—He is the God of the
   human heart:
That is His name and that is His memorial to all eternity.

— CHAIM NAHMAN BIALIK, 1873-1934

For years I sought the Many in the One,
I thought to find lost waves and broken rays,
The rainbow's faded colours in the sun—
The dawns and twilights of forgotten days.

But now I seek the One in every form,
Scorning no vision that a dewdrop holds,
The gentle Light that shines behind the storm,
The Dream that many a twilight hour enfolds.

— EVA GORE-BOOTH, 1870-1926

It is a great thing, an exceeding great thing, in the time of this exile to be joined to God in the divine light by a mystical and denuded union. This takes place where a pure, humble, and resigned soul, burning with ardent love, is carried above itself by the grace of God, and through the brilliancy of the divine light shining on the mind, it loses all consideration and distinction of things, and lays aside all, even the most excellent images, and all liquefied by love, and, as it were, reduced to nothing, it melts away into God. It is then united to God without any medium, and becomes one spirit with Him, and is transformed and changed into Him, as iron placed in the fire is changed into fire, without ceasing to be iron. It becomes one with God, yet not so as to be of the same substance and nature as God. . . .

The soul, having entered the vast solitude of the Godhead, happily loses itself; and enlightened by the brightness of most lucid darkness, becomes through knowledge as if without knowledge, and dwells in a sort of wise ignorance. And although it knows not what God is, to whom it is united by pure charity, although it sees not God as He is in His glory, it yet learns by experience that He infinitely transcends all sensible things, and all that can be apprehended by the human intellect concerning Him. It knows God by this intimate embrace and contact better than the eyes of the body know the visible sun. . . .

When through love the soul goes beyond all working of the intellect and all images in the mind, and is rapt above itself, utterly leaving itself, it flows into God: then is God its peace and fullness. It loses itself in the infinite solitude and darkness of the Godhead; but so to lose itself is rather to find itself. The soul is, as it were, all God-coloured, because its essence is bathed in the Essence of God.

— Louis of Blois, sixteenth century

Man of Song and Man of Science,
Truly you are as people on the outside of a house,
And one of you sees only that it is made of stone, and its windows
   of glass, and that fire burns in the hearth,
And the other of you sees that the house is beautiful and very
   human,
But I have gone inside the house,
And I live with the host in that house
And I have broken bread with him, and drunk his wine,

And seen the transfiguration that love and awe make in the brain . . .
For that house is the world, and the Lord is my host and my
  Father:
It is my Father's house. . . .
Enough? I see what is enough!
Machinery is enough for a Scientist,
And Beauty is enough for a Poet;
But in the hearts of men and women, and in the thirsty hearts of
  little children
There is a hunger, and there is an unappeasable longing,
For a Father and for the love of a Father . . .
For the root of a soul is mystery,
And the Night is mystery,
And in that mystery men and women open inward into Eternity,
And know love, the Lord.
Blessed be his works, and his angels, and his sons crowned with his
  glory!

— JAMES OPPENHEIM, 1882-1932

In the year that King Uzziah died I saw also the Lord sitting upon a
throne, high and lifted up, and His train filled the temple.

Above it stood the seraphims: each one had six wings; with twain
he covered his face, and with twain he covered his feet, and with
twain he did fly.

And one cried unto another, and said, Holy, holy, holy, is the
LORD of hosts: the whole earth is full of His glory.

And the posts of the door moved at the voice of him that cried,
and the house was filled with smoke.

Then said I, Woe is me! for I am undone; because I am a man
of unclean lips, and I dwell in the midst of a people of unclean lips:
for mine eyes have seen the King, the LORD of hosts.

Then flew one of the seraphims unto me, having a live coal in his
hand, which he had taken with the tongs from off the altar:

And he laid it upon my mouth, and said, Lo, this hath touched
thy lips; and thine iniquity is taken away, and thy sin purged.

Also I heard the voice of the Lord, saying, Whom shall I send,
and who will go for us? Then said I, Here am I; send me.

— THE BIBLE, Isaiah 6:1-8

When the spirit loses itself and is merged with Godhood pure and simple, then all its grandeur and perfection must not be interpreted as the transformation of its earthly substance into Godhood, as if its very self were God . . . but it is due to the losing of itself to what it beholds . . . Then God has become all things to the spirit, and for the spirit; all things, as it were, have become God. For all things give reply to it in their capacity of being in God, and yet each thing remains what it is by nature.

—Suso, 1300?-1366

The Soul. What is that sweet thing that comes sometimes to touch me at the thought of God? It affects me with such vehemence and sweetness that I begin wholly to go out of myself and to be lifted up, whither I know not. Suddenly, I am renewed and changed; it is a state of inexpressible well-being. My consciousness rejoices. I lose the memory of my former trials, my soul rejoices, my mind becomes clearer, my heart is enflamed, my desires are satisfied. I feel myself transported into a new place, I know not where. I grasp something interiorly as if with the embraces of love. I do not know what it is, and yet I strive with all my strength to hold it and not to lose it. I struggle deliciously to prevent myself leaving this thing which I desire to embrace for ever, and I exult with ineffable intensity, as if I had at last found the goal of all my desires. I seek for nothing more. I wish for nothing more. All my aspiration is to continue at the point I have reached. Is it my Beloved? Tell me, I pray thee, if this be He, that when He return, I may conjure Him not to depart, and to establish in me His permanent dwelling-place?

The Man. Yes, it is truly the Beloved who visits thee. But He comes invisible, hidden, incomprehensible. He comes to touch thee, not to be seen; to intimate His presence to thee, not to be understood; to make the taste of Him, not to pour Himself out in his entirety; to draw thy affection, not to satisfy thy desire; to bestow the first-fruits of His love, not to communicate it in its fullness. Behold in this the most certain pledge of thy future marriage: that thou art destined to see Him and to possess Him eternally, because He already gives himself to thee at times to taste; with what sweetness thou knowest. Therefore in the times of His absence thou shalt console thyself; and during His visits thou shalt renew thy courage which is ever in need of heartening. We have spoken at great length, O my soul. I ask thee to think of none but Him, love none but Him, listen to none but Him, to take hold of none but Him, possess none but Him.

The Soul. That indeed is what I desire, what I choose; that is what I long for from the depths of my heart.

—Hugh of St. Victor, 1096?-1141

I hear and behold God in every object, yet understand God not in the least,
Nor do I understand who there can be more wonderful than myself.

Why should I wish to see God better than this day?
I see something of God each hour of the twenty-four, and each moment then,

In the faces of men and women I see God, and in my own face in the glass,
I find letters from God dropped in the street—and every one is signed by God's name,
And I leave them where they are, for I know that others will punctually come forever and ever.

—Walt Whitman, 1819-1892

Love all God's creation, both the whole and every grain of sand. Love every leaf, every ray of light. Love the animals, love the plants, love each separate thing. If thou love each thing thou wilt perceive the mystery of God in all; and when once thou perceive this, thou wilt thenceforward grow every day to a fuller understanding of it: until thou come at last to love the whole world with a love that will then be all-embracing and universal.

—Fëdor Dostoevski, 1821-1881

As rivers seek a sea they cannot fill
But are themselves filled full in its embrace,
Absorbed, at rest, each river and each rill;
        Grant us such grace.

—Christina Georgina Rossetti, 1830-1894

One of the devout who had deeply plunged his head into the cowl of meditation, and had been immersed in the ocean of visions, was asked, when he had come out of that state, by one of his companions, who had desired to cheer him up: "What beautiful gift hast thou brought us from the garden in which thou hast been?"

He replied: "I intended to fill the skirts of my robe with roses, when I reached the rose-tree, as presents for my friends, but the perfume of the flowers intoxicated me so much that I let go the hold of my skirts."

—Saadi, 1184?-1291

A messenger of Hope comes every night to me,
And offers for short life, eternal liberty.

He comes with western winds, with evening's wandering airs,
With that clear dusk of heaven that brings the thickest stars.
Winds take a pensive tone, and stars a tender fire,
And visions rise, and change, that kill me with desire.

Desire for nothing known in my maturer years,
When Joy grew mad with awe, at counting future tears.
When, if my spirit's sky was full of flashes warm,
I knew not whence they came, from sun or thunderstorm.

But, first, a hush of peace, a soundless calm descends:
The struggle of distress, and fierce impatience ends;
Mute music soothes my breast—unutter'd harmony,
That I could never dream, till earth was lost to me.

Then dawns the Invisible; the Unseen its truth reveals;
My outward sense is gone, my inward essence feels:
Its wings are almost free—its home, its harbour found;
Measuring the gulf, it stoops and dares the final bound.

Oh! dreadful is the check—intense the agony—
When the ear begins to hear, and the eye begins to see;
When the pulse begins to throb, the brain to think again;
The soul to feel the flesh, and the flesh to feel the chain.

—Emily Brontë, 1818-1848

For God is Himself the *Being of all Beings,* and we are as gods in Him through whom He revealeth Himself.

— JAKOB BÖHME, 1575-1624

· II ·

He that planted the ear, shall He not hear?
He that formed the eye, shall He not see?

— THE BIBLE, Psalm 94:9

The ancient truth of the mystic is nothing else than *the truth about originality,* about what it is to own one's own soul. The knowledge of God as the worshipper has it is the opposite of everything that can ever become merely traditional in religion. No matter how true an idea of God religion may hand on, the true idea may constitute a wall which keeps God out, if it is adopted as an idea simply—that is to say, as a repetition of other men's insights, as a universal idea. God, who is truly said to explain man to himself, must explain *me* to *myself.* What I require to find in a god is that "This is what I have wanted; this what I have been meaning all the time; the world as I now see it is a world in which I as a primitive, various, infinitely discontented will can completely live and breathe." This is what the mystic is trying to make plain—that the idea, as a universal, is not sufficient for any man to live by.

Hence the chief burden of his revelation (as if of the idea's own never-resting conscience) is that religion must exist as experience and not as idea only. There is nothing in sensation which physical science cannot exhaust, except the experience of having sensations: in the same way, there is nothing in the mystic experience not expressible in idea, except the experiencing itself. This is the chief part of the mystic knowledge which cannot be otherwise known, namely that the mystic experience is possible. Monotonously and age after age, men rediscover and reannounce this invariant truth, as if they were calling on men to exist, to live, to save their souls. And what is it to save one's soul, if not to be original in this sense (and in what follows from it)? From this point of view the reiteration of the mystic is justified.

— WILLIAM ERNEST HOCKING, 1873-

Every moment is the message of God's will; every external event, everything outside us, and even every involuntary thought and feeling within us is God's own touch.

— DOM JOHN CHAPMAN, 1865-1933

The religious spirit is in us. It preceded the religions, and their task as well as that of the prophets, of the initiated, consists in releasing, directing, and developing it. This mystical aspiration is an essentially human trait. It slumbers at the bottom of our souls awaiting the event, or the man capable, in the manner of an enzyme, of transforming it into true mysticism, into faith.

— PIERRE LECOMTE DU NOÜY, 1883-1947

In mystic states we both become one with the Absolute and we become aware of our oneness. This is the everlasting and triumphant mystical tradition, hardly altered by differences of clime or creed. In Hinduism, in Neoplatonism, in Sufism, in Christian mysticism, in Whitmanism, we find the same recurring note, so that there is about mystical utterances an eternal unanimity which ought to make a critic stop and think, and which brings it about that the mystical classics have, as has been said, neither birthday nor native land. Perpetually telling of the unity of man with God, their speech antedates languages, and they do not grow old. . . .

It must always remain an open question whether mystical states may not possibly be superior points of view, windows through which the mind looks out upon a more extensive and inclusive world.

— WILLIAM JAMES, 1842-1910

How rich, O Lord, how fresh Thy visits are!
'Twas but just now my bleak leaves hopeless hung
    Sullied with dust and mud;
Each snarling blast shot through me, and did share
Their youth and beauty; cold showers nipped and wrung
Their spiciness and blood.
But since Thou didst in one sweet glance survey

Their sad decays, I flourish and once more
 Breathe all perfumes and spice;
I smell a dew like myrrh and all the day
Wear in my bosom a full sun; such store
 Hath one beam from Thy eyes.
But, ah my God, what fruit hast Thou of this?
What one poor leaf did ever I let fall
 To wait upon thy wreath?
Thus Thou all day a thankless weed dost dress,
And when Thou hast done, a stench or fog is all
 The odour I bequeath.

     — HENRY VAUGHAN, 1622-1695

The most beautiful and most profound emotion we can experience is the sensation of the mystical. It is the dower of all true science. He to whom this emotion is a stranger, who can no longer wonder and stand rapt in awe, is as good as dead. To know that what is impenetrable to us really exists, manifesting itself as the highest wisdom and the most radiant beauty which our dull faculties can comprehend only in their most primitive forms—this knowledge, this feeling is at the centre of true religiousness.

     — ALBERT EINSTEIN, 1879-

I confess, then, though I say it in my foolishness, that the Word has visited me, and even very often. But although He has frequently entered into my soul, I have never at any time been sensible of the precise moment of His coming. I have felt that He was present; I remember that He has been with me; I have sometimes been able even to have a presentiment that He would come; but never to feel His coming or His departure. For whence He came to enter my soul, or whither He went on quitting it, by what means He has made entrance or departure, I confess that I know not even to this day . . . It is not by the eyes that He enters, for He is without colour; nor by the ears, for His coming is without sound; nor by the nostrils, for it is not with the air but with the mind that He is blended; nor again does He enter by the mouth, not being of a nature to be eaten or drunk; nor lastly is He capable of being traced by the touch, for He is intangible.

You will ask, then, how, since the ways of His access are thus incapable of being traced, I could know that He was present. But He is living and full of energy, and as soon as He has entered into me He has quickened my sleeping soul, has aroused and softened and goaded my heart, which was in a state of torpor and hard as stone. He has begun to pluck up and destroy, to plant and to build, to water the dry places, to illuminate the gloomy spots, to throw open those which were shut close, to inflame with warmth those which were cold, as also to straighten its crooked paths and make its rough places smooth, so that my soul might bless the Lord and all that is within me praise His Holy Name. Thus, then, the Bridegroom-Word, though He has several times entered into me, has never made His coming apparent to my sight, hearing, or touch. It was not by His motions that He was recognised by me, nor could I tell by any of my senses that He had penetrated to the depths of my being. It was, as I have already said, only by the movement of my heart that I was enabled to recognise His presence, and to know the might of His power by the sudden departure of vices and the strong restraint put upon all carnal affections. From this discovery and conviction of my secret faults I have had good reason to admire the depths of His wisdom; His goodness and kindness have become known in the amendment, whatever it may amount to, of my life; while in the renewal of the spirit of my mind, that is, of my inward man, I have perceived in some degree the loveliness of His beauty, and have been filled with amazement at the multitude of His greatness, as I meditated upon all these things.

But when the Word withdrew Himself, all these spiritual powers and faculties began to droop and languish, as if the fire had been withdrawn from a bubbling pot; and this is to me the sign of His departure. Then my soul is necessarily sad and depressed until He shall return and my heart grow warm within me, as it is wont, which indeed is the indication to me that He has come back again.

After having, then, such an experience of the Word, what wonder that I should adopt for my own the language of the Bride, who recalls Him when He has departed, since I am influenced by a desire, not indeed as powerful, but at least similar to hers. As long as I live that utterance shall be in my mind, and I will employ, for the recalling of the Word, that word of recall which I find here in the word "Return." And as often as He shall leave me, so often shall He be called back by my voice; nor will I cease to send my cries, as it were, after Him as He departs, expressing the ardent desire of my heart that He should return, that He should restore to me the joy of

His salvation, restore to me Himself. I confess to you, my sons, that I take pleasure in nothing else in the meantime, until He is present who is alone pleasing to me.

— St. Bernard of Clairvaux, 1091-1153

This solitary response to reality is the deepest religious experience one can have. It is turning from the periphery of life to the core of existence. In this solitary moment it is as if one entered into the scheme of things. He penetrates the outer glare and comes into a sombre retreat where perspective is steady and clear. But the solitary view does more than intensify the subjective focus; it illumines the objective reference. . . . It deafens one's ears to folk noises and fills them with the sound of vastness. It stirs one from the mood of living to a sense of life in its immensities. Solitariness makes one world-conscious. And in becoming world-conscious he becomes God-conscious.

I have known solitary moments such as these to bring me a peculiarly intimate understanding of the moment of life. It was as if I were momentarily lifted from the scene of details to a lone plateau where a broader vista was possible. The universe as an entity seemed to be moving through space-time, an earnest, living organism of huge dimensions, pulsating with innumerable life-activities, yet, like a massive liner at sea, plowing its own course through waves of time, whither, there was no knowing. There is a feeling of eternity or timelessness that comes over one in such a glimpse of the total course of things that seems to give dignity and worth to the temporal passage of events. . . .

Contemplating this vast, on-going process of life in this intimate way makes one vividly aware of the great community of cosmic activities which sustain and promote life. The cosmos becomes a community, near and neighborly. It is, indeed, a vivid awareness of God.

— Bernard Meland, 1899-

CHAPTER FOURTEEN

If a Man Loveth Not

His Brother

*Have we not all one father? Hath not one God created us?
Why do we deal treacherously every man against his
brother?*

— THE BIBLE, Malachi 2:20

·I·

HE THAT loveth not knoweth not God; for God is love. . . .

If a man say, I love God, and hateth his brother, he is a liar: for
he that loveth not his brother whom he hath seen, how can he love
God whom he hath not seen?

— THE BIBLE, I John 4:8, 20

I believe in God, who is for me spirit, love, the principle of all
things. I believe that God is in me, as I am in Him. I believe that the
true welfare of man consists in fulfilling the will of God. I believe
that from the fulfillment of the will of God there can follow nothing but that which is good for me and for all men. I believe that the
will of God is that every man should love his fellow-men, and
should act toward others as he desires that they should act toward
him. I believe that the reason of life is for each of us simply to grow

262

in love. I believe that this growth in love will contribute more than any other force to establish the Kingdom of God on earth. To replace a social life in which division, falsehood and violence are all-powerful, with a new order in which humanity, truth and brotherhood will reign.

—COUNT LEO TOLSTOY, 1828-1910

The character of combined ultimacy and intimacy is the hallmark of religion.

—C. C. J. WEBB, 1865-

If a person were in such a rapturous state as St. Paul once entered, and he knew of a sick man who wanted a cup of soup, it would be far better to withdraw from the rapture for love's sake and serve him who is in need. . . . We ought to get over amusing ourselves with such raptures for the sake of that better love, and to accomplish through loving service what men most need, spiritually, socially, or physically. . . . St. Thomas Aquinas says that the active life is better than the contemplative, for in it one pours out the love he has received in contemplation. Yet it is all one; for what we plant in the soil of contemplation we shall reap in the harvest of action and thus the purpose of contemplation is achieved. . . . In contemplation, you serve only yourselves. In good works, you serve many people.

—MEISTER ECKHART, 1260?-?1327

SCENE.—*An audience room in the Sultan's palace.*

SALADIN [*giving directions at the door*]. Here, introduce the Jew, whene'er he comes,—
He seems in no great haste. . . .

[NATHAN *enters.*]

Draw nearer, Jew; yet nearer; here, quite by me,
Without all fear.
SALADIN. Remain that for thy foes!
SALADIN. Your name is Nathan?
NATHAN. Yes.

SALADIN. Nathan the Wise?

NATHAN. No.

SALADIN. If not thou, the people call thee so.

NATHAN. May be, the people.

SALADIN. Fancy not that I
Think of the people's voice contemptuously;
I have been wishing much to know the man
Whom it has named the Wise. . . .

NATHAN. Doubtless, then, you would learn what, on my journey,
I noticed of the motions of the foe,
Who stirs anew. If unreserved I may—

SALADIN. Neither was that the object of my sending:
I know what I have need to know already.
In short, I willed your presence—

NATHAN. Sultan, your order.

SALADIN. To gain instruction quite on other points.
Since you are a man so wise,—tell me, which law,
Which faith, appears to you the better?

NATHAN. Sultan,
I am a Jew.

SALADIN. And I am a Mussulman:
The Christian stands between us. Of these three
Religions only one can be the true.
A man like you remains not just where birth
Has chanced to cast him, or, if he remains there,
Does it from insight, choice, from grounds of preference.
Share, then, with me your insight,—let me hear
The grounds of preference, which I have wanted
The leisure to examine,—learn the choice
These grounds have motived, that it may be mine.
In confidence I ask it. How you start,
And weigh me with your eye! It may well be
I'm the first sultan to whom this caprice,
Methinks not quite unworthy of a sultan,
Has yet occurred. Am I not? Speak, then,—speak.
Or do you, to collect yourself, desire
Some moments of delay? I give them you.—
[SALADIN *steps into the room to which* SITTAH *had retired.*]

NATHAN. Strange! How is this? What wills the sultan of me?
I came prepared with cash,—he asks truth. Truth?
As if truth, too, were cash,—a coin disused,
That goes by weight,—indeed, 'tis some such thing;—

But a new coin, known by the stamp at once,
To be flung down and told upon the counter,
It is not that. Like gold in bags tied up,
So truth lies hoarded in the wise man's head,
To be brought out.—Which, now, in this transaction,
Which of us plays the Jew? He asks for truth,—
Is truth what he requires, his aim, his end? . . .
I must be cautious. Yet to drive him back,
And be the stubborn Jew, is not the thing;
And wholly to throw off the Jew, still less.
For, if no Jew, he might with right inquire,
Why not a Mussulman?—Yes,—that may serve me.
Not children only can be quieted
With stories.—Ha! he comes;—well, let him come.
    SALADIN [*returning*]. I'm not too quick?
Thou hast bethought thyself as much as need is?—
Speak, no one hears.
    NATHAN. Might the whole world but hear us!
    SALADIN. Is Nathan of his cause so confident?
Yes, that I call the sage,—to veil no truth;
For truth to hazard all things, life and goods.
    NATHAN. Ay, when 'tis necessary, and when useful.
    SALADIN. Henceforth I hope I shall with reason bear
One of my titles,—"Betterer of the world
And of the law."
    NATHAN. In truth, a noble title.
But, Sultan, ere I quite unfold myself,
Allow me to relate a tale.
    SALADIN. Why not?
I always was a friend of tales well told.
    NATHAN. Well told,—that's not precisely my affair.
    SALADIN. Again so proudly modest?—Come, begin.
    NATHAN. In days of yore, there dwelt in the East a man
Who from a valued hand received a ring
Of endless worth: the stone of it an opal,
That shot an ever-changing tint: moreover,
It had the hidden virtue him to render
Of God and man beloved, who, in this view,
And this persuasion, wore it. Was it strange
The Eastern man ne'er drew it off his finger,
And studiously provided to secure it
For ever to his house? Thus he bequeathed it,

First, to the most beloved of his sons,—
Ordained that he again should leave the ring
To the most dear among his children,—and,
That without heeding birth, the favorite son,
In virtue of the ring alone, should always
Remain the lord o' th' house.—You hear me, Sultan?
   SALADIN. I understand thee,—on.
   NATHAN. From son to son,
At length this ring descended to a father
Who had three sons alike obedient to him;
Whom, therefore, he could not but love alike.
At times seemed this, now that, at times the third
(Accordingly as such apart received
The overflowings of his heart), most worthy
To heir the ring, which, with good-natured weakness,
He privately to each in turn had promised.
This went on for a while. But death approached,
And the good father grew embarrassed. So
To disappoint two sons, who trust his promise
He could not bear. What's to be done? He sends
In secret to a jeweller, of whom,
Upon the model of the real thing,
He might bespeak two others, and commanded
To spare nor cost nor pains to make them like,
Quite like the true one. This the artist managed.
The rings were brought, and e'en the father's eye
Could not distinguish which had been the model.
Quite overjoyed, he summons all his sons,
Takes leave of each apart, on each bestows
His blessing and his ring, and dies.—Thou hear'st me?
   SALADIN. I hear, I hear. Come, finish with thy tale;—
Is it soon ended?
   NATHAN. It is ended, Sultan;
For all that follows may be guessed of course.
Scarce is the father dead, each with his ring
Appears, and claims to be the lord o' th' house.
Come questions, strife, complaint,—all to no end;
For the true ring could no more be distinguished
Than now can—the true faith.
   SALADIN. How, how?—is that
To be the answer to my query?
   NATHAN. No,

But it may serve as my apology,
If I can't venture to decide between
Rings which the father got expressly made,
That they might not be known from one another.
    SALADIN. The rings,—don't trifle with me; I must think
That the religions which I named can be
Distinguished, e'en to raiment, drink, and food.
    NATHAN. And only not as to their grounds of proof.
Are not all built alike on history,
Traditional or written? History
Must be received on trust,—is it not so?
In whom now are we likeliest to put trust?
In our own people surely, in those men
Whose blood we are, in them who from our childhood
Have given us proofs of love, who ne'er deceived us,
Unless 'twere wholesomer to be deceived.
How can I less believe in my forefathers
Than thou in thine? How can I ask of thee
To own that thy forefathers falsified,
In order to yield mine the praise of truth?
The like of Christians.
    SALADIN. By the living God!
The man is in the right,—I must be silent.
    NATHAN. Now let us to our rings return once more.
As said, the sons complained. Each to the judge
Swore from his father's hand immediately
To have received the ring, as was the case;
After he had long obtained the father's promise
One day to have the ring, as also was.
The father, each asserted, could to him
Not have been false: rather than so suspect
Of such a father, willing as he might be
With charity to judge his brethren, he
Of treacherous forgery was bold to accuse them.
    SALADIN. Well, and the judge,—I'm eager now to hear
What thou wilt make him say. Go on, go on.
    NATHAN. The judge said, "If ye summon not the father
Before my seat, I cannot give a sentence.
Am I to guess enigmas? Or expect ye
That the true ring should here unseal its lips?
But hold,—you tell me that the real ring
Enjoys the hidden power to make the wearer

Of God and man beloved: let that decide.
Which of you do two brothers love the best?
You're silent. Do these love-exciting rings
Act inward only, not without? Does each
Love but himself? Ye're all deceived deceivers,—
None of your rings is true. The real ring,
Perhaps, is gone. To hide or to supply
Its loss, your father ordered three for one."
    SALADIN. Oh, charming, charming!
    NATHAN. "And," the judge continued,
"If you will take advice, in lieu of sentence,
This is my counsel to you,—to take up
The matter where it stands. If each of you
Has had a ring presented by his father,
Let each believe his own the real ring.
'Tis possible the father chose no longer
To tolerate the one ring's tyranny;
And certainly, as he much loved you all,
And loved you all alike, it could not please him,
By favoring one, to be of two the oppressor.
Let each feel honored by this free affection
Unwarped of prejudice; let each endeavor
To vie with both his brothers in displaying
The virtue of his ring; assist its might
With gentleness, benevolence, forbearance,
With inward resignation to the Godhead;
And if the virtues of the ring continue
To show themselves among your children's children
After a thousand thousand years, appear
Before this judgment-seat,—a greater one
Than I shall sit upon it, and decide."—
So spake the modest judge.
    SALADIN. God!
    NATHAN. Saladin,
Feel'st thou thyself this wiser, promised man?
    SALADIN. I, dust,—I, nothing,—God?
    NATHAN. What moves thee, Sultan?
    SALADIN. Nathan, my dearest Nathan, 'tis not yet
The judge's thousand thousand years are past,—
His judgment seat's not mine. Go, go, but love me.

— GOTTHOLD EPHRAIM LESSING, 1729-1781

Lord, make me an instrument of Thy peace,
Where hate rules, let me bring love,
Where malice, forgiveness,
Where disputes, reconciliation,
Where error, truth,
Where doubt, belief,
Where despair, hope,
Where darkness, Thy light,
Where sorrow, joy!
O Master, let me strive more to comfort others than to be comforted,
To understand others than to be understood,
To love others, more than to be loved!
For he who gives, receives,
He who forgets himself, finds,
He who forgives, receives forgiveness,
And dying, we rise again to eternal life.

— Attributed to St. Francis of Assisi, 1182-1226

We desire but the good of the world and the happiness of the nations; yet they deem us a stirrer up of strife and sedition worthy of bondage and banishment; that all nations should become one in faith and all men as brothers; that the bonds of affection and unity between the sons of men should be strengthened; that diversity of religion should cease, and differences of race be annulled. . . . Yet so it shall be; these fruitless strifes, these ruinous wars shall pass away, and the "Most Great Peace" shall come. . . . Yet do we see your kings and rulers lavishing their treasures more freely on means for the destruction of the human race than on that which would conduce to the happiness of mankind. These strifes and this bloodshed and discord must cease, and all men be as one kindred and one family. . . . Let not a man glory in this, that he loves his country; let him rather glory in this, that he loves his kind.

— Bahaullah, 1817-1892

· II ·

Six things the Lord hates,
Seven are an abomination to Him:

Haughty eyes, a lying tongue,
And hands that shed innocent blood;
A mind that plots mischievous schemes,
Feet that are quick to run after evil;
A false witness who utters lies;
And he who sows discord among brothers.

— THE BIBLE, Proverbs 6:16-19

Father of all! in every age,
    In every clime adored,
By saint, by savage, and by sage,
    Jehovah, Jove, or Lord!

Thou Great First Cause, least understood,
    Who all my sense confined
To know but this, that Thou art good,
    And that myself am blind!

Yet gave me, in this dark estate,
    To see the good from ill;
And, binding nature fast in fate,
    Left free the human will.

What conscience dictates to be done,
    Or warns me not to do,
This teach me more than hell to shun,
    That, more than heav'n pursue.

What blessings Thy free bounty gives,
    Let me not cast away;
For God is paid when man receives,
    To enjoy is to obey.

Yet not to earth's contracted span
    Thy goodness let me bound,
Or think Thee Lord alone of man,
    When thousand worlds are round.

Let not this weak, unknowing hand
    Presume Thy bolts to throw,
And deal damnation round the land
    On each I judge Thy foe.

If I am right, Thy grace impart
    Still in the right to stay;
If I am wrong, oh, teach my heart
    To find the better way!

Save me alike from foolish pride,
    And impious discontent,
At aught Thy wisdom has denied,
    Or aught Thy goodness lent.

Teach me to feel another's woe,
    To hide the fault I see;
That mercy I to others show,
    That mercy show to me.

Mean though I am, not wholly so,
    Since quickened by Thy breath;
O lead me wheresoe'er I go,
    Through this day's life or death.

This day be bread and peace my lot:
    All else beneath the sun,
Thou knowest if best bestowed or not,
    And let Thy will be done.

To Thee, whose temple is all space,—
    Whose altar, earth, sea, skies,—
One chorus let all beings raise!
    All nature's incense rise!

        — ALEXANDER POPE, 1688-1744

May I be no man's enemy, and may I be the friend of that which is eternal and abides. May I never quarrel with those nearest me; and if I do, may I be reconciled quickly. May I never devise evil against any man; if any devise evil against me, may I escape uninjured and without the need of hurting him. May I love, seek, and attain only that which is good. May I wish for all men's happiness and envy none. May I never rejoice in the ill-fortune of one who has wronged me. When I have done or said what is wrong, may I never wait for the rebuke of others, but always rebuke myself until I make amends. . . . May I win no victory that harms either me or my opponent. . . . May I reconcile friends who are wroth with one another. May I, to the extent of my power, give all needful help to my friends and to all who are in want. May I never fail a friend in danger. When visiting those in grief may I be able by gentle and healing words to soften their pain. . . . May I respect myself. . . . May I always keep tame that which rages within me. . . . May I accustom myself to be gentle, and never be angry with people because of circumstances. May I never discuss who is wicked and what wicked things he has done, but know good men and follow in their footsteps.

— Attributed to EUSEBIUS

Imagine a circle and in the middle of it a center; and from this center forthgoing radii-rays. The farther these radii go from the center, the more divergent and remote from one another they become; conversely, the nearer they approach to the center, the more they come together among themselves. Now suppose that this circle is the world: the very middle of it, God; and the straight lines (radii) going from the center to the circumference, or from the circumference to the center, are the paths of the life of men. And in this case also, to the extent that the saints approach the middle of the circle, desiring to approach God, do they, by so doing, come nearer to God and to one another . . . Reason similarly with regard to their withdrawing—when they withdraw from God, they withdraw also from one another, and by so much as they withdraw from one another do they withdraw from God. Such is the attribute of love; to the extent that we are distant from God and do not love Him, each of us is far from his neighbor also. If we love God, then to the extent that we approach to Him through love of Him, do we unite in love with our neighbors; and the closer our union with them, the closer is our union with God also.

— ABBA DOROTHEUS, seventh century

We therefore hope in Thee, O Lord our God, and in the coming of Thy kingdom, when Thy unity and supremacy will be realized throughout the world, and all men will be bound together in a common fealty to Thy law of righteousness. On that day men will be ashamed of that exclusive and arrogant self-worship whereby nations, races and religious communions profane Thy name. They will all renounce such idolatries and acknowledge Thy sole sovereignty,

O God of the spirits of all flesh. Then will men recognize, in the soul of every nation, race and religion, a manifestation of Thy divine spirit and will accord to every human society the equal right to serve Thee with whatever gifts Thou hast bestowed upon it. Nation will not lift up sword against nation, neither will men learn warfare any more. For the earth shall be filled with the knowledge of Thee, as the waters cover the sea.

—SABBATH PRAYER BOOK
(Jewish Reconstructionist Foundation)

Quaint, outlandish heathen gods
Black men fashion out of rods,
Clay and brittle bits of stone,
In a likeness of their own,
My conversion came high-priced;
I belong to Jesus Christ,
Preacher of humility;
Heathen gods are naught to me.
Father, Son and Holy Ghost,
So I make an idle boast;
Jesus of the twice-turned cheek,
Lamb of God, although I speak
With my mouth thus, in my heart
Do I play a double part.
Even at Thy glowing altar
Must my heart grow sick and falter,
Wishing He I served were black,
Thinking then it would not lack
Precedent of pain to guide it,
Let who would or might deride it;
Surely then this flesh would know
Yours had borne a kindred woe.
Lord, I fashion dark gods, too,
Daring even to give You
Dark despairing features where,
Crowned with dark rebellious hair,
Patience wavers just so much as
Mortal grief compels, while touches
Quick and hot, of anger, rise
To smitten cheek and weary eyes.

Lord, forgive me if my need
Sometimes shapes a human creed.

— COUNTEE CULLEN, 1903-1946

The nearest way to God
Leads through love's open door;
The path of knowledge is
Too slow for evermore.

— ANGELUS SILESIUS, 1624-1677

We have heard it affirmed . . . that at the heart of this universe there is personality which is at once the source of life and the goal of life. If that affirmation is valid, then a series of things must follow therefrom, and it is along the line of these that I think the quest for fulfilment, the quest of God, drives one.

First of all, if God is the source of all life, if from Him emanates all creation, then there must be an underlying unity for all of them, and wherever one digs in honestly, living up to the limit of the light that one has at the particular time, one does make contact with that unity. . . .

If there is the unity of which we are thinking, the next thing which comes out of that is an essential kinship of all the creations of all the people in the world and if that kinship is true, is genuine, then I can never be the kind of person that I ought to be until everybody else is the kind of person that everybody else ought to be. . . .

If I need every one else, then by the same process I must be sensitive to the needs of other people. Human need is infinite but when I respond to it to the limit of my power and become thereby painfully conscious of my own inadequacy, I seem to send my soul through the air and the sky and the sea in quest of an infinite energy that I may release for an infinite task.

— HOWARD THURMAN, 1899-

Brother, you say there is but one way to worship and serve the Great Spirit. If there is but one religion, why do you white people differ so much about it? Why are not all agreed, as you can all read the Book?

Brother, we do not understand these things. We are told that your religion was given to your forefathers and has been handed down from father to son. We also have a religion which was given to our forefathers and has been handed down to us, their children. We worship in that way. It teaches us to be thankful for all the favors we receive, to love each other, and to be united. We never quarrel about religion.

Brother, the Great Spirit has made us all, but He has made a great difference between His white and His red children. He has given us different complexions and different customs. To you He has given the arts. To these, He has not opened our eyes. We know these things to be true. Since He has made so great a difference between us in other things, why may we not conclude that He has given us a different religion according to our understanding? The Great Spirit does right. He knows what is best for His children; we are satisfied.

Brother, we do not wish to destroy your religion or take it from you. We only want to enjoy our own.

—RED JACKET, 1758?-1830

The basis of fellowship between believers of different spiritual families is friendship and the love of charity. . . . It is the implications of love itself that supply us with the guiding idea we need and that make manifest for us the "analogical" likeness of practical thought. . . .

It is obvious in fact that, if I am right in what I have said, the primary and fundamental likeness between us is the acknowledgment of the fundamental and primordial ethical value of the law of brotherly love, however much this law may have different theological and metaphysical connotations for us, according to the religion or school of thought to which we belong. For the Christian it corresponds to and raises to divine levels a fundamental though terribly thwarted tendency of our nature. It is the second commandment, which forms but one with the first: the commandment to love our neighbour as ourselves. "I feel," wrote Gandhi in a note on the *Satyagraha* in 1920, "that nations cannot be one in reality, nor can their activities be conducive to the common good of the whole humanity, unless there is this definite recognition and acceptance of the law of the family in national and international affairs, in other words, on the political platform. Nations can be called civilized, only to the extent that they obey this law." That, I also believe, is the truth.

Now this very law of brotherly friendship in practice has many implications. The first truth it implies, and which underlies all the rest, is that our existence is directed towards God and that, in accordance with the first commandment, we must love God above everything. How indeed can the law of love have *absolute* value, transcending all the conflicts and discords which flourish among men, unless all men, whatever their race or colour, their class, their nation, their social conditions, their natural shortcomings, receive from an Absolute above the world the bond creating between them a more fundamental and far-reaching communion than all their diversities, and unless they are created to love first and foremost this Absolute in which all things live and move and have their being? We see only too readily that, in the great contemporary movements in which God is in practice denied, whether by virtue of an atheism that refuses to admit His existence or by virtue of a pseudo-theism that blasphemes His nature, love and charity are alike rejected as weaknesses and as the worst enemies either of the State or of the Revolution. The theorists of these movements make that abundantly clear in their writings.

The second implication is on the one hand the holiness of truth and on the other hand the eminent value of good will. If man can bend the truth to his own desires, will he not also want to bend other men in like manner? Those who despise charity are also those who think that truth depends, not on *what is*, but on what at each moment serves most effectively their party, their greed, or their hate. And those who despise charity also despise good will. The word to them seems pale and dangerously liberal. . . . Real, authentic good will indicates the sacred mystery which spells salvation for men and which makes it possible to say of a man that he is purely and simply good. It enables men to go out of themselves to meet their neighbours halfway. That is why the pharisees and the fanatics, walled up in their whited sepulchres, wherein they would like to enclose the whole world, are not only suspicious of good will; they detest the very idea.

The third implication contained in fraternal amity is the dignity of the human person with the rights it implies and the realities on which it is based. I refer to the spirituality of the human soul and its eternal destiny. In the text from which I have already quoted, Gandhi also pointed out that, "It [*Satyagraha*] is called also soul-force, because a definite recognition of the soul within is a necessity, if a *Satyagrahi* is to believe that death does not mean cessation of the struggle, but a culmination." I as a Christian know very well on what my faith in the immortality of the soul and the dignity of the human person is based. I read in the Gospels: *What doth it profit a man if he gain the whole world and lose his own soul?* I read also that the hairs on each of our heads are counted, and that the angels who see the face of the Father watch over each of the children of men, who are equal in that dignity, and that we must love our enemies. . . . It is not community of race, of class, or of nation; it is the love of charity that makes us what we ought to be, members of the family of God, of the only community where each person, drawn out from his fundamental loneliness, truly communicates with others and truly makes them his brothers, by giving himself to them and in a certain sense dying for them. Nothing that has ever been said points out more profoundly the mystery and dignity of the human person. Who is my neighbour? The man of my blood? Of my party? The man who does me good? No. It is the man to whom I show mercy, the man to whom is transmitted through me the universal gift and love of God, who makes the rain from heaven fall upon both the good and the wicked.

The existence of God, the sanctity of truth, the value and necessity of good will, the dignity of the person, the spirituality and immortality of the soul: these, and all the other implications bound up with them which I shall not mention here, correspond to spontaneous perceptions of our reason and to primary tendencies of our nature; but they are not understood in an identical and univocal way by believers in the various religions of humanity. Thus Christianity and Buddhism have different conceptions of the human person; the survival of the soul has a different meaning for those who believe in personal immortality and in the resurrection of the body and those who believe in transmigration; the sanctity of truth appears in a different light according to the fashion in which both revelation and human reason are conceived; the value of good will has different connotations for the Catholic who believes in sanctifying grace, for the Orthodox who believes in the sanctifying uncreated Spirit but not in created grace, for the Protestant who believes that the merits of Christ are imputed to an essentially corrupt nature, for the Israelite who believes in the Law, for the Moslem who believes in salvation by the mere profession of Islamic faith; and this difference is still greater as between these religious groups and the religious groups who believe in Karma. As regards the existence of God itself, I do not think that Buddhism rejects, as is often stated, the existence of God, nor that it is in reality an atheistic religion. I believe that this apparent atheism comes from the fact that Buddhism has developed historically as a kind of mystical destruction of the Brahmanic affirmation, so that the Buddhist ascesis and Nirvana are, as it were, like a vast apophatic or negative theology, standing alone in emptiness. But this example does serve to cast light on the extent to which the idea of God may differ among believers of the various religions. It should be added that those who believe that they are non-believers may, in their practical lives, by choosing as the aim of their activity the authentic moral good, choose God, and may do so by virtue of God's grace, without their knowing God in a consciously and conceptually formulated manner.

All this goes to show that there is nothing *univocal* between the various paths travelled by men, and that practical good fellowship is not based on a common minimum of doctrinal identity. . . . The coming together of such men to co-operate for the good of human society is not based upon an equivocation. It is based upon "analogical" likeness as between the practical principles, motions, and progressions implied in their common acceptance of the law of love, and corresponding to the primary inclinations of human nature.

And why should I, a Christian, according to whose faith a single Name has been given to men through whom they can be saved, even in the temporal order, why should I disguise the fact that this community of analogy itself supposes a *primum analogatum* purely and simply true; and that implicitly and ultimately everything which is authentic love, working in the world for the reconciliation of men and the common good of their life here below, tends, under forms more or less perfect, more or less pure, toward Christ, who is known to some, unknown to others?

— JACQUES MARITAIN, 1882-

The greatest ethic of all, because all-embracing, is the Golden Rule, and it is traceable from early historic times as the product of the social faculty. In the Egyptian *Book of the Dead*, the words repeated by the deceased on entering the Judgment Hall of Osiris are but an extended version of the Rule, and the ethic of Egypt was equal to any of modern times. In the Christian religion it takes the form of the command: "Do unto others as you would they should do unto you." In the Hindu *Vedas* it is embodied in "Let him not do evil to others who desires not that sorrows should pursue him." Confucius stated it in "Is not 'reciprocity' such a word? What you want done to yourself, that do to others." The Greeks had a word for it when Socrates said: "You should do to others what you think I should be to you." It is reflected in the Zoroastrian *Zend-Avesta:* "Hear with your ears what is best, perceive with your mind what is pure." Cicero has: "Nature ordains that a man should wish the good of every man, whatever he may be, and for this reason—that he is a man," while Mohammed alludes to Reciprocity when he said: "Do good, for God loveth those who do good."

— PERCIVAL MACLEOD YEARSLEY, 1867-

Pure religion and undefiled before God and the Father is this, To visit the fatherless and widows in their affliction, and to keep himself unspotted from the world.

— THE BIBLE, James 1:27

· III ·

"Sire," announced the servant to the King, "the saint Narottam has never deigned to enter your royal temple.

"He is singing God's praise under the trees by the open road. The temple is empty of worshippers.

"They flock round him like bees round the white lotus, leaving the golden jar of honey unheeded."

The King, vexed at heart, went to the spot where Narottam sat on the grass.

He asked him, "Father, why leave my temple of the golden dome and sit on the dust outside to preach God's love?"

"Because God is not there in your temple," said Narottam.

The King frowned and said, "Do you know, twenty millions of gold went to the making of that marvel of art, and it was consecrated to God with costly rites?"

"Yes, I know it," answered Narottam. "It was in that year when thousands of your people whose houses had been burned stood vainly asking for help at your door."

"And God said, 'The poor creature who can give no shelter to his brothers would build my house!'

"And he took his place with the shelterless under the trees by the road.

"And that golden bubble is empty of all but hot vapour of pride."
The King cried in anger, "Leave my land."
Calmly said the saint, "Yes, banish me where you have banished
my God."

— Sir Rabindranath Tagore, 1861-1941

It is almost a truism amongst us that our age has lost the sense of
God. There can be little doubt about the fact. As a nation we are
probably more moral, more humane, more sincere and honourable,
than ever before. Beauty and truth are active ideals in our land as
they have never yet been. The standards of civilization are higher
and cleaner. But we have undoubtedly lost the sense of God, and
that fact is more significant and more disquieting than any other.

Two questions push themselves insistently before our minds when
we ponder this fact. We want to know what it means, and also what
is its cause. What is it that we have lost, and how or why have we
lost it? The first of these questions is not difficult to answer. The
sense of God is the sense that the world as a whole is personal. This
is the very heart of all religious experience. To the man with the
sense of God alive in his soul the world is neither a mechanical system nor an evolving organism. It is something made by Someone,
and brought to life by Someone, controlled, indwelt, loved by an
infinite Person who is its meaning and its reality and its good. It is
this capacity to feel the personality of the Universe, this readiness to
talk with it, rejoice and sorrow with it, work with it and love it,
that we have lost. To talk of the world in terms of energy and radia-
tion, of stresses and velocities, is natural to us. To realise that it
grows and develops like a tree from a seed, revealing new qualities
and realising new potentialities at each new stage of its history,
through the countless ages of the geologist's time-scale—that too is
familiar and easy. But to talk of the universe as organised and in-
formed by a beneficent purpose, as "groaning and travailing in pain,
waiting for the manifestation of the sons of God," seems to us fantastic, a little ridiculous, at the best a pleasant metaphor, at the worst
a gross anthropomorphism. That is what it means to have lost the
sense of God.

Why have we lost it? I imagine because we have idolised the impersonal. Modern science with its craving for mass-generalisation,
and modern industrialism with its cult of mass-production, have

tended to crush our interest in the individual. We think in crowds, in groups, in classes. Our schemes of redemption are not aimed at the salvation of men and women, but of varieties and species of the genus homo—minorities, the oppressed races, the unemployed. So it has come about that we can scarcely, even in our everyday contacts, treat each other and value each other as persons. We lose the arts of friendship, the joys of quiet communion, the adventures of intimate conversation. Our psychologists have turned us into curious and intricate mechanisms full of psychological kinks and subconscious complexes. It is difficult for us to believe in our own souls, apart altogether from their immortality. We have been so bewitched by the evolutionists that we can only believe in the past and the future, in the past because it is no longer, in the future because it is not yet. The universal we can bow before and reverence, because it is abstract and unactual. But the present, the living actual, the concrete individual, escapes us and seems altogether unimportant.

Is it any wonder that we have lost the sense of God? "If any man love not his brother whom he hath seen, how can he love God whom he hath not seen?" The brotherhood of Man is a mere phrase that can only become real as the brotherhood of men who shake hands and share their secrets. So long as the cult of the impersonal receives the homage of our imagination, so long as the craving for anonymity rules our desires, we cannot be ourselves, and we cannot brook that others should be themselves. If we are to regain the sense of God, we must first regain the sense of our unique human reality. We must re-establish in our heart the reverence for what is personal. We must relearn the subtleties of human fellowship and friendship. For the sense of God is not the sense of the infinite, but the sense of the dominion of personality.

— JOHN MACMURRAY, 1891 -

We cannot know whether we love God, although there may be strong reasons for thinking so, but there can be no doubt about whether we love our neighbour or no. Be sure that in proportion as you advance, in fraternal charity, you are increasing in your love of God, for His Majesty bears so tender an affection for us, that I cannot doubt He will repay our love for others by augmenting, in a thousand different ways, that which we bear for Him.

— ST. THERESA, 1515-1582

My heart has become capable of every form.
It is a pasture for gazelles and a convent for Christian monks;
And a temple for idols, and the pilgrim's Ka'ba;
And the tables of the Torah and the book of the Koran.
I follow the religion of Love,
Whichever way his camels take.

— JALAL-UD-DIN RUMI, 1207-1273

Even the professed enemies of God may bear unconscious witness
to him, if they organize their lives about some really significant
cause or ideal; and such people may be far less godless than some
who loudly profess belief in God and yet live essentially self-
centered lives.

— WALTER MARSHALL HORTON, 1895-

If we suppose a large family of children who, on any particular day,
or particular occasion, made it a custom to present to their parents
some token of their affection and gratitude, each of them would
make a different offering, and most probably in a different manner.
Some would pay their congratulations in themes of verse and prose,
by some little devices, as their genius dictated, or according to what
they thought would please; and, perhaps, the least of all, not able to
do any of those things, would ramble into the garden or the field
and gather what it thought the prettiest flower it could find, though
perhaps it might be but a single weed. The parents would be more
gratified by such a variety than if the whole of them had acted on a
concerted plan and each had made exactly the same offering. This
would have the cold appearance of contrivance, or the harsh one of
control. But of all unwelcome things, nothing would more afflict the
parent than to know that the whole of them had afterwards gotten
together by the ears, boys and girls, fighting, reviling, and abusing
each other about which was the best or the worst present.

Why may we not suppose that the great Father of all is pleased
with variety of devotion; and that the greatest offense we can act
is that by which we seek to torment and render each other miserable? For my own part, I am fully satisfied that what I am now
doing, with an endeavor to conciliate mankind, to render their
condition happy, to unite nations that have hitherto been enemies, and

to extirpate the horrid practice of war, and break the chains of slavery and oppression, is acceptable in his sight, and being the best service I can perform, I act it cheerfully.

— THOMAS PAINE, 1737-1809

In the West you observe, watch, and act. In the East we contemplate and commune, and suffer ourselves to be carried away by the spirit of the universe. In the West you wrest from nature her secrets, you conquer her, she makes you wealthy and prosperous, you look upon her as your slave, and sometimes fail to realize her sacredness. In the East nature is our eternal sanctuary, the soul is our everlasting temple, and the sacredness of God's creation is only next to the sacredness of God himself. In the West you love equality, you respect man, you seek justice. In the East love is the fulfillment of the law, we have hero worship, we behold God in humanity. In the West you establish the moral law, you insist upon propriety of conduct, you are governed by public opinion. In the East we aspire, perhaps vainly aspire, after absolute self-conquest, and the holiness which makes God its model. In the West you work incessantly, and your work is your worship. In the East we meditate and worship for long hours, and worship is our work. Perhaps one day . . . the Western and the Eastern man will combine to support each other's strength and supply each other's deficiencies. And then that blessed synthesis of human nature shall be established which all prophets have foretold, and all the devout souls have sighed for.

— PROTAP CHUNDER MOZOOMDAR, 1840-1905

The ideal ends to which we attach our faith are not shadowy and wavering. They assume concrete form in our understanding of our relations to one another and the values contained in these relations. We who now live are parts of a humanity that extends into the remote past, a humanity that has interacted with nature. The things in civilization we most prize are not of ourselves. They exist by grace of the doings and sufferings of the continuous human community in which we are a link.

Ours is the responsibility of conserving, transmitting, rectifying, and expanding the heritage of values we have received that those who come after us may receive it more solid and secure, more widely accessible and more generously shared than we have received it. Here are all the elements for a religious faith that shall not be confined to sect, class, or race. Such a faith has always been implicitly the common faith of mankind. It remains to make it explicit and militant.

— JOHN DEWEY, 1859-1952

CHAPTER FIFTEEN

And to Enjoy Him Forever

> *The Stoics say, "Retire within yourselves, there will you find your rest"; which is not true. Others say, "Go out of yourselves, seek your happiness in diversion"; nor is that true, for sickness may come.*
>
> *Happiness is neither without us nor within us; it is in God, both without us and within us.*
>
> — BLAISE PASCAL, 1623-1662

· I ·

RELIGION is the first thing and the last thing, and until a man has found God, and been found by God, he begins at no beginning, he works to no end. He may have his friendships, his partial loyalties, his scraps of honor, but all these fall into place, and life falls into place, only with God. Only with God, who fights through men against Blind Force and Might and Non-Existence; who fights with men against the confusion and evil within us and without, and against death in every form; who loves us as a great captain loves his men, and stands ready to use us in his immortal adventure against waste, disorder, cruelty, and vice; who is the end, who is the meaning, who is the only King.

The moment may come while we are alone in the darkness under the stars, or while we walk by ourselves or in a crowd. It may come upon the sinking ship or in the tumult of the battle. There is no saying when it may come. For it comes as the dawn comes, through whatever clouds and mists. It comes as the day comes to the ships

285

that put to sea. But after it comes, our lives are changed. Before the coming of the true King, the inevitable King, the King who is present when just men foregather, this blood-stained rubbish of an ancient world shrivels like paper thrust into a flame. Thereafter one goes about like one who was lonely and has found a lover, like one who was perplexed and has found a solution. One is assured that there is a Power that fights against the confusion and evil of the world. There comes into the heart an enduring happiness and courage.

— H. G. WELLS, 1866-1946

God is the One in Whom all is lost and yet the One in Whom all is found.

— EDWARD CAIRD, 1835-1908

God is the denial of denials.

— MEISTER ECKHART, 1260?-?1327

Thou hast made us for Thyself, and our heart is restless until it finds repose in Thee.

— ST. AUGUSTINE, 354-430

The Spirit of the Lord God is upon me; because the Lord hath anointed me to preach good tidings unto the meek; He hath sent me to bind up the broken-hearted, to proclaim liberty to the captives, and the opening of the prison to them that are bound;

To proclaim the acceptable year of the Lord, and the day of vengeance of our God; to comfort all that mourn;

To appoint unto them that mourn in Zion, to give unto them beauty for ashes, the oil of joy for mourning, the garment of praise for the spirit of heaviness; that they might be called trees of righteousness, the planting of the Lord, that He might be glorified.

— THE BIBLE, Isaiah 61:1-3

· II ·

I have made Thee my refuge, my terror and trembling,
  And when straitly besieged I have made Thee my tower,
When to left and to right I have sought for a helper,
  I could look for dear life to no aid but Thy power.
More than all earthly treasure I have made Thee my portion,
  Through all cares the delight and desire of my days,
In the flood of Thy love I have rapture eternal
  And prayer is but an occasion for praise.

— SOLOMON IBN-GABIROL, 1021?-?1058

How, then, shall we lay hold of that Life and Power, and live the life of prayer without ceasing? By quiet, persistent practice in turning of all our being, day and night, in prayer and inner worship and surrender, toward Him who calls in the deeps of our souls. Mental habits of inward orientation must be established. An inner, secret turning to God can be made fairly steady, after weeks and months and years of practice and lapses and failures and returns. It is as simple an art as Brother Lawrence found it, but it may be long before we achieve any steadiness in the process. Begin now, as you read these words, as you sit in your chair, to offer your whole selves, utterly and in joyful abandon, in quiet, glad surrender to Him, who is within. In secret ejaculations of praise, turn in humble wonder to the Light, faint though it may be. Keep contact with the outer world of sense and meanings. Here is no discipline in absentmindedness. Walk and talk and work and laugh with your friends. But behind the scenes, keep up the life of simple prayer and inward worship. Keep it up throughout the day. Let inward prayer be your last act before you fall asleep and the first act when you awake. And in time you will find, as did Brother Lawrence, that "those who have the gale of the Holy Spirit go forward even in sleep."

— THOMAS R. KELLY, 1893-1941

The foundation of devoutness, the root of perfect service, is that man clearly sees and finds truly confirmed what his duty is in his world, and on what he should turn his gaze and his striving in all he busies himself with, all the days of his life. For behold, what our sages, blessed be their memory, have taught, is this, that man was created only to delight in the Lord, to rejoice is the glory of His Presence, for that is the true delight, and among all blissful things the most blissful. . . .

And if you go into this matter more deeply, you will see that the world was created for man's use. He, however, stands on a dangerous brink, for if he permits himself to be drawn toward the world, if he moves away from his Creator, behold, he grows corrupt and corrupts the world along with him. But if he governs himself and clings to his Creator, and uses the world only as a tool to help him to serve his Creator, he is lifted up, and the world is lifted with him. For it is uplifting to all creatures that they are the helpers of perfect man, who is hallowed with His holiness, blessed be He. . . .

Thus we see that the basic meaning of the life of man in this world is only to keep the commandments, to worship God, and to withstand trials—nothing but this. And the pleasures of this world are there only to be a help to him and a tool, so that he may be tranquil and circumspect, and bend his heart to this service he is in duty bound to perform. And it is right that man turn wholly to the Creator, blessed be He, that he have no other goal in his doing, be it great or small, than to approach Him, blessed be He, than to break through any dividing wall that stands between him and his Maker (and everything of material nature is such a wall), until he strives straight toward Him, blessed be He, as the iron to the magnet. And let him follow everything of which he can possibly think that it may be a means to this approach, let him seize upon it and not relinquish it. But let him flee, as one flees from fire, all that he thinks might hinder him in this pursuit. As it is said: "My soul cleaves unto Thee; Thy right hand holdeth me fast." For his coming into the world is only for one purpose, to attain this nearness by saving his soul from everything that hinders and harms it.

— Moses Hayyim Luzatto, 1707-1747

As I analyze myself I find several things happening to me as a result of these two months of strenuous effort to keep God in mind every minute. This concentration upon God is strenuous, but everything else has ceased to be so. I think more clearly, I forget less frequently. Things which I did with a strain before, I now do easily and with no effort whatever. I worry about nothing, and lose no sleep. I walk on air a good part of the time. Even the mirror reveals a new light in my eyes and face. I no longer feel in a hurry about anything. Everything goes right. Each minute I meet calmly as though it were not important. Nothing can go wrong excepting one thing. That is that God *may slip from my mind* if I do not keep on my guard. If He is there, the universe is with me. My task is simple and clear.

— FRANK LAUBACH, 1884-

The word, to worship, means to stoop and bow down the body with external gestures; to serve in the work. But to worship God in spirit is the service and honor of the heart; it comprehends faith and fear in God. The worshipping of God is two-fold, outward and inward —that is, to acknowledge God's benefits, and to be thankful unto Him.

— MARTIN LUTHER, 1483-1546

The habits of those who love God are too many to be enumerated, and so I shall speak of those which occur to me.

These are the men who have knowledge of their God, who perceive that He delights in them and leads them, that He guides them and sustains them. And so it becomes clear to them, and they trust in it, that all their concerns and impulses are guided according to the decision of the Creator, exalted be He, and according to His desire. Thus they desist from choosing one thing and preferring it to another, and are certain that their Creator will choose for them what is good and right.

When you deal with them, they seem to you the brothers of modesty; when you talk with them, they appear to you as sages; when you question them, as scholars; when you sin against them, as the meek. You see their forms: they are bathed in light. And if you search their hearts, you will find a heart broken before God. In communing with Him, they are at home; in the business of the world, they are silent. Their hearts are filled with the love of God, but not with desire for the doing of men, and not with pleasure in their talk. They spurn the road of corruption and go on the most elect of all paths. It is their merit that suffering departs, that rain falls; and that men and beasts have water is their merit, because they have denied their bodies forbidden union, they have kept their hands from all manner of indulgences, and their souls have fled from what is forbidden in order to go the good and straight path. And so by suffering only few days, they attain to high rank, and acquire both worlds; they garner both kinds of good, and they receive both advantages in full. As it is said in the psalm: "Happy is the man that feareth the Lord, that delighteth greatly in His commandments," and so to the end. And an extraordinary thing about them is that in their eyes the commandments that their Creator summons them to do are too few, in comparison to the duties that would be in measure with the good He has done for them, or in comparison to what their souls have assumed in the way of effort, and striving, and enduring, and patience, in order to cling in his service. . . . And so they serve the Creator by doing commandments of reason, by extraordinary discipline, and by a good spiritual conduct of life; and by these things they add to the known commandments, because they have pure hearts devoted to God. And so they learn the ways of the prophets and the habits of the devout, in order thus to seek the approval of God, and in order to be accepted by Him.

— BAHYA IBN-PAKUDA, eleventh century

The Lord is my light and my salvation; whom shall I fear? The Lord is the strength of my life; of whom shall I be afraid?

When the wicked, even mine enemies and my foes, came upon me to eat up my flesh, they stumbled and fell.

Though an host should encamp against me, my heart shall not fear: though war should rise against me, in this will I be confident.

One thing have I desired of the Lord, that will I seek after; that I may dwell in the house of the Lord all the days of my life, to behold the beauty of the Lord, and to enquire in His temple.

For in the time of trouble He shall hide me in his pavilion: in the secret of his tabernacle shall he hide me; He shall set me up upon a rock.

— THE BIBLE, Psalm 27

· III ·

Man's perfect happiness consists in a perfect knowledge of God; an imperfect knowledge of God is not sufficient for man's true happiness.

— ST. THOMAS AQUINAS, 1225?-1274

All that unites us to God, all that causes us to taste Him, to delight in Him, to rejoice in His glory, and to love Him so purely that we find our happiness in Him, and, not satisfied with reflections, with thoughts, with affections and resolutions, leads us solidly to the practice of detachment from self and from created things; all this is good, all this is true prayer. We must take care not to torment our heads, or over-excite our hearts; but to take whatever offers itself to the soul's sight with humility and simplicity, without those violent efforts which are rather imaginary than real and well grounded; allowing ourselves to be drawn gently to God, abandoning ourselves to the promptings of our own spirit.

— JACQUES BÉNIGNE BOSSUET, 1627-1704

Your enjoyment of the World is never right, till you so esteem it, that everything in it, is more your treasure than a King's exchequer full of Gold and Silver. And that exchequer yours also in its place and service. Can you take too much joy in your Father's works? He is Himself in everything. Some things are little on the outside, and rough and common, but I remember the time when the dust of the streets were as pleasing as Gold to my infant eyes, and now they are more precious to the eye of reason.

Your enjoyment of the world is never right, till every morning you awake in Heaven; see yourself in your Father's Palace; and look upon the skies, the earth, and the air as Celestial Joys: having such a reverend esteem of all, as if you were among the Angels. The bride of a monarch, in her husband's chamber, hath no such causes of delight as you.

You never enjoy the world aright, till the Sea itself floweth in your veins, till you are clothed with the heavens, and crowned with the stars: and perceive yourself to be the sole heir of the whole world, and more than so, because men are in it who are everyone sole heirs as well as you. Till you can sing and rejoice and delight in God, as misers do in gold, and Kings in sceptres, you never enjoy the world.

Till your spirit filleth the whole world, and the stars are your jewels: till you are as familiar with the ways of God in all Ages as with your walk and table: till you are intimately acquainted with that shady nothing out of which the world was made: till you love men so as to desire their happiness, with a thirst equal to the zeal of your own: till you delight in God for being good to all: you never enjoy the world.

— THOMAS TRAHERNE, 1637?-1674

We are like a choir of singers standing round the conductor, who do not always sing in time, because their attention is diverted to some external object. When they look at the conductor, they sing well and are really with him. So we always move round the One. If we did not, we should dissolve and cease to exist. But we do not always look towards the One. When we do, we attain the end of our existence, and our rest; and we no longer sing out of tune, but form in truth a divine choir round the One.

— PLOTINUS, 205?-270

In our very laudable enthusiasms over action and social morality and class equality and hygienic conditions and international policies and tangible results, we are beginning to forget the inner life of the soul, the quiet turning of the spirit back upon itself, which in the rhythmic life of man is quite as important as is the outward-going impulse. In our safe and sane and sober fear of emotionalism and sentimentality, we seem tempted to disown the spiritual nature which is part of our human heritage. The glow of feeling, the sense of the Infinite, the intuition of a Beyond, the aspiration for the more than earthly, these are and always must be an important, if not an essential, part of religion. And they are genuinely human as well,— as genuinely natural *ends* as are the biological processes of digestion, assimilation, and reproduction. It is certainly of great importance that we should consider what we and our slum friends shall eat and what we shall drink and wherewithal we shall be clothed; but there are one or two other things which it is well to seek, and perhaps the "kingdom of God" is one of them. And while many will respond that the "kingdom of God" consists just in the proper physical and social conditions, I cannot forget that one who spoke with some authority on this matter said, "The kingdom of God is within you."

In short, every age has need of "the contemplative life," and ours is no exception to the rule. It might, in fact, be maintained that our twentieth century stands in special need of it. When, indeed, could its importance be more properly emphasized than at a time when

Activity is the shibboleth of theory and Efficiency the motto of practice, when we are brought up to feel that at every moment we must be working or else we must be amused, and taught to believe that most real values are to be appraised in terms of economic productivity? Even social justice and college settlements and industrial democracy and international amity are not enough to satisfy the full warm life of the soul. The soul needs a larger draft of air, a less circumscribed horizon, than even these excellent things can give. It needs a chance for spreading its wings, for looking beyond itself, beyond the immediate environment, and for quiet inner growth, which is best to be found in that group of somewhat indefinite but very real experiences—aspiration, insight, contemplation—which may well be called the mystic life.

— JAMES BISSETT PRATT, 1875-1944

The Lord raise up that in thee, which is of him; and so guide and order thy heart, that it may long and cry after him, and be heard and satisfied by him.

— ISAAC PENINGTON, 1617-1680

How that presence is felt, it may better be known by experience than by any writing; for it is the life and the love, the might and the light, the joy and the rest of a chosen soul. And therefore he that hath soothfastly once felt it, he may not forbear it without pain; he may not undesire it, it is so good in itself and so comfortable . . .He cometh privily sometimes when thou art least aware of Him, but thou shalt well know Him ere He go; for wonderfully He stirreth and mightily He turneth thine heart into beholding of His Goodness, and doth thine heart melt delectably as wax against the fire into softness of His love, and this is the voice that He soundeth.

— WALTER HILTON, died 1395

When with the help of God my self is purified,
To go to God I need not wander far and wide.

— ANGELUS SILESIUS, 1624-1677

· IV ·

He is the Way.
Follow Him through the Land of Unlikeness;
You will see rare beasts, and have unique adventures.

He is the Truth.
Seek Him in the Kingdom of Anxiety;
You will come to a great city that has expected your return for
  years.

He is the Life.
Love Him in the World of the Flesh;
And at your marriage all its occasions shall dance for joy.

— W. H. AUDEN, 1907-

It is good that we have sometimes some troubles and crosses; for
they often make a man enter into himself, and consider that he is
here in banishment, and ought not to place his trust in any worldly
thing.

It is good that we be sometimes contradicted, and that men think
ill or inadequately; and this, although we do and intend well.

These things help often to the attaining of humility, and defend us
from vainglory: for then we are more inclined to seek God for our
inward witness, when outwardly we be contemned by men, and
when there is no credit given unto us.

And therefore a man should settle himself so fully in God, that he
need not to seek many comforts of men.

— GERHARD GROOTE, 1340-1384

The great thing is to resign all your interests and pleasures and comfort and fame to God. He who unreservedly accepts whatever God
may give him in this world—humiliation, trouble, and trial from
within or from without—has made a great step towards self-victory;
he will not dread praise or censure, he will not be sensitive; or if he
finds himself wincing, he will deal so cavalierly with his sensitive-
ness that it will soon die away. Such full resignation and unfeigned
acquiescence is true liberty, and hence arises perfect simplicity.

Blessed indeed are they who are no longer their own, but have given themselves wholly to God!

— FRANÇOIS FÉNELON, 1651-1715

Like chapters of prophecy my days burn in all their revelation,
And my body in their midst is like the thick lump of metal intended
    for smelting.
And over me stands my God, the blacksmith, and strikes with all
    might:
Each wound cut in me by time opens a lesion,
And casts forth the imprisoned flame in sparks of moments.
This is my sentence and destiny till evening on the road.
And when I return to thrust the smitten lump of my body upon the
    bed,
My mouth is an open wound.
All naked I then speak with my God: You have worked hard,
Now night has come; desist—let us both rest.

— URI ZEVI GREENBERG, 1894-

Though it is true that in Buddhism, in Judaism, and in Christianity the thought of God as a sure refuge is to be found in different forms, the salvation which those religions offer is not a mere escape. The believer is offered, so to speak, a stand outside the world from which he can confront and overcome the otherwise overwhelming evils of this world. At their highest, the spiritual religions have summoned men to confront life's problems rather than to evade them, and have given men courage and hope for the conflict. It would be a strange misreading of the message of the Buddha and still more of that of the Christ to imagine that either minimized or concealed the evil and hardship of the world. Spiritual religion has claimed to be both an interpretation and a conquest of reality.

—W. R. INGE, 1860-1952

O soul, canst thou not understand
Thou art not left alone,
As a dog to howl and moan
His matter's absence? Thou art as a book

Left in a room that He forsook,
But returns to by and by,
A book of His dear choice,—
That quiet waiteth for His Hand,
That quiet waiteth for His Eye,
That quiet waiteth for His Voice.

— MICHAEL FIELD
(Katharine Bradley, 1846–1914, and Edith Cooper, 1862–1913)

· v ·

So long as the bee is outside the petals of the lily, and has not tasted the sweetness of its honey, it hovers round the flower emitting its buzzing sound; but when it is inside the flower, it noiselessly drinks its nectar. So long as a man quarrels and disputes about doctrines and dogmas, he has not tasted the nectar of true faith; when he has tasted it, he becomes quiet and full of peace.

— RAMAKRISHNA, 1834-1886

And one of the scribes came, and having heard them reasoning together, and perceiving that he had answered them well, asked him, Which is the first commandment of all?

And Jesus answered him, The first of all the commandments is, Hear, O Israel; the Lord our God is one Lord:

And thou shalt love the Lord thy God with all thy heart, and with all thy soul, and with all thy mind, and with all thy strength: this is the first commandment.

And the second is like, namely this, Thou shalt love thy neighbour as thyself. There is none other commandment greater than these.

And the scribe said unto Him, Well, Master, thou hast said the truth: for there is one God; and there is none other but He:

And to love Him with all the heart, and with all the understanding, and with all the soul, and with all the strength, and to love His neighbour as himself, is more than all whole burnt offerings and sacrifices.

And when Jesus saw that he answered discreetly, He said unto him, Thou art not far from the Kingdom of God.

— THE BIBLE, Mark 12:28-34

In western Colorado there are mountain torrents which for un-
counted centuries have come tumbling down through gorges that
they have worn for themselves and have made their way to the sea,
leaving dry and barren the naturally fertile steppes through which
they flow. But in recent years men have directed these torrents out
upon the steppes, through channels that subdivide endlessly, like the
arteries of the human body, till every square foot of soil over wide
areas has the requisite moisture, and all the land has become wonderfully fruitful. Nor have the mountains and the glaciers lost any of
their grandeur through the fact that now they nourish a new abun-
dance of life.

Similarly, there is much religious passion in the world which is
simply following the channels worn long ago, leaving great tracts
of human society barren and desolate for lack of the fructification
it might impart. If creative social intelligence were recognized as
affording suitable channels for this religious passion, it might be
flowing out over these desolate tracts of human life and, penetrating to every part of them, redeem them to great fruitfulness and
beauty. Nor need the ancient sublimities of faith be in the least
diminished thereby.

— Eugene William Lyman, 1872 - 1948

Wherewith shall I come before the Lord, and bow myself before
the high God? Shall I come before Him with burnt offerings, with
calves of a year old?

Will the Lord be pleased with thousands of rams, or with ten
thousands of rivers of oil? Shall I give my firstborn for my transgression, the fruit of my body for the sin of my soul?

He hath shewed thee, O man, what is good; and what doth the
Lord require of thee, but to do justly, and to love mercy, and to
walk humbly with thy God?

— The Bible, Micah 6:6-8

It is known and certain that the love of God does not become closely
knit in a man's heart till he is continuously and thoroughly possessed
by it and gives up everything else in the world for it; as God commanded us: "with all thy heart and with all thy soul" (Deuteronomy
6:5). We love God only with the knowledge with which we know

Him, and as is the measure of the knowledge, so is the measure of
the love: if little, little; if much, much.

—Maimonides, 1135-1204

Now let us mark: Where men are enlightened with the true light,
they perceive that all which they might desire or choose, is nothing to that which all creatures, as creatures, ever desired or chose
or knew. Therefore they renounce all desire and choice, and com-
mit and commend themselves and all things to the Eternal Goodness. Nevertheless, there remaineth in them a desire to go forward
and get nearer to the Eternal Goodness; that is, to come to a clearer
knowledge, and warmer love, and more comfortable assurance, and
perfect obedience and subjection; so that every enlightened man
could say: "I would fain be to the Eternal Goodness, what his own
hand is to a man." And he feareth always that he is not enough so,
and longeth for the salvation of all men. And such men do not call
this longing their own, nor take it unto themselves, for they know
well that this desire is not of man, but of the Eternal Goodness; for
whatsoever is good shall no one take unto himself as his own, seeing
that it belongeth to the Eternal Goodness only. . . .

For a true lover of God, loveth him or the Eternal Goodness alike,
in having, and in not having, in sweetness and in bitterness, in good or
evil report, and the like, for he seeketh alone the honour of God, and
not his own, either in spiritual or natural things. And therefore he
standeth alike unshaken in all things, at all seasons.

—Theologia Germanica

As the love of God is man's highest happiness and blessedness, and
the ultimate end and aim of all human actions, it follows that he
alone lives by the Divine law who loves God not from fear of
punishment, or from love of any other object, such as sensual pleasure, fame, or the like; but solely because he has knowledge of God,
or is convinced that the knowledge and love of God is the highest
good. The sum and chief precept, then, of the Divine law is to love
God as the highest good, namely, as we have said, not from fear of
any pains and penalties, or from the love of any other object in
which we desire to take pleasure. The idea of God lays down the
rule that God is our highest good—in other words, that the knowl-

edge and love of God is the ultimate aim to which all our actions should be directed. The worldling cannot understand these things, they appear foolishness to him, because he has too meagre a knowledge of God, and also because in this highest good he can discover nothing which he can handle or eat, or which affects the fleshly appetites wherein he chiefly delights, for it consists solely in thought and the pure reason. They, on the other hand, who know that they possess no greater gift than intellect and sound reason, will doubtless accept what I have said without question.

—BARUCH SPINOZA, 1632-1677

The more God is in all things, the more He is outside them. The more He is within, the more without.

—MEISTER ECKHART, 1260?-?1327

· VI ·

O God, grant us the serenity to accept
What cannot be changed;
The courage to change what can be changed,
And the wisdom to know one from the other.

—REINHOLD NIEBUHR, 1892-

Almighty God, who art the Father of our spirits and the Guardian of our lives, we pray Thee for comfort and courage in this hour. We know that Thou art ever with us, for we cannot be where Thou art not. In the labors of the day as in the watches of the night, on sea and land and in the air, in far countries, among strange peoples, Thy presence is known, and Thy blessing, like the sun and rain, a gift from out Thy hand. So we do take heart in every lot, and fear not the peril of any hour.

We pray Thee for those we love and who love us, that they may be sheltered from all distress of mind, body, or estate. Keep them tenderly within Thy loving care, and teach them to be not anxious nor afraid. Help us to be worthy of their trust, to be secure from all temptations unto sin, and to be glad in their gift to them of clean hands and pure heart.

We pray Thee for our country, that she may be ever true to the ideals of liberty which we have been summoned to serve and save. Guard her shores from every foe, her people from undue suffering and loss, her rulers from lust of power and dominion. Grant this nation, in this hour of her travail, a new birth of freedom, that government of the people, for the people, and by the people may not perish from the earth.

— JOHN HAYNES HOLMES, 1879-

Give me Thy grace, good Lord,
To set the world at nought,
To set my mind fast upon Thee.
And not to hang upon the blast of men's mouths.
To be content to be solitary,
Not to long for worldly company,
Little and little utterly to cast off the world,
And rid my mind of all the business thereof.
Not to long to hear of any worldly things,
But that the hearing of worldly phantasies may be to me displeasant.
Gladly to be thinking of God,
Piteously to call for His help,
To lean unto the comfort of God,
Busily to labour to love Him.
To know mine own vility and wretchedness,
To humble and meeken myself under the mighty hand of God,
To bewail my sins passed,
For the purging of them, patiently to suffer adversity.
Gladly to bear my purgatory here,
To be joyful of tribulations,
To walk the narrow way that leadeth to life.

— SIR THOMAS MORE, 1478-1535

God, if I worship Thee in fear of hell,
Burn me in hell.
And if I worship Thee in hope of Paradise,
Exclude me from Paradise;
But if I worship Thee for Thine own sake,
Withhold not Thine everlasting Beauty.

— RABIAH, 717?-801

Who dwelleth in that secret place,
Where tumult enters not,
Is never cold with terror base,
    Never with anger hot:
For if an evil host should dare
    His very heart invest,
God is his deeper heart, and there
    He enters in to rest.

When mighty sea-winds madly blow,
    And tear the scattered waves,
Peaceful as summer woods, below
    Lie darkling ocean caves:
The wind of words may toss my heart,
    But what is that to me!
'Tis but a surface storm—Thou art
    My deep, still, resting sea.

— GEORGE MACDONALD, 1824-1905

O Lord, grant us to love Thee; grant that we may love those that love Thee; grant that we may do the deeds that win Thy love. Make the love of Thee be dearer to us than ourselves, than our families, than wealth, and even than cool water.

— MOHAMMED, 570-632

The prayers I make will then be sweet indeed,
If Thou the spirit give by which I pray;
My unassisted heart is barren clay,
That of its native self can nothing feed;
Of good and pious works Thou art the seed
That quickens only where Thou say'st it may.
Unless Thou show to us Thy own true way,
No man can find it: Father! Thou must lead;
Do Thou then breathe those thoughts into my mind
By which such virtue may in me be bred
That in Thy holy footsteps I may tread;
The fetters of my tongue do Thou unbind,

That I may have the power to sing to Thee,
And sound Thy praises everlastingly!

— MICHELANGELO, 1475-1564

God be in my head,
And in my understanding;
God be in mine eyes,
And in my looking;
God be in my mouth
And in my speaking;
God be in my heart,
And in my thinking;
God be at my end and at my departing.

— SARUM PRIMER

INDEX OF AUTHORS

ABOUT THE EDITOR

CARL HERMANN VOSS was born in Pittsburgh, Pennsylvania in 1910, and received the degrees of Doctor of Philosophy and Bachelor of Arts from the University of Pittsburgh. His graduate studies were pursued in Elsinore, Denmark and Geneva, Switzerland, and at several American universities; he earned his Bachelor of Divinity degree at the Union Theological Seminary in New York City. As a parish minister, he has served churches in Raleigh, North Carolina; Pittsburgh, Pennsylvania; and Brooklyn, New York. As an executive, he was a member of the staff of the Church Peace Union and the World Alliance for International Friendship through Religion.

At present, he is chairman of the executive council of the American Christian Palestine Committee and a member of the faculty of the New School for Social Research in New York City.

Dr. Voss was assisted in the preparation of this book by his wife, Dorothy Grote Voss, an attorney at law. They live in New York City with their young daughter, Carlyn.